ELEVATION
B:
S
A
C

Michael I. Posey

Everything You Need To Know About Buying Mountain Property

It is one thing to not know the answers, quite another to not know the questions.

How to go about finding the perfect property to fulfill your second home, vacation home, retirement home dreams in the mountains.

Copyright © 2012 Michael I. Posey
All rights reserved.
ISBN: 1478234113
ISBN 13: 9781478234111
Library of Congress Control Number: 2012912690
CreateSpace, North Charleston, SC

This book is dedicated to my wife, Sonia, who has the patience and love to put up with my two careers, and to my three children, Taylor, Hannah, and Leila, who are a reminder to me every day of the true essence of life...I love you all.

Acknowledgments

The most enjoyable aspect of achieving anything worthwhile is the furthering of the friendships that inevitably occur during the process. I have been helped, urged on, supported, and uplifted...and alternatively...kidded, chided, and verbally abused. Mostly, I have had a lot of fun writing this book, and I wanted to give those that so richly deserve it the thanks and recognition that they are due.

First and foremost, I want to thank Jason and Julie Gilliland of Site Design Studio in Asheville, North Carolina, for their patient review of each and every chapter in the book. If that wasn't enough, they also provided the illustrations and the photography that put an additional layer of explanation and interpretation to the narrative. Their efforts were extraordinarily productive in complementing the written word through their visual enhancements of the points that I was trying to convey.

Secondly, I am indebted to my good friend, Rolando Paez, at Buena Vista Construction, for providing me with a great deal of the practical wisdom that served as a jumping off point for a number of the chapters in the book. He is, without a doubt, the best builder I have come across here in the mountains of western North Carolina.

I would also like to express my sincere gratitude to the following for their review and assistance with more specific topics where their expertise was critical to the finished product:

To Craig Justus at the Van Winkle Law firm, for his help with the chapter on "The Paper Chase," particularly regarding the excerpted sections on Covenants, Conditions, and Restrictions.

To Shane Valliere at Ace Construction, for his assistance with the very sexy subject of septic/drain field systems for residential use.

To Brian Greene of Greene Brothers Well Drilling, for his advice and review of the sections on deep well drilling to access potable water sources for residential use.

To John Witherspoon at Conservation Advisors, Inc., who is at the forefront of consulting firms that specialize in the sometimes complicated process of private landowners dedicating conservation easements for the preservation of our natural habitat and ecosystems. Many thanks for the review of all of Chapter Eight.

To Gene Adams at Webb Insurance, whose explanations regarding the world of property insurance were key to that discussion.

To Michael James at Blue Ridge Consulting, whose extensive knowledge of acoustics gave me more insight into noise pollution issues than I ever thought possible.

To Will Gentry at Bunnell Lammons Engineering, for furthering my education on the geotechnical investigation process and for the use of one of their proprietary reports as an exhibit in the book.

To the North Carolina Geological Survey, for their assistance with the various topographic map illustrations that should help to further the reader's understanding of that topic.

Finally, so many thanks to my family for support and encouragement. I lean on all of you more than I should and will surely return the favor...right after I finish my next book...

List of Illustrations, Photos, and Exhibits

Illustrations

Illustration 2.1	Driveway Switchbacks	16
Illustration 2.2	Slab-on-Grade	20
Illustration 2.3	Crawl Space	21
Illustration 2.4	Partial Basement	23
Illustration 2.5	Full Walkout Basement	25
Illustration 2.6	Pedestal Foundation	28
Illustration 2.7a	Steep Slope Vegetation Removal	31
Illustration 2.7b	Gentle Slope Vegetation Removal	32
Illustration 3.1	Portion of a Plat Map	50-51
Illustration 3.2a	Topographic Map – Plan View without Relief	55
Illustration 3.2b	Topographic Map – Plan View with Relief	56
Illustration 3.2c	Topographic Map – Oblique Perspective View	57
Illustration 3.3	Flood Zone Map	99
Illustration 4.1	Road/Utility Section	133

Photos

Photo 2.1	Crawl Space	22
Photo 2.2	Partial Basement	24
Photo 2.3	Full Walkout Basement	26
Photo 2.4	Pedestal Foundation	29

Photo 2.5	Well-drilling Rig... 34
Photo 2.6	Retaining Walls—Boulder 37
Photo 2.7	Retaining Walls—Stone Masonry 38
Photo 2.8	Back Porch View.. 42
Photo 4.1	Drain Field Installation.................................... 142

Exhibits

Exhibit 3.1	Soil/Site Evaluation Report.....................104-106
Exhibit 3.2	Property Owners Association Budget............ 86
Exhibit 3.3	Form 12-T: Offer to Purchase and Contract—Vacant Lot/Land.................107-115
Exhibit 3.4	Geotechnical Report 116-127
Exhibit 7.1	Asheville Accolades 244-252
Exhibit 7.2	One-day-only Sales Event—Ad 204
Exhibit 7.3	One-day-only Sales Event—Ad 205
Exhibit 7.4	One-day-only Sales Event—Ad 206
Exhibit 7.5	One-day-only Sales Event—FAQ 213-214
Exhibit 7.6	Site Plan 217
Exhibit 7.7	One-day-only Sales Event—Vital Information Sheet.............................218-220
Exhibit 7.8	One-day-only Sales Event—Contract Form 222-225
Exhibit 8.1	Land Trusts in North Carolina...............270-279

About the Author

Michael Posey was born in Auburn, New York, in 1958, was raised in Boca Raton, Florida, and spent the majority of his career in construction and real estate development along the Gold Coast of Florida from Miami to West Palm Beach, until he moved to Asheville, North Carolina, in 2005. Prior to moving to Asheville, Michael spent the previous ten years as the COO and VP of Development on Fisher Island, the private island of residences and resort/club amenities located just off the southern tip of Miami Beach.

He is a graduate of St. Andrew's School in Boca Raton, Florida, and earned a bachelor's degree from the University of Virginia in Charlottesville, Virginia, and both a bachelor's and master's degree from the University of Florida's School of Construction Management in the College of Architecture.

He is married to Sonia Santana and has three children, Taylor, Hannah, and Leila, all of whom reside in Asheville.

He continues to develop residential real estate in the western North Carolina area, with his current focus on Sunset Falls at Bald Creek, a three hundred-acre community located just outside of Waynesville, North Carolina, in the picturesque farming community of Crabtree in Haywood County.

Michael can be reached at bluemountainquill@gmail.com, where he welcomes your thoughts and comments on the book, particularly from those who may have had their own noteworthy experiences buying property here in the mountains. Additionally, Michael invites your suggestions regarding topics that readers may feel were omitted or ideas that readers believe may not have been given their due coverage.

Contents

Acknowledgments v
List of Illustrations, Photos, and Exhibits ix
About the Author xi

Chapter One: Introduction 1
It is one thing not to know the answers—quite another not to know the questions

Chapter Two: Do Your Due Diligence—Part I 13
Site characteristics and their impact on the viability of the land for your intended home

Chapter Three: Do Your Due Diligence—Part II 49
The "Paper Chase"—documentation and investigation

Chapter Four: Where's the Beef? 129
The community's infrastructure and municipal services

Chapter Five: Outside Influences 155
External variables that can impact the homesite purchasing decision and quality of life inside the community

Chapter Six: The Brokerage Community..................................**177**
Internet-based marketing and community information websites, land listing sites, land brokers, conventional brokers, and developer sales staff

Chapter Seven: Buyer Beware!..**197**
The "One-Day-Only Sales Event"

Chapter Eight: Conservation Easements........................**253**
Property ownership, habitat preservation, and economic benefits

Chapter Nine: Epilogue..**281**
Some closing thoughts

CHAPTER ONE

Introduction

"It is one thing not to know the answers—quite another not to know the questions"

In the fall of 2011, I sat on the porch of a mountain home that some of my very good friends had built as a sort of "friends and family" shared residence in our new community. They were gracious enough to allow us, as the developers, to use it for "Discovery Weekends" for clients who had an interest in the homesites in our community and who wanted to experience the neighborhood and the local environment over a weekend stay. Perched in an Adirondack chair at about forty-one hundred feet in elevation, I was looking out upon an incredible October view, the closer layers of sloping mountain faces within the viewscape bathed in every hue of yellow, orange, red, and purple that nature could offer. Farther away toward the sunset were layers of intersecting ranges and ridgelines, mostly bluish but with gray and off-white mists obscuring the clarity in places. The highest peaks exceeded six thousand feet in elevation, beyond which was the soft glow of the setting sun. I sat there for some time, immersed in a wonderful serenity of almost no sound at all, except for the occasional chatter of birds and an autumn breeze forging its divided pathways through the woods. The view was simply awesome, the atmosphere unmatched in its peacefulness, the solitude almost hypnotic.

As much as I wanted to stay until the colors of the sunset had given way to nightfall, I needed to get back to my family in Asheville, and I had the always pleasant drive back to the "big city" to think about things. Lately, I had been a bit preoccupied with the demise of a couple of very well-respected residential developers, one who had already succumbed to a foreclosure action, and the other who was traveling down that same inevitable path—with clearly just a matter of time before the reality of five years of a devastating real estate market took its final toll. The quality of their communities, the integrity of their characters, the strength of their business plans—none of it mattered as they rode this particular roller coaster down to the bottom, a bottom which seemed like it could never quite be reached. It was just amazing to me that development teams that had done almost everything right were throwing in the towel (or rather being removed from the game), when just five short years ago, they were riding on a crest so high that any notion that a bottom could even exist was never part of the dialogue. As I was driving through the countryside, I was having one of those moments where you feel compelled to do something to rectify a situation, right the wrong, fix the inequity, and bring the perpetrators to justice. Okay, so what was I going to do about the state of the world's collapsed real estate market that had been created via the subprime mortgage mess, collateralized debt obligations, credit default swaps, and other arcane financial instruments, the impacts of which no one really understood until it was far too late? Well, pretty much nothing, if I approached it from that angle.

As I thought about it further, I realized what was really bothering me more than anything else. It wasn't the precipitous decline of the good guys that bothered me so much; it was a different scenario that took place at the same time that was really eating at me. During those boom years, other developers, if you could even call them that, who had done just about everything wrong that one could do wrong, had enjoyed an almost equal amount of comparative success as the good guys. They too were belly-up at this point, in fact, well before this point, but the difference was that they left an inordinate amount of pain in their wake, pain that in many cases was absorbed primarily by the individuals who purchased homesites from them. I had heard so many horror stories recounted by folks who had purchased a lot for their planned retirement, vacation, or second home that could simply not come to fruition now because they were the victims of circumstances well beyond their knowledge and control. Perhaps, I thought, I couldn't do a thing about the havoc that Wall Street had wrought, but what if I could help the individual buyers to successfully navigate their way through the land purchase process? If I could put myself in the shoes of the buyers (which wasn't difficult, because I had been doing exactly that almost every day as a developer), maybe I could at least help by providing them with the information and resources they needed to minimize the risk inherent in the purchase of a homesite.

When I got home that day, I immediately went to my computer and pulled up a couple of the major booksellers' websites and started a search within book titles, focusing on keywords and phrases such as "how to buy land in the mountains" and similar variations. I was kind of stunned as I found almost nothing that covered what I intended to cover in the book that I was imagining. I thought, is this because nobody is interested in the topic, or is this because nobody ever thought to write about it? I suppose I won't know that for sure until this book goes to market.

There are some seventy-eight million baby boomers who were born from 1946 to 1964 who have just recently entered their retirement years or are quickly approaching them. For those who are ready to leave the job market for good, part of that process may include the acquisition of a parcel of land on which to build their retirement home. For those not quite ready to retire, who have been fortunate enough to achieve a comfortable level of wealth, a vacation home or second home may be a part of the equation. Wherever they may be in that stage of their lives, many couples envision not only the dream of their own escapes to paradise but also the aspiration of a legacy to leave to their extended families. For many in this sizable generation, the Blue Ridge and Smoky Mountains region (i.e., western North Carolina, eastern Tennessee, northern Georgia, northwestern South Carolina, and southwestern Virginia) provides a very attractive setting in which to accomplish those dreams of escaping to a more peaceful and less stressful lifestyle. This book is written through the lens of my development experience in this region of the country, though I believe that much of the information and lessons herein are applicable to land purchases in any mountainous, rural region of the country.

The inevitable first step in the property search process in our increasingly digital world is, of course, the Internet (see Chapter Six), where a number of websites that cater to property-seeking baby boomers enjoy hundreds of thousands of hits and visitors in pursuit of that effort. Some are just curious, but others are beginning an earnest and determined search to find a paradise that they have long imagined and are ready to realize. These websites provide a very valuable initial service, but the bottom line is that those in search of a rural, mountain homesite—whether within a subdivided community or as a stand-alone purchase outside of a planned neighborhood—need to assume the ultimate responsibility for attaining their goals.

This book is about the process involved in making sure that your dream does not become a nightmare. It is intended to serve as a blueprint that, if followed diligently, will go a very long way to ensuring that the property you purchase will accommodate the home you wish to build, whenever that may be. It is a book that is predicated on the assumption that you are buying a homesite—that is, the land on which to *eventually* build a home, which seems to be the preferred strategy for at least four reasons that come to mind:

1. From a financial and timing perspective, many buyers view the effort as a two-step process:
    a) the purchase of the homesite first, to take advantage of today's prices while the buyers prepare for their future retirement; and
    b) the design and the construction of the home later, at the time they retire.

2. From a practical perspective, one of the things that you will learn in this book is that mountainous topography will dictate many of the design aspects of the home. In other words, once you have picked a homesite, you can then start designing the home. It doesn't work the other way around; you don't pick out a house plan and then try to plop it down on the homesite. You can do that in Florida and Texas and Arizona and Kansas, where the topography is essentially flat and has little, if any, design implications; you can't do that here in the mountains (see Chapter Two).

3. Related to the practical issue of design in item #2, for many individuals and couples, this may be the last house that they own during the active years of their later adulthood. They would much prefer to live those years in a home that not only meets their needs but also meets their wants in every way. That usually entails having a custom home designed and built specifically for them, which provides them with the freedom and flexibility to accommodate all of their wishes. The alternative is to buy an existing home, which may address many of their wants and needs but will inevitably fall short of that which they can achieve with their own design.

4. From the perspective of what the market typically offers here in the mountains, new developments, which many buyers desire, are typically in the business of selling homesites. I think this is partially because of the three items above, but it is also driven by two other factors:
    a) Developers here are typically good at planning residential developments and managing the construction of the infrastructure and amenities, but they are simply not set up from a personnel and expertise standpoint to include home construction as part of their business model. They happily yield this segment of the business to the homebuilder.
    b) Having said that, unfortunately many of the homebuilders here are simply not very well capitalized; they don't have the financial resources to build speculatively and then bear the carrying costs, should the home not sell quickly upon its completion.

Introduction

The market trends that I have witnessed at the start of this millennium make it abundantly clear that it isn't just the "boomers" who are drawn to realizing their dream of a change to a different lifestyle here in the mountains. A notable percentage of another forty-five to fifty million Americans who were born in the 1965–1980 era, Generation X as they are called, are themselves toying with the thought of relocation, but at a different stage in their lives and for different reasons. This is a generation that seems more attuned to the nucleus of family, espouses a work/life balance, and is exceedingly comfortable with the tools of technology. These three traits work together to make this same geographic region more appealing to them as well. There is the prospect of raising their children in an environment where childhood is celebrated, not expedited, where outdoor recreation and adventure is the weekend focus—not additional time at the office and hanging out at the mall—and where volunteerism and service to the community is valued more than the consumption of what the community has to offer. This is a generation built on a sense of independence, self-reliance, and resourcefulness, and many of these people are comfortably able to work from the home with the many advances in technology. They are just as apt to prefer to buy a homesite first—while they rent their first home here—and begin the design process to conceive and create a residence that addresses the particular needs of their family.

This book is also, to a great extent, focused upon the quotation at the beginning of this chapter: *"It is one thing to not know the answers—quite another to not know the questions."* I have repeated this adage so many times in my life that I am sure there are more than a few of my colleagues and associates who have grown weary of hearing it. It has served me well to remember it, and it is my sincere hope that after you have read this book, you will be armed, maybe not with all of the answers, but at least with all of the questions. You can do without knowing the answers if you know the questions and have the willpower and perseverance to find the answers. If you know the questions, the answers will come, but no answer can ever come to the question that's never asked. In almost every tale of woe I have heard, it is the question that wasn't asked that raised its ugly head down the road.

Most of the second home buyers in this region of the southeast come from well outside the area, generally from more metropolitan areas that are comparatively flat in topography, well-served by centrally supplied, municipally served utility systems of all kinds, and served by a real estate development industry that is more highly regulated in order to protect their heavy populations. Because many mountain communities have none of these attributes, an unfortunate "void" exists in buyers' experiences that leaves them unprepared, without the tools and ammunition to seek out property from a position of knowledge and strength.

For example:

- If you've never experienced building a home that is served by a deep well for its source of potable water and by a septic tank and drain field for its wastewater needs, both of which are subject to very specific criteria dictated by the attributes of the land, how do you know what questions to ask when buying that land? (See Chapters Two, Three, and Four.)
- If you've never experienced building a home that may be situated on topography ranging from 10 percent to 40 percent in slope and blanketed in old-growth forest and granite

Introduction

outcroppings, how do you know what questions to ask about the proper siting of the home when buying that land? (See Chapters Two and Three.)
- If you're not familiar with the area, the culture, and the surrounding "lay of the land," how do you know what questions to ask that will lead you to a location and community that is right for you? (See Chapter Five.)
- If a developer or salesperson for a development is not being forthright about the information you need in order to make an informed decision, how will you know what you are *not* being told? (See Chapter Seven.)

From my perspective, more informed and knowledgeable buyers are the catalyst for the improvement of the second home, vacation home, and retirement home residential market in this area. If buyers are smarter, then developers have to provide a product—a homesite—that is responsive to that increased knowledge by improving the quality of the product and by disclosing the factual information that has a material impact on the buyer's decision to purchase. In addition, an increase in the scope and sophistication of statutory regulations by local governments can also play a significant role in improving the real estate development industry. (See Chapter Seven.) The lack of an appropriate level of land development regulations in some jurisdictions invites inexperienced, undercapitalized, and disreputable developers to thrive at the expense of the consumer and ultimately at the expense of the entire region.

Chapter Eight is a bit of a departure from Chapters Two through Seven in that land conservation, the primary focus of the chapter, isn't necessarily or even typically on the radar screen of many buyers. It is difficult enough to reach the plateau of success that affords one the opportunity to acquire a second home property. Clearly, it is the scaling of an additional set of financial rungs altogether that provides the freedom to purchase a tract of land large enough to consider the conservation of it (as opposed to the development of it) in perpetuity.

The sheer beauty of these Southern Appalachian Mountains attracts the interest of what may seem on the surface to be two mutually exclusive endeavors, development and conservation. Those interests generate two types of land transactions here on a very regular basis: the acquisition of large tracts of land by developers and individuals and secondly, the placement of conservation easements, by various land conservancies and land trusts, over large tracts of land that have significant habitat conservation value. Interestingly, western North Carolina in particular has become a fertile ground for the active and cooperative efforts of landowners and land conservationists to work in harmony to preserve as much land as possible while still allowing, in some cases, a limited degree of low impact development to take place.

When a region that is so rich in natural beauty and resources becomes a hotbed of in-migration and population growth, there is no singular source of political willpower or purse strings that can stop the train's forward movement. I give much credit to the land conservancies and trusts and the heightened ecological concerns of both the long-term residents of the area and the newcomers, who realize this and who have found a way to work hand-in-hand to conserve significant portions of the privately owned land here. Even if you don't have the wherewithal to be a direct source for these conservation efforts, you can play your part through demanding that developers be better stewards of their land by doing a better job of employing development practices that protect the land, and by volunteering with the countless nonprofit firms and groups in the area who are keenly focused on the preservation of our environment, our habitat, and our natural resources.

With the above thoughts in mind, I invite you to read ahead to hopefully benefit from some experience and insight that you may find useful in making a guided and informed decision, should you decide to relocate to the mountains. More than anything else, I hope that you enjoy reading this book as much as I have enjoyed writing it.

CHAPTER TWO

Do Your Due Diligence – Part I

Site characteristics and their impact on the viability of the land for your intended home

The Question:
What are the factors and variables regarding the physical attributes of the land that I need to analyze and understand in order to make an informed purchase of a mountain property?

TOPOGRAPHY

As a prospective homesite buyer, it is essential that you understand the impact of the topography of a given tract of land in the mountains. Topography is the configuration of the mountain's surface, including its relief and the position of its natural and human-made features. In this context, "relief" refers to the variations in elevation of an area of the mountain's surface. There are other more common terms that you might hear as substitutions for topography, such as "slope," "incline," "grade," "steepness," "contour," and "elevation." Topography is collectively all of these terms combined. From a practical perspective, it is the reason that you may or may not see your neighbors' homes from your window. It may be the major factor impacting the view (or obstruction) of sunrise or sunset. It will define how you handle the control and direction of storm water as it travels through your property. It might affect the ability to efficiently collect the sun's rays for passive solar heating. It may very well be the basis for your decision to choose CATV or to opt for satellite-sourced television signal reception. These are all practical lifestyle decisions that are never or rarely impacted by topographic factors and influences in flatter terrain. They are, however, significantly impacted in mountainous terrain.

Topography can affect the following, among other things: the most advantageous location for the home, the location and path of the driveway that will access the home, the orientation of the home to capture the views, the configuration of the home and its foundation type, the extent of the removal of vegetation required to provide the desired views, the location of the well that will provide the source for potable water, the location of the drain field area that will serve the wastewater disposal needs, and finally, the need for retention structures such as boulder walls and stone masonry walls to retain the earth.

Let's look at these variables individually.

1. The most advantageous location of the home

A viable homesite in what may appear to be difficult topography should have at least one area of the tract that is defined by a flat to gentle slope (from 0 to 15 percent) that can be easily graded to a level expanse capable of accommodating the size of the intended home's foundation or "building envelope." The existence of a rounded ridge, sometimes called a nose or finger ridge, is an excellent site characteristic if it is comprised of suitable soil (not solid rock) that can be graded effectively and inexpensively to a flattish contour in order to create a generous building pad area. If you happen to be fortunate enough to have more than one such area, then the other factors discussed here will impact the final decision of which alternative is chosen on which to locate the home. If the parcel of land has no area that fits this description, but you are otherwise infatuated with the property for a host of other valid reasons, don't fret; item four below should help to alleviate those concerns to some degree.

2. The location and path of the driveway that will access the home

Just because you may have found the perfect location for the home on the lot, that does not necessarily mean that you can find an appropriate access route from the main frontage road to the house pad. Difficult topography could easily result in a number of switchbacks (turns in the driveway that allow you to climb in elevation at a more gradual and safer pace), thereby lengthening the road and increasing the overall site preparation costs. (See Illustration 2.1.) Solid rock within the most advantageous path may need to be blasted, and retaining walls may need to be erected on the cut slope (the "high" side of the driveway) to hold back the earth. Large and prized old-growth hardwood trees may need removal, for which the homeowner's association (HOA) may not grant permission. All of these parameters should be evaluated, preferably with a design consultant, general contractor, and site contractor who are familiar with the community, as well as with a representative from the developer. If budget is a concern, it is critical that an acceptable driveway route be flagged and approved and that the cost impacts are understood as part of the due diligence process.

Everything You Need To Know About Buying Mountain Property

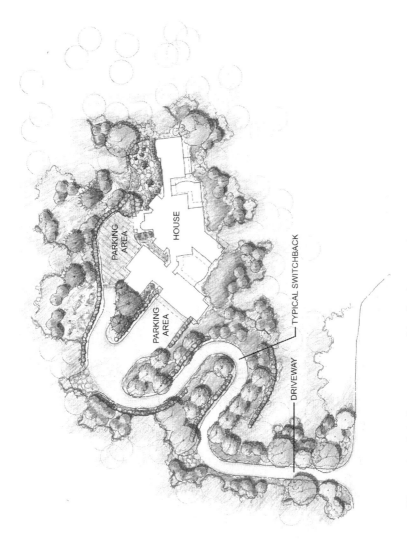

Illustration 2.1: driveway switchbacks that may be necessary in difficult topography

3. Orientation of the home to capture the views

The orientation of the home, the primary direction to which the main elements of the house point, is essential to capturing the spectacular views that draw so many second home buyers to the mountains. The multiplicity of views is no different conceptually than the variation in views that a coastal condominium might afford: ocean vistas and sunrises or sunsets, party boats and yachts meandering down the Intracoastal Waterway, the lights and excitement of downtown sights at night. Differing locations of a condominium unit within the same building will offer equally differing views of the horizon to which the unit is oriented. The same holds true for mountain vistas: the horizon can include sunrises or sunsets, long-range views of distant mountains or closer mid-range views where autumn colors will be breathtaking, nighttime views of the twinkling lights of nearby towns, lake or river views, pasture/pastoral views, farm views, etc. Beauty, as they say, is in the eye of the beholder, and that holds equally true for the variations within the horizon of mountain vistas that can capture the imagination. The point is that the property you choose should have the topographical characteristics that will allow you to orient the home's primary view corridors in the direction of the horizons and landscapes that you value the most.

4. The configuration of the home and its foundation type

The size of the building pad area that you can reasonably and efficiently create, which is a function of the existing topography, can have a significant effect on the configuration of the home as well as its foundation system. From a foundation perspective, the following alternatives are presented in the order of increasing topographical slope, starting with a flat building pad.

a) On a predominantly flat piece of land (0–10 percent slope) where the size of the building pad is practically limitless, there is no need to have a crawl space or basement of any kind if neither is desirable. Your foundation and your first floor slab can essentially be one and the same; this is commonly referred to as a "slab-on-grade." (See Illustration 2.2)

b) In gentle to moderately sloping topography (10–20 percent slope), a crawl space may be advisable, which is a nonhabitable airspace that may range in height from two to three feet at the shallowest portion to perhaps eight or nine feet at the deepest portion. (See Illustration 2.3 and Photo 2.1.) Crawl spaces allow you to transition the differential in the slope of the land (from the lowest end to the highest end of the land at the home's perimeter foundation) without the necessity of filling that space through expensive earthmoving operations. Crawl spaces also have the added benefit of providing enclosed (but not conditioned) space for storage and for the location of mechanical equipment that would otherwise need to be located within the living space of the home.

c) In the next category of steepness, let's call it moderately sloping topography (20–30 percent slope), a partial basement may be the best alternative. (See Illustration 2.4 and Photo 2.2.) This option involves both an unfinished crawl space area, where the shallower height of the foundation isn't adequate for a full height living space, and a finished basement area, where the height can accommodate useable living space.

d) In moderate to steep topography (30–45 percent slope), a full "walkout" basement may be the best alternative. (See Illustration 2.5 and Photo 2.3)
In this scenario, you have created an entire lower level floor of the home that is partially below grade; however, the lowest side of the basement is fully above grade, allowing you to "walk out" to the rear yard.

e) Finally, in steep topography (greater than 45 percent slope), the approach may not be to create a below grade, enclosed space of any kind but rather to elevate the entire house on a foundation system of vertical structures (columns or pedestals) that ignores any attempt to utilize the exiting topography. (See Illustration 2.6 and Photo 2.4) This involves extending columns vertically from the existing ground level up to an elevation where the first floor can be set upon those columns, resulting in a completely elevated first floor with open space below it.

A paramount issue here is to understand that each of these foundation systems generally progresses in expense, from the least costly at foundation type "a" to the most expensive at foundation type "e." *This is not, however, by any means, to suggest that the least expensive is best and the most expensive is the worst.* It is intended to inform you of what you might expect as a design element for the foundation portion of the home, so that you can understand and incorporate that element into the overall budget, function, and use of the home.

The second element in the title of this section is the configuration of the home. We have discussed the foundation, but I think it is equally important to discuss the impact on the rest of the home

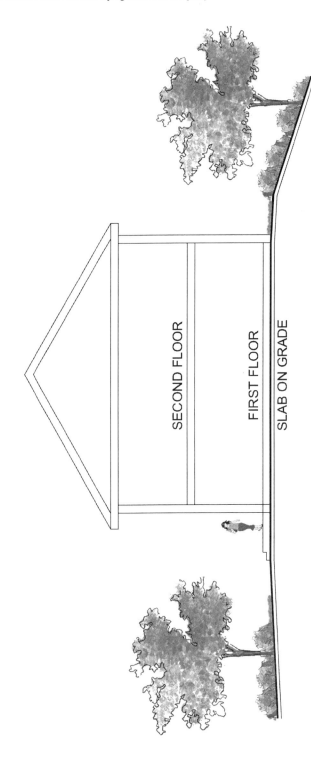

Illustration 2.2: slab-on-grade foundation type.

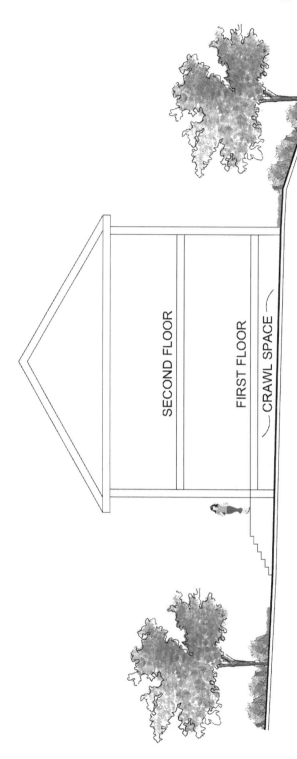

Illustration 2.3: crawl space foundation type

Photo 2.1: the outward appearance of a crawl space foundation type

Do Your Due Diligence – Part I

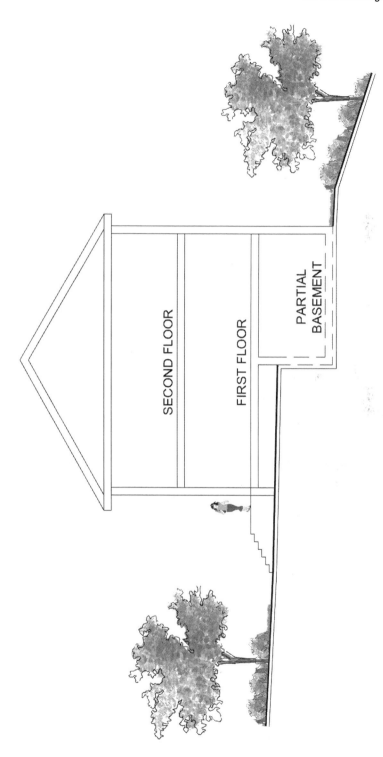

Illustration 2.4: a partial basement foundation type

Everything You Need To Know About Buying Mountain Property

Photo 2.2: the outward appearance of a partial basement foundation type

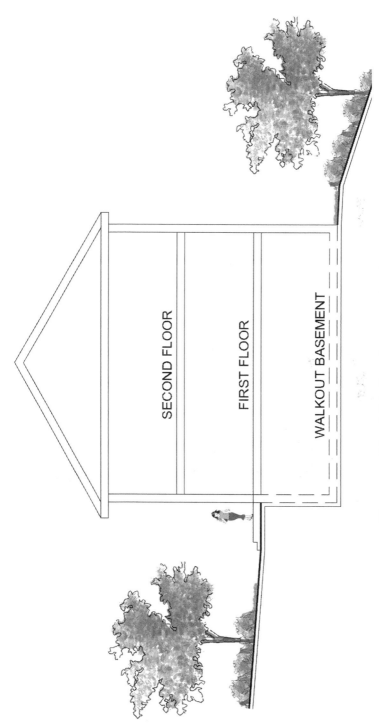

Illustration 2.5: a full walkout basement foundation type

Photo 2.3: the outward appearance of a full walkout basement type

resulting from a small or large building pad area (foundation). Simply stated, if you try to "fit" a particular amount of square footage onto varying foundation sizes, the smallest foundation will force you to build a multistory home, and the largest foundation might at least allow you to build perhaps a one-story home. Now a whole series of design questions starts to come into play. If multistory, what rooms go on what floors? Where do the stairs go? What rooms get exterior deck space? What rooms will get the best view? Where does the chimney from the first floor travel through the second floor to get through the roof? If more than one floor, will you want an elevator as you get older?

The idea that should be becoming clear to you now is that the attributes of a homesite in the mountains, in many respects, will define the design of the home. Again, the focus of this book is predominantly on how to go about buying land for the dream home that you want to build. However, I can't stress enough that you must avoid thinking of the land purchase and at least the conceptual home design as being two separate events. Do not make the mistake of being emotionally attached to the specific, detailed design of a home in advance of finding a homesite, unless you are willing to have the design of the home take precedence over the selection of the homesite. In my experience, the homesite should be selected first, and then the concept of the home you have in mind should be rearranged to fit the layout that the topography dictates.

5. **The extent of the removal of vegetation required to provide the desired views**

Topography plays a key role here because the faster that the sloping mountainside falls away from the house (i.e., the steeper the topography below the house, in the direction of the primary view),

Everything You Need To Know About Buying Mountain Property

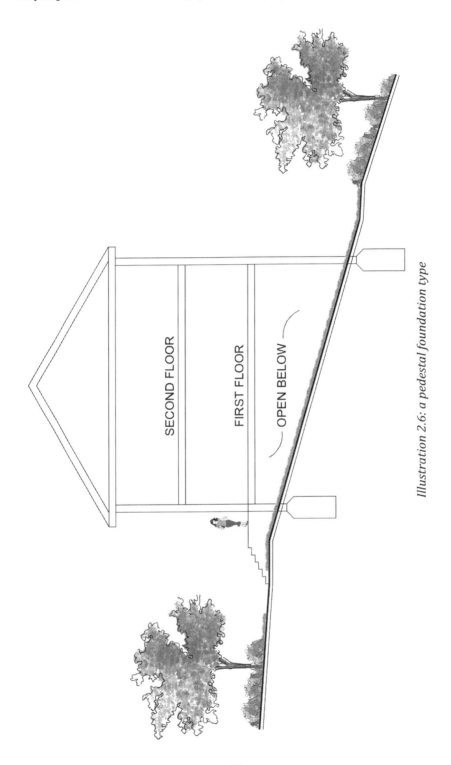

Illustration 2.6: a pedestal foundation type

Do Your Due Diligence – Part I

Photo 2.4: the outward appearance of a pedestal foundation type

the easier it will be to cut in that view corridor. (See Illustration 2.7a and 2.7b.) In other words, if the ground elevation slopes away steeply from the building pad, fewer trees will need to be removed, because the treetops will be below the view angle within a fairly short distance from the house; the fewer the trees that need to be removed to provide the desired view, the fewer the dollars that need to be spent to remove them. Moreover, both the community benefits and you benefit from minimizing the removal of the natural habitat that provides so much of the beauty in the first place.

There is one very important point to consider in the discussion of both orientation and view. It is perhaps somewhat counterintuitive to consider a visit to tour properties in the dead of winter. It is cold, probably overcast, windy, and downright unpleasant for some to trudge through a possible blanket of snow in these less than ideal conditions. However, the winter months are absolutely the best time to tour property, when the deciduous trees are completely defoliated. You can see with absolute clarity the exact views that may be available and can negotiate at that time regarding the developer's and the HOA's conceptual approval of the selective removal of enough trees within the corridor to expose the view.

It is best to keep in mind that most responsible developers have to continually balance the buyer's desire to uncover and expose the views, which give the property much of its perceived value and enjoyment, with the need to protect and preserve as much of the natural surroundings as possible. It is a difficult balance to achieve, because the competing demands of respecting the environment, on the one hand, are in direct opposition to the buyer's desire for unobstructed, stunning views on the other. Most developers know they have found an acceptable balance when neither party's interest is completely satisfied.

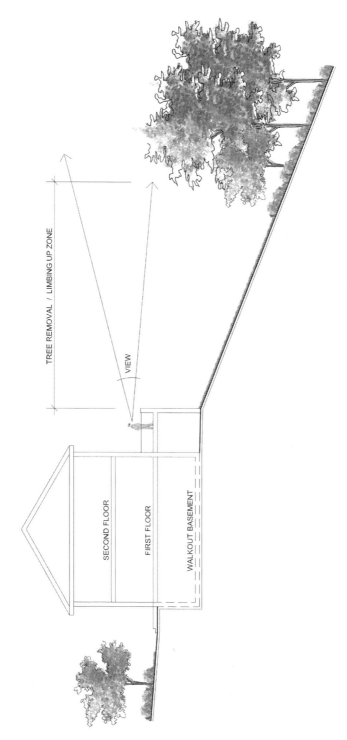

Illustration 2.7a: the decrease in vegetation required to be removed to open the views in steeper slopes

Everything You Need To Know About Buying Mountain Property

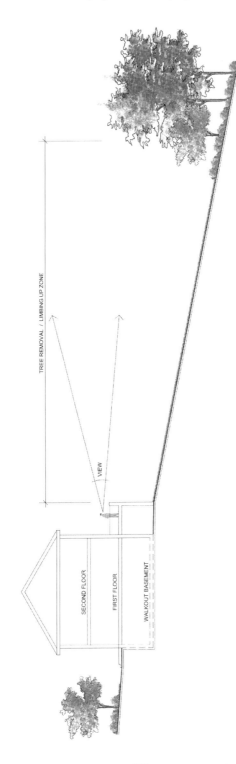

Illustration 2.7b: the increase in vegetation required to be removed to open the views in gentler slopes

Do Your Due Diligence – Part I

6. **The location of the well that will provide the source for domestic (potable) water**

The farther the well from the house the more expensive.

A large percentage of vacation home properties is located within rural enclaves that are situated well beyond the reach of public water systems. This means that unless the homesite is served by a "community well" that is internal to the development itself, which is quite atypical, you will be required to secure a domestic water source from within your own property, through the drilling of a deep well. (Please see Chapter Four for a more in-depth discussion of deep well issues.) From a logistical standpoint of coordinating with site topography, you need to be aware that a deep well needs to be located not only to conveniently serve the home (i.e., supply piping from the well needs to travel a practical route to the home), but also to be conveniently accessible by the well-drilling equipment and the vehicle on which this equipment is mounted. This is no small concern, because the well-drilling apparatus is large, bulky, and unwieldy, and it is incapable of either traveling through or setting up on areas that are anything but reasonably level with structurally sound ground conditions. (See Photo 2.5.) It may be that these restrictions on the rig's mobility require an installation location at a significant distance from the house, requiring a larger pump, increased electrical requirements, and greater lengths of supply piping to the home, all of which impact the costs associated with the delivery of water to the home.

Another important parameter, from a regulatory standpoint, is that local codes typically require the well to be located no less than one hundred feet from the closest point of any septic system tank, drain field, and designated repair area, whether any of those septic system components are on your property or your neighbor's property. The code requirement is for obvious reasons—to maintain a safe

Photo 2.5: well-drilling rig set up and ready to go

distance between the source of drinking water and the contaminants found within the effluent that the drain fields are intended to filter and disperse. The point here is that you do not have the freedom to place the well wherever you might please. The practical issue of access for the installation, combined with regulatory issues designed to ensure the purity of the water, dictate that the well be placed in an area that meets both parameters, which in turn may have a significant impact on site costs.

7. **The location of the drain field area that will serve the wastewater disposal needs**

For reasons analogous to the above scenario for sourcing water—the lack of a centralized system that extends to rural areas—wastewater disposal systems in many second home communities are also the responsibility of the homesite buyer within the confines of his or her own property. Unless a community wastewater system has been constructed, which is typically not the case, the homeowner will be required to construct his or her own on-site wastewater treatment system. (Please see Chapter Four for a more detailed presentation of septic/drain field systems.) Having a septic tank and drain field area to disperse the effluent is typical. A drain field location authorized by the local county health department is actually a requirement of the platting process in most county jurisdictions. That means that a homesite within a planned community cannot be transferred (sold) without the health department's approval of the septic facilities, which includes the specific location of the drain field. The topography of the site has a considerable impact on the location of the drain field, and, although its location has already been determined by the health department and is not a decision that the buyer needs to make, its location impacts all of the remaining site elements. The drain field area cannot be disturbed other than the disturbance required to install it. It cannot be located less than one hundred feet from any deep well, including the wells on the adjacent lots. It cannot have any structure built on it - not the home, the garage, the driveway, retention walls, or any other constructed element. It must be left in its natural state.

8. The need for retention structures

One of the common site requirements that results from the final layout and construction of all of the various site elements that serve the home and the location of the home itself is the erection of retaining structures/walls to hold back (retain) the natural elevations of the earth once the "unnatural" improvements have been put in place. (See Photos 2.6 and 2.7.) For example, when you construct a basically flat-surfaced driveway into a mountainside that is sloped to some degree, there may be certain lengths of the drive that are cutting across the slope (as opposed to rising or falling with the slope). If any portion of the driveway happens to run in close proximity to a neighbor's property line (a not unusual circumstance), you may not have the luxury of creating a sloped bank on the high side of the drive without encroaching on your neighbor's property line. If no other alternative seems viable for the driveway location, you can address the problem with a stone-clad masonry wall or perhaps a boulder wall, if the required height is substantial. These retention structures allow you to create an immediate change in elevation—from high at the top of the wall to low at the base of the wall—in situations where you do not have enough width of land to transition gradually.

Photo 2.6: a boulder wall that allows for the immediate change in elevation necessary to safely separate a descending driveway from the house (Photo courtesy of Sunset Falls at Bald Creek)

Photo 2.7: a stone masonry wall that retains the descending topography of the yard from the driveway (Photo courtesy of Sunset Falls at Bald Creek)

There is quite a variety of circumstances that might render the need for retaining walls in addition to the above example: the proximity of the driveway to the house, the creation of a flat area for gardens, a BBQ pit area or play area, the protection of the drain field area, and the protection of wetlands or streams, just to name a few. Again, their advantage lies in their ability to allow for an immediate change in elevation when there are restraints on the amount of land with which one has to work, such that a gradual slope will not accommodate the necessary change in elevation. It should be noted that retention walls have the added bonus, if constructed artistically, of providing very aesthetically pleasing elements that should dramatically complement the architecture of the home. Native stone and boulders, properly constructed, serve not only the structural purpose for which they are intended, the retention of the earth, but also provide architectural elements that serve to enhance the natural beauty of the surrounding landscape into which they are crafted.

In summary, the challenging topography of mountainous terrain, combined with the need to provide for on-site water and sewer facilities, creates a "puzzle" of interacting elements, all of which depend on each other and must be coordinated with each other. The ultimate goal is to locate the puzzle pieces in a logical and cost efficient manner to maximize the function that each of those elements serves. As part of that endeavor, you may want to seriously consider retaining a design firm that specializes in the site planning of these elements to provide you with a conceptual site plan that reflects your interests, prior to closing on the homesite. Consider it a very inexpensive insurance policy to protect you from the risk that you may not be able to achieve your desired design on the land that you have chosen.

9. Elevation, travel time, and weather conditions

This is a topic that, though not exactly internal to the attributes of the homesite itself, like the other eight topics, is significant, nonetheless, and can be the *most important* issue for many individuals. When potential buyers are asked for the most relevant attribute in their "must have list" of key features, "long range mountain views" is easily the most often repeated necessity. It may also be the necessity that is the most easily given up, once they fully understand what comes with that view.

Most sizable developments here in the mountains rise at least one thousand feet from bottom to top, and some even two thousand feet and more. In order to access the homesites with the most spectacular views, it is a given that one will need to make the vertical climb to reach those upper elevations. That takes time. The roads need to be constructed pursuant to the safe slope subdivision ordinances that govern them. The more safe the slope, the greater the time it takes to get from bottom to top. It would be wonderful if we could just put in the roads like ski lifts—straight up the side of the mountain—but we can't. And so with each safe traverse from one switchback to the next, you climb the mountain safely and hopefully still in one piece by the time you get to the top. In typical mountain topography, with a well-built, safe-slope roadway system, it may take six or seven minutes to climb a thousand feet. Some buyers are surprisingly taken aback by that time frame, as though they somehow imagined that you simply arrive at four thousand feet upon entrance into the community. From my perspective and that of those who choose to buy the homesites with stunning views, the drive to the top is simply one of the pleasures of getting there, and the views are the reward. Compare it to, say, a seven-minute drive in New York City or Atlanta or Miami, where you might get from one stoplight to the next, in between a few honks and a middle finger salute or two.

In addition to the longer drive home, be prepared for the weather to be a bit dicier as well. In a winter storm, it can actually be sleeting or even raining at the bottom of a mountain and snowing on the top. It can be thirty-six degrees at the bottom of the mountain and twenty-six degrees at the top. The wind might be blowing at 12 mph at the bottom of the mountain and 27 mph at the top. That's just the way it is. Again, some folks enjoy all that nature has to offer (to a point, of course), and some prefer the more predictable and even-keeled norms of a given climate.

Finally, if you don't already have one, if you're going to buy property in mountainous terrain and particularly at the upper elevations, get yourself a four-wheel drive or all-wheel drive vehicle. This is not an option; this is a must. And be prepared, occasionally, to replace the brake pads that wear out more quickly from the daily descents down the mountain...a very small price to pay, in my opinion, for all that beauty off your back porch. (See Photo 2.8)

Additional Reading: The following is an excellent article that Ms. Stephanie Pankiewicz of the firm, LandDesign, and Mr. Jason Gilliland of the firm, Site Design Studio, have graciously allowed me to reprint here, as its content—residential development in steep slope environments—is apropos to the topics explored in this chapter.

Reevaluating the Steep Slope Debate

The quality and quantity of hillside development has aroused a vigorous and intense debate in western North Carolina, with many people using the term "steep slope" as a catch-all phase to describe what is perceived as "improper" mountain development.

Photo 2.8: the awesome views from the back elevated terrace of a home situated at 4100 feet in elevation on relatively steep terrain (Photo courtesy of Sunset Falls at Bald Creek)

Such generalization is overly simple. Rather than the incline, what is often most upsetting are the environmentally damaging land-clearing disturbances that result in erosion, run-off and sedimentation that can harm local water resources. As upsetting and emotional for many is the negative impact on community views (view sheds), particularly as related to construction near ridge lines or predominant peaks that often is further exposed by clear-cutting of trees and under-story vegetation.

Reacting to these concerns, some local governments have responded by threatening or issuing moratoriums on all development (which has the potential to slow down the area's economic growth), or they create regulations focused mainly on the average slope within a minimum lot size. Area citizens, seasonal residents, real estate professionals, builders, developers, design consultants, politicians, environmentalists and other groups representing a variety of interests need to better articulate and agree upon the specific issues at the heart of this discussion in order to seek a fair and workable solution that allows proper development while maintaining the scenic and environmental qualities that make Western North Carolina an unique and beautiful region.

On the surface of this dialogue, the slope percentage allowed on a parcel or lot seems a straightforward way for local governments to control development so that construction occurs in a positive manner.

However, the variety of opinions and perspectives readily illustrate that "steep slope" does not have a commonly accepted definition. Any review of recent ordinances and laws being proposed for western North Carolina mountain jurisdictions indicates a wide range of standards used as the basis for discussion. Environmental groups tend to consider any grade over 15 percent as steep slope, while builders and developers contend that up to 30–33 percent is acceptable for a standard residential foundation.

Most of the regulations either enacted or under consideration by local governments focus on slopes of 25 percent and higher. The Safe Artificial Slope Construction Act (NC House Bill 1756), currently under consideration, would require a plan prepared by a qualified engineer for any development that occurs on grades greater than 40 percent or in "landslide hazard areas" as mapped by the North Carolina Geological Survey.

Interpreting Slope

Adding to the confusion is the difficulty in interpreting and visualizing these degrees of slope, particularly as they relate to building sites. A 33 percent slope, for example, extended over the 30-foot width of an average home footprint involves a drop of just 10 feet.

From the standpoint of affordable construction, including the costs of site excavation and grading, this would allow for a direct front access to the first floor entry and a walkout basement that maximizes land use and adds value to a home. An easy way to demonstrate this is to place a tape measure on top of a yardstick and extend it out 10 feet to the ground, which illustrates a 3:1 ratio or 33 percent slope. Constructability above this percent is often more difficult, leading to taller foundations and intensive tree clearing.

Land planners, such as civil engineers and landscape architects, can provide proper planning and site evaluation techniques for development, regardless of the parcel size or slope. As part of a preliminary site evaluation, a slope analysis map can be prepared that accurately depicts slopes based on a minimum of five-foot contour intervals.

Using topographic survey information, the grade ranges within the site can be mapped in order to highlight slopes 33 percent and below. This should be verified by the planner through a physical investigation (i.e., site visit) of the property.

Additional data can be provided through a geotechnical report, prepared by a qualified professional that certifies a site is geologically suitable for its proposed use and provides recommendations for safe, stable grading and development.

An environmental expert may also perform a stream and wetlands survey to make certain such features are properly identified and protected. Based on this information, a land planner can identify "building envelopes" or the pockets of land within the site that are suitable for development and construction purposes. This approach makes certain the structures in the development are positioned in response to the characteristics of the site rather than arbitrarily placed based on a lot size or slope gradient.

This building envelope then dictates the size of the structure that can be built, generally within an area measuring approximately 100 by 100 feet. In practice, the use of a suitable building area, or envelope, is no different than a suburban lot with defined front, side and rear-yard setbacks that dictate where a structure can be built. In the case of a mountain development, the identification of building envelopes within individual parcels can ensure proper density, eliminate slope-related issues, and limit clearing of trees and vegetation.

The identification of building envelopes also maintains natural drainage patterns, protects stream corridors and wetlands, and contributes to preservation of open spaces within a development, further minimizing environmental impact. The utilization of Best Management Practices (BMP) and Low Impact Design (LID) methods can mitigate erosion, sediment and storm water impacts. Preferably, these should be applied to each specific building envelope as well as the overall development, which enhances their effectiveness.

The town of Waynesville adopted this approach recently in its new Hillside Conservation Development design standards and regulations. In its documents, the town noted that the regulations were mandatory "to implement a vision for development within hillside areas, in essence, to blend structures into the surrounding landscape offering an aesthetically pleasing community which places emphasis on enhancement and preservation of the Town of Waynesville's natural beauty and mitigate adverse impacts to the environment."

The town's policy outlines specific requirements for building envelopes and architecture, the latter establishing aesthetic criteria for building style and materials. Structures also are to be positioned within the building envelope "in response to access, slope, unique vegetation, landforms and orientation toward vistas."

Protecting Views

This relationship to vistas points to an issue that has become one of the more critical and contentious components of the current steep slope controversy. Sensitivity to the community view shed has aroused significant concern and emotional response among citizens who resent the visible intrusion of structures on the higher elevations.

A major cause is clear-cutting, which often is utilized primarily to provide access to an individual view corridor, a highly valued feature of life in the mountains. However, this also exposes the property/structure to others, which can be perceived as detrimental to the overall community view shed.

One workable answer might be to require selective trimming that can provide the desired view without unnecessary exposure. This may involve "limbing up" trees to open up views, rather than cutting the trees down. Attention also should be given to preserving the native under-story vegetation that can shield properties from view and reduce opportunities for erosion and run-off. The inclusion of a registered landscape architect and certified arborist into the planning process can help make certain that the correct approaches are used to both allow for generous views while maintaining the overall beauty of the site.

Another solution is increased use and enforcement of design guidelines, such as those established by the town of Waynesville or prepared by private developers to dictate the range of items that characterize a development or even a single home.

The first requirement of the document should be proper site analysis and identification of suitable building envelopes. The design guidelines, whether prepared by a developer or set by local government, then can make certain that views are protected, structures are suitable in scale and composition to the site, including the height of the overall structure and the height of the foundation.

They also can ensure that damage to the land is minimized even as far as requiring the use of existing logging roads for access (improved to current roadway standards) and/or shared driveways. Design guidelines also can specify acceptable building materials (non-reflective, for example) and even colors, such as natural earth tones to better blend into the surrounding environment.

Setting well-thought out standards for steep slope development is imperative to protect the beauty of the North Carolina mountains while allowing for growth. In many cases, the preservation of views and protection of the natural environment are the greatest concerns.

A common understanding of slope percentages, proper site analysis, and investigation and application of design guidelines are excellent tools that planners, developers and citizens can utilize in order to achieve a mutually acceptable solution.

Everything You Need To Know About Buying Mountain Property

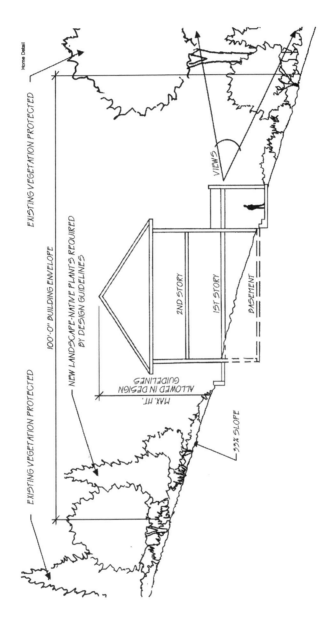

Figure 1 – Typical Building Envelope Cross-Section prepared by LandDesign, Inc.

CHAPTER THREE

Do Your Due Diligence—Part II

The "Paper Chase"—documentation and investigation

**The Question:
What documentation and information should I request from the developer/seller to review prior to signing a purchase agreement for a homesite within a community, and what further investigation should I conduct on my own?**

1. The Plat (or Plat Map or Plat Survey)

A plat is a map or survey, recorded in the official records of the county in which the property is located, of an entire subdivision, including every homesite and all of the common areas within the development. (See Illustration 3.1)

Due to the sizes of these communities, there may be multiple pages or maps, each one covering a certain portion of the community. When taken together, they represent the entire map of the whole community, and you need to make sure that the particular homesite that you are interested in buying is duly reflected on one of those sheets. The

Everything You Need To Know About Buying Mountain Property

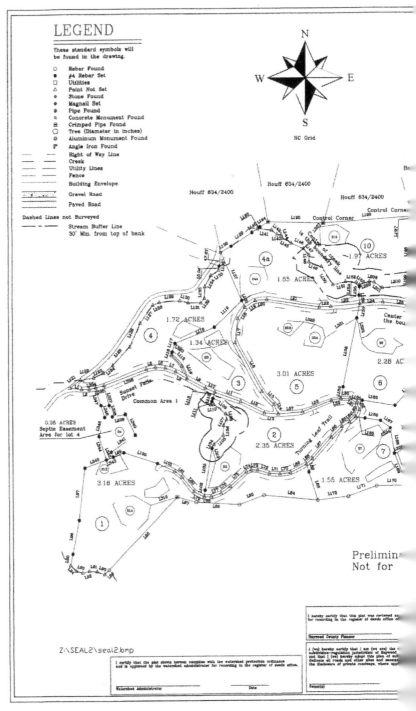

Illustration 3.1: Portion of a plat map

Do Your Due Diligence—Part II

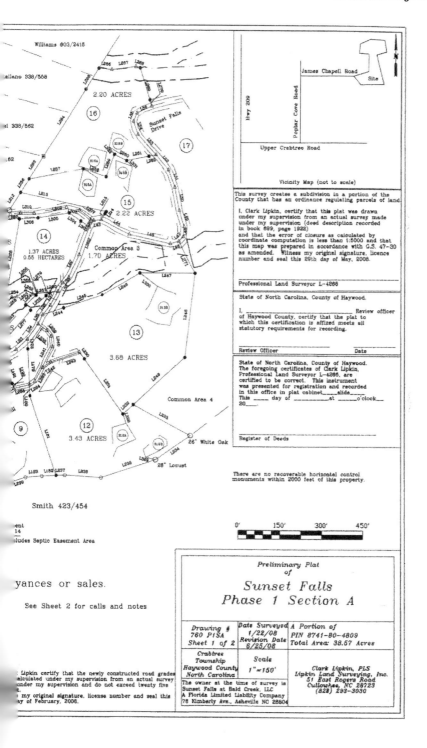

plat shows the exact boundaries of each and every lot and of each and every common space serving the community. It also may show various easements and rights-of-way, typically dedicated to utility providers; encumbrances such as greenway buffers around streams and wetlands (a good thing); and encroachments (usually a bad thing) such as a sliver of a neighbor's septic field that "encroaches" or travels within the boundaries of the adjacent homesite that you are looking to purchase. The plat of your lot is a very important document for you to obtain, prior to closing, for a couple of reasons.

The first is that it graphically reflects what it is that you are buying and what and where the impacts are by others who have certain rights to your property or have applied certain restrictions to your property. For example, the power company and the phone company have the right to come onto your property where their easements are located in order to construct, restore, repair, and otherwise maintain their facilities in good working order. They also have the right to restrict you from building or placing anything within the boundaries of that easement that would negatively impact their services or prevent them from properly maintaining their services. Most easements are good things, giving the providers of the utility services that you want for your home the ability to provide them freely. Some easements are not good things, like an access easement that your future neighbor might have to travel through the middle of your property, right through the living room of the home you were planning to build there.

The second reason that the plat is so important is that it is a recorded document, a document that is recorded or legally recited in the official public record books of the county having jurisdiction. This means that the law will rely on this document, should there be any dispute regarding the exact boundaries of ownership and the rights that others may have via recorded easements and other encumbrances clearly reflected on the plat. This is not to say that the plat will necessarily reflect all such impacts and rights of others to and on your property. There may be other easements and encumbrances that exist on separate recorded documents that are not shown on the plat. The firm that you engage to write the title insurance policy will be sure to unearth any and all documents that exist in the public records that affect the property. The important point is to *get a copy of the recorded plat—understand it—have your attorney review it.* Let your attorney advise you on the impacts to your land. Your job is to understand how the impacts affect what you want to build and where you want to build it.

2. A Topographic Survey

The best way to understand what a topographic survey is and what it intends to show is to imagine that you are up in a hot-air balloon, looking straight down on a particular piece of property. You have no problem seeing the extent of the two-dimensional horizontal area of the land below you, but you can't make out the third dimension, the change in vertical height of the ups and downs of the various ridges and valleys, hills and dales, etc. A topographic survey addresses this problem of adding a third dimension to a two-dimensional map by showing what are known as "contour lines," each of which represents a specific elevation, typically a certain distance above sea level. (See Illustrations 3.2a, 3.2b, and 3.2c.) It isn't really the distance above sea level that is intrinsically important, but the distance in elevation change from each contour line to the adjacent contour line and the spacing between each line. For example, many topographic maps of an individual homesite are done on "two-foot centers," meaning that each contour line that the survey locates is two feet higher (if above) or lower (if below) than the adjacent contour line. If the contour lines get very close together in an area of the topographic map, then the terrain is steeper in this area. If the contour lines are more spread out, then that portion of the survey is indicative of flatter terrain.

It may take you a bit of time and practice to fully understand topographic surveys three-dimensionally, but just trust that any good developer should have a builder and site contractor available to assist you who should have no problem interpreting the topographic survey while walking the site with you. The goal in obtaining this document prior to closing the transaction is to get a very educated feel for the best location for the foundation of the home and the driveway and a comfort level for the magnitude of potentially significant site costs involved in earthmoving and retention walls, if the terrain dictates their need.

3. Health Department Approvals for Drain Field and Well Locations

In most counties, a precondition to plat approval (and thus, to the developer's legal right to sell homesites) is the health department's evaluation and approval of the septic/drain field system. (See Exhibit 3.1 in the Appendix at the end of this chapter.)

The approval is preliminary in nature, meaning that the final approval is given when a home is actually being permitted for construction, but it does give an authorization for a drain field location and type and for the maximum number of bedrooms that the future home can have. Even though you are only purchasing the land at

Do Your Due Diligence—Part II

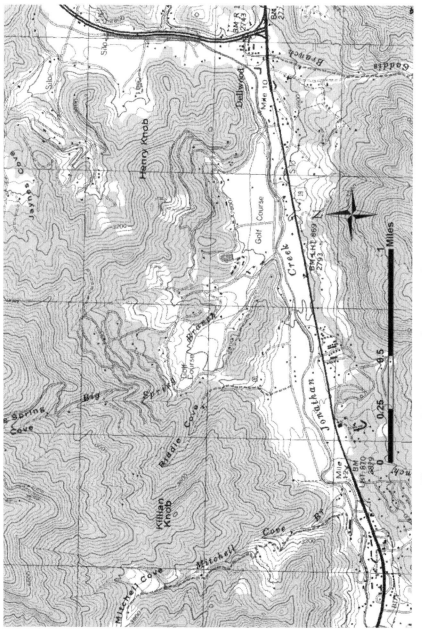

Illustration 3.2a: Topographic map – plan view without relief

Everything You Need To Know About Buying Mountain Property

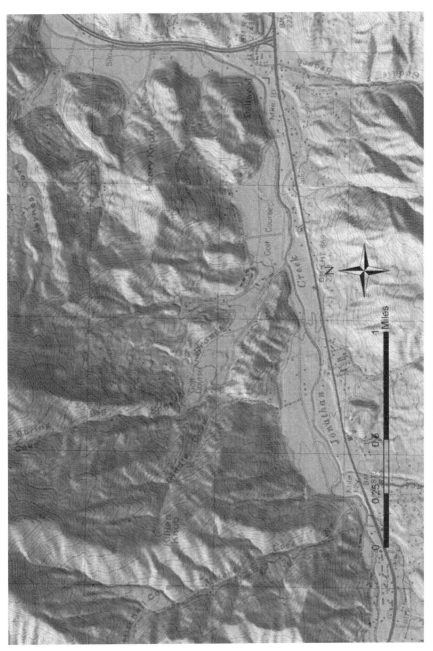

Illustration 3.2b: Topographic map – plan view with relief

Do Your Due Diligence—Part II

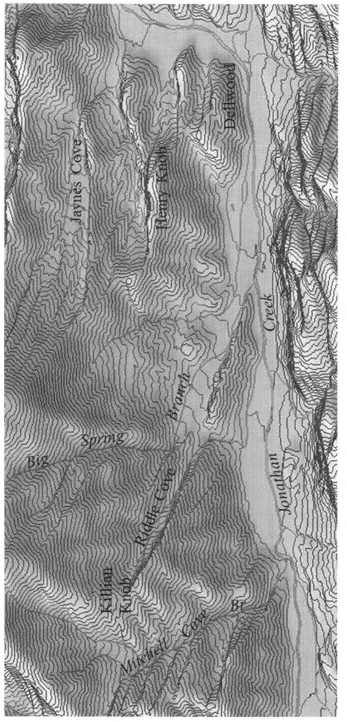

Illustration 3.2c: Topographic map – oblique perspective view.

this time, the health department is actually doing you a huge regulatory favor by doing the legwork in advance of your purchase, to assure you that your homesite can indeed accommodate a drain field area that will serve a future home of enough bedrooms to suit your plans and family needs.

Oftentimes, the health department's approval will also show an acceptable location for the drilled well that will become the source of your family's domestic water needs. These health department approvals for the drain field and well locations, combined with the information from the plat and topographic survey, will provide you and your architect with all of the "pieces to the puzzle" to allow you to logistically lay out all of the elements of your future home. The ability to coordinate the pieces allows you to design the site and the home in a manner that is feasible and practical and which, further, makes the most sense financially.

All of these efforts can and should be accomplished as part of the due diligence process, prior to ever closing on the acquisition of the homesite. Engaging an architect or planning firm to assist you is a very worthwhile endeavor that can be accomplished in a comfortable time frame prior to closing. It makes no sense to discover that a parcel of land will not accommodate your future plans for a home after you have already purchased it. The investment is usually far too large for most people to risk a piecemeal engagement in due diligence efforts. You may certainly decide to build later—but you should confirm now that you *can* build later and that you can build the home you want to build.

4. The Covenants, Conditions, and Restrictions, (also known as the CCR's, the Protective Covenants, the HOA Documents, or the POA Documents)

The covenants, conditions, and restrictions comprise a set of documents that govern certain aspects of almost all newly subdivided residential communities, and they are recorded in the public records of the county in which the community is located. The fact that they are recorded means that they are legally binding documents that "run with the land," as they say, i.e., are binding upon all of the parties that own a homesite within the community that is subject to these governing documents. The CCRs outline, often in very specific language, how the HOA will operate and the various rules and regulations by which all homeowners must abide. There is typically a collection of related documents that make up a complete set of CCRs:

- the covenants, conditions, and restrictions
- the articles of incorporation
- the by-laws
- the rules and regulations
- the legal description of the property
- amendments (if any)

For our purposes, we're going to focus on the CCRs and the rules and regulations. These two documents contain language that may have potentially significant impacts on you personally and on how you want to live in your own neighborhood. These are the documents that contain the language that may have a practical impact on your decision to buy or not buy—or to buy, but with perhaps some added language to the purchase agreement to clarify issues of concern to you within the language of those documents.

Prior to jumping into the specifics of the areas within the documents that are a potential cause for concern, let me offer the following two pieces of advice. Covenants are, by and large, a good thing for the large majority of the buyers who become subject to them. Their very purpose, intent, and impact are reflected in a particular change over time in the terminology used to reference them. They used to be called "restrictive covenants," and now they are more often referred to as "protective covenants." That is because, from a marketing and connotation perspective, people would much rather feel that they are being "protected" and not "restricted," and that is really the purpose of the documents—to protect your investment financially and to protect your right to peacefully enjoy your investment from the nuisance that can sometimes be your neighbor. The notion of restrictive versus protective is of course in the eye of the beholder. If you want to do something that the documents do not permit, then you are apt to feel that you are being restricted. On the other hand, your neighbors probably feel as though they are being protected from your indiscretions. Suffice it to say that the covenants are intended to allow what reasonable people—i.e., the bulk of the population—would want for themselves and their neighbors and to disallow what those same reasonable people would find distasteful, unattractive, unpleasant, or a nuisance. If you are a very independent sort who has a strong inclination to live by your own set of rules and regulations, different from those by which the rest of the world lives, I would advise in all candor that you look for property that is not subject to a traditional set of CCRs. You will probably value your freedom there more than the protections you will have relinquished elsewhere.

The second nugget of help is this: if you really are in love with a community and a particular homesite within that community, and if there is language within the covenants by which you believe you cannot abide, at least make the effort with the developer to voice your concerns, to see if the person is willing to address those concerns to your satisfaction. Covenants are renowned for having inappropriate or inapplicable language within them that even the developer has neglected to catch and modify or delete. Covenants are, after all, initially generated from a lawyer's database of his or her most current set of covenants for a similar type of property. At the time that the development is just starting to take shape and the developer is anticipating the sales process, the developer's attorney will ask a number of questions, the answers to which will form the basis of customizing the covenants to the community in question. It is not at all unusual that the draft of documents sent over to the developer for review is not examined with a truly fine-tooth comb by the developer, and language ends up staying in that should have been removed or, at the very least, modified to suit this specific community. A developer's failure to review every article and every paragraph of the documents can result in the loss of a sale to a potential buyer who is simply too shy to question the content of the language. This is an unfortunate and unnecessary loss for both the developer and for the buyer, who might otherwise have gone through with the purchase had he or she known that the developer may have been willing and able to address the concerns through clarifying the meaning of the language.

If you find language within the covenants that is unacceptable to you, the best way to discuss and negotiate an addendum to the purchase agreement with the developer is to focus on the *intent* of the language. I often find that when the buyer understands what I am trying to achieve with the language—what activities, habits, situations, and conflicts I am trying to control or prevent—the person then understands that he or she has no intention or desire to violate them, and we have the basis for an understanding. Conversely, when I am able to understand the buyer's intent, and I can conclude that his or her intentions are honorable and not in conflict with the spirit of the language, then I can find new language we can both agree on, to add to the purchase agreement, that satisfies both of our concerns.

I want to be clear here that I am not suggesting that the developer has the right to add or delete language from the covenants on an individual basis with each buyer. Quite to the contrary, every buyer who purchases a homesite that is subject to a set of covenants has the right to expect the enforcement of those covenants. The developer certainly does have the right to make certain amendments to the covenants during the developer's period of control; however, such amendments shall equitably affect all buyers in the community. My point above is that oftentimes the developer can clarify the *meaning* of the language within the covenants, in an effort to arrive at an understanding with the buyer as to the *intent* of language, thereby securing the sale of a homesite that benefits both the developer and the buyer.

As almost all legal documents are wont to do over time, a set of CCRs has become thicker and thicker in order to address each and every new legal case and decision that comes down the pike. It is beyond the scope of importance to cover all of the topics that one might find. Accordingly, I have focused on the ten most arguable and contentious areas from my own experience with buyers. I have also tried to elucidate some examples of how a clearer understanding of the purpose and spirit of language in the covenants can be reconciled to the needs of the buyer, to arrive at compromises that are acceptable to both parties. Keep in mind that it is the concept and notion of "reasonableness" that is typically the overriding factor when it comes to the interpretation of covenants, should a dispute arise in the future.

a. Restrictions on Animals and Pets

Some of the more common restrictions in a set of covenants are those placed on the things that many hold so near and dear to their hearts, their pets. Specific rules may restrict the types of animals that may be owned, the quantity of animals that may be kept, the particular housing of the animals within the homeowner's property, and the requirement for restraint of animals, particularly within the common areas of the community. You will not be able to devote a portion of your yard to a small pig farm; you will not be able to breed dogs commercially on your property as a primary business; you will not be able to leave your bloodhounds outside all night if they moan, whine, and bark to come inside; and you will not be allowed to let your man-eating, alpha male canine roam the community untethered and free to attack whatever moves. To find out what you reasonably can do, here is a sample of a paragraph you may find in a set of covenants that is intended to address concerns about animals and pets:

Animals and Pets

Raising, breeding, or keeping animals, livestock, or poultry of any kind, except as permitted by Declarant on specifically designated Lots, shall be strictly prohibited. No animals of any kind shall be kept by any Owner or Occupant upon any portion of the Community, with the exception being that a reasonable number of generally recognized house pets (not to exceed three), may be kept in Dwellings, subject to rules and regulations adopted by the Association. All pets shall be registered, licensed, and inoculated as required by law. It is provided that such pet or pets are kept or maintained solely as domestic pets and not for any commercial purpose. It is further provided that dog houses, kennels, fenced runs or pens for the outside housing of any pet shall be subject to the approval of the ARC, which it may grant or deny in its sole discretion.

No pet shall be allowed to make an unreasonable amount of noise, to endanger the health or safety of other Owners or Occupants, or to become a nuisance. Pets shall be under leash at all times when walked or exercised in any portion of the Common Area, and the owner of any pet shall clean up after said pet. Upon the written request of any Owner or Occupant, the Board may conclusively determine, in its sole and absolute discretion, a particular pet is a generally recognized house pet or such pet is a nuisance. The Board shall have the right to require the owner of a particular pet to remove that pet from the Community if it is found to be a nuisance or to be in violation of these Rules. The Board shall also have the right, subject to the Governing Documents, to fine any Owner or Occupant for his or her violation(s) of these Rules, and that Owner or Occupant shall be liable to the Association for the cost of repair of any damage to the Common Area caused by that pet. Any such fine or cost of repair shall be added to and become a part of that portion of any Assessment next coming due to which such Dwelling and its Owner are subject.

You will note that the language restricts the maximum number of pets to three. Now, will I or the community care if you have four house cats that relieve themselves in litter boxes and rarely venture outside? No. I will care much more (and so will your neighbors) if you have just one unspayed large tomcat that is left outside on a regular basis and howls a wail of a mating call throughout the wee hours of the morning. If we can agree that your four cats are all neutered and will stay inside or, if outside, will be reasonably contained, etc., then I'm sure we can arrive at some language by which we both can abide.

b. **Renting Your Home**

There is rarely, if ever, an absolute restriction on renting your home out to others; however, there is quite often a stipulated minimum duration of time for which you can rent it, coupled with a maximum number of times per year that you can rent it to a different party. Here is a paragraph that is typical:

Renting and/or Leasing
Lease or rental of a Dwelling for Single Family Residential purposes will also not be considered to be a violation of this covenant so long as the lease (a) is for not less than the entire Dwelling and all the Improvements thereon, and (b) is otherwise in compliance with Rules and Regulations as may be promulgated and published from time to time by Declarant or the Board. **All leases or rental agreements shall be in writing and shall be for a duration of six (6) months or more unless, for good cause shown, the Board permits, in writing, a shorter term.** *Upon request, the Owner shall provide Declarant and the Board with copies of such lease or rental agreement. Any Occupant will in all respects be subject to the terms and conditions of this Declaration and the Rules and Regulations adopted hereunder.*

Let's talk about intent again. The developer is not trying to prohibit you from making money, but to the contrary, would love for you to stay as financially healthy as you possibly can, so that your home doesn't go into foreclosure and become an eyesore for the community. The developer is, however, justifiably concerned about the transient use of properties within the community by outsiders who have no vested interest in the neighborhood. First and foremost, renters have no emotional or financial connection to the community and thus are a much greater risk to neglect or even abuse the owner's property or the common areas or both, and they are far less inclined to live within the rules of the community, since there are often no repercussions for them if they do not. Secondly, short stays are typically vacation stays, which may entail lots of partying and carousing into the night, at the expense of the sleeping habits of the neighbors (unless, of course, they're invited). Thirdly, if the community is gated but not manned, it means more potentially untrustworthy folks having access codes to the community if they have been entrusted with them, which can easily jeopardize the security of the residents. So the clear intent, from the developer's perspective, is to not give rise to the nuisances that strangers (renters) can become through a risky relaxation of the rental rules.

Part of what makes this language a nonstarter for some prospects is that they intend to use the future home solely as a vacation home, meaning variable and occasional use on their part. Many find the supplemental income generated by the freedom to rent it out—on whatever terms they wish—to be a major financial incentive to buying the property in the first place. They may fully intend to place it on the Internet through a website such as Vacation Rental by Owner or to place it in the hands of a local brokerage/rental management firm in order to maximize the income. If you do plan to utilize your property this way, you need to become very familiar with the language on rental restrictions before you buy, if the community is subject to a set of covenants, conditions, and restrictions.

c. **The Ability to Subdivide**

You may have the idea that a great investment strategy would be to purchase a larger lot than you really need and, at an opportune time in the future, subdivide it into two or even more lots. You may be able to recapture some of, all of, or even more than the original acquisition cost of the land, depending on the strength of the market and the relative success of the community. Unfortunately, there is typically a prohibition against the buyer subdividing any of his or her property in the future without the developer's consent. There are two primary reasons for this: (1) the developer does not want to lose control of good planning and civil engineering practices by having a homeowner, who is inexperienced in the codes, intricacies, and details of development, compromise the integrity of the infrastructure of the community; and 2) the developer has no interest in competing with additional homesites coming onto the market in his or her own community. A standard paragraph addressing this issue might be as follows:

<u>Subdividing, Combination and Boundary Relocation</u>
No Lot shall be subdivided, or its boundary lines relocated, for any purpose other than to merge an additional Lot or part thereof so as to create a Lot larger than the original Lot without the written consent of the Declarant during the Declarant Control Period or thereafter the Association; provided, however, Declarant hereby expressly reserves to itself, its successors or assigns, the right to re-plat, combine or subdivide any Lot or Lots, shown on the recorded plats, prior to the conveyance thereof, in order to create a modified Lot or Lots. These restrictions herein apply to each Lot which may be so created. Following the combination of two Lots into one larger Lot, only the exterior boundary lines of the resulting larger Lot shall be considered in the interpretation of this Declaration. Once combined, the resulting larger Lot may only be subdivided with the written consent of Declarant or the Board. The Board, in its sole discretion, shall determine what effect, if any, the combination or subdivision of a platted Lot has on the Assessments for that modified Lot.

One interesting note that can be inferred from the language is that a developer, as a rule, has no objection to a buyer combining adjacent homesites to make one larger one. In the event that you wish to pursue a combined purchase, if the covenants do not state otherwise, I would strongly suggest that you add language to the purchase agreement that recognizes your purchase as that of a singular lot for the purpose of HOA dues, so that you are not charged more than the HOA dues for one homesite. The developer may require that the multiple lots be replatted as one lot to afford you this benefit, which I would do in a heartbeat if I were the buyer. In fact, I would make it part of the negotiation that the developer pay for and complete the replat as a precondition to closing.

d. **Rules Regarding the Operation and Storage of Motor Vehicles, Trailers, Boats, etc.**

Here is a fairly standard paragraph addressing this issue:

Motor Vehicles, Trailers, Boats, Etc.
Each Owner will provide for parking of automobiles off the streets and roads within the Community. There will be no outside storage or parking upon any portion of the Community of any mobile home, trailer (either with or without wheels), motor home, tractor, truck (other than pick-up trucks), commercial vehicles of any type, camper, motorized camper or trailer, boat or other watercraft, boat trailer, motorcycle, motorized bicycle, motorized go-cart or any other related forms of transportation devices, except in a Dwelling's garage. Any permitted parking of a mobile or motor home within a garage will not be construed as permission for any person to occupy such mobile or motor home, which is strictly prohibited. Furthermore, although

not expressly prohibited hereby, the Board may at any time prohibit or write specific restrictions with respect to the operating of mobile homes, motor homes, campers, trailers of any kind, motorcycles, motorized bicycles, motorized go-carts, all terrain vehicles (ATVs) and other vehicles upon any portion of the Community, if in the opinion of the Board, such prohibition or restriction will be in the best interests of the Community. Such policies may change from time to time with changing technology. The storage of any such vehicles within a garage will be permitted, even if operating the same is prohibited. No Owners or other Occupants of any portion of the Community will repair or restore any vehicle of any kind upon or within a property subject to this Declaration except (a) within enclosed garages, or (b) for emergency repairs, and then only to the extent necessary to enable the movement thereof to a proper repair facility.

It is quite common to have a prohibition on the exterior storage of motorized vehicles of any kind. I find this to be overly burdensome and unnecessary. The prevailing sentiment for most homeowners in these more rural settings is that they should be permitted to park a maximum of two vehicles (cars or noncommercial trucks) on a daily basis within the driveway area of their property, outside of the garage space. I would agree that trailers, boats, commercial trucks, ATV's, etc., can be somewhat of an eyesore, particularly when they are not kept up in good condition. However, what I think is reasonable is not the point here. The point is to read and understand this language, and if you anticipate a potential problem, but really love the community and homesite, then be sure to try to negotiate some acceptable language with the developer for an addendum to the purchase agreement.

As an example, perhaps you have a large RV that cannot fit into a garage. Suppose also that you're interested in a perimeter lot, one that is located on the outer perimeter of the development, with no community neighbor behind you. Your home design will allow a space behind the garage for the RV, out of the sight and view corridor of anyone in the community, including your neighbors. Is this a valid request? I would think so. As a developer, my concern is that I not allow an individual to compromise the enjoyment of his or her neighbors and others in the community. Every rule cannot address every situation, so some situations need to be looked at individually for the details of how they do or do not impact the community. Some developers will take a hard stand, preferring not to have to spend their time assessing the justification; it's just easier to say no and avoid the time and effort in authoring language that will reflect the intent of both parties. My view is that the essence of getting deals done is the willingness to compromise, as long as the integrity of the community is not threatened.

e. **Restrictions on the Building of Multiple Structures on One Homesite**

Most of the current covenants for single-family residential neighborhoods do not allow for more than one primary structure—the main home—and one unattached structure—typically a garage, perhaps with living quarters above the garage. The practical purpose behind this restriction is to prevent the housing of multiple families within the confines of a singular lot. Additionally, it prevents the possible usage of the property for "hobbies" that can easily grow into mini-commercial and manufacturing enterprises, which are clearly not allowed and are so noted in other areas of the covenants. Multiple families and commercial enterprises tend to become a nuisance to the rest of the community through overburdening the community with a disproportionate share of traffic and noise and the negative visual impact of multiple buildings that have the potential to overwhelm the lot and destroy its curb appeal.

It is interesting to note that covenant language has now become common that specifically disallows the construction of a secondary structure in advance of the primary structure. This language came about in response to individuals who built the garage and living quarters above it and then never built the primary home; this left what appeared to be a garage with no residence. It is human nature that we always want to blame lawyers for "over-lawyering" a document; unfortunately, it's the small minority of people with bad intent that creates the problem in the first place. Every bad apple creates another paragraph of legalese that burdens all of us at some time in our lives. Here is some typical language that addresses the issues of multiple structures:

*Number of **Structures**[1] on Lots*

Unless otherwise provided in a Supplemental Declaration, no structure on a Lot will be constructed other than one (1) Single-Family Dwelling and one (1) accessory building, which may include a detached private garage, servant's quarters, or guest house, provided a single structure may incorporate all of said uses and provided such Dwelling or accessory building does not overcrowd the Lot and is not used for any activity normally conducted as a business. Such accessory building may not be constructed prior to the construction of the main building. A guest suite or like facility may be included as part of the main building or accessory building, but said suite may not be

---

[1] A "**Structure**" shall mean anything artificially erected or installed on or under a Lot, including, but not limited to, any building, outbuilding, lampposts, driveway lights, fence, wall, swimming pool, tennis court, detached antennae, satellite dishes, mailboxes, fuel tanks, dog lots, or play sets.

rented or leased except as part of the entire premises including the main Dwelling in accordance with the provisions of this Declaration. Notwithstanding the above, all of the above-mentioned structures shall be subject to the approval of the Architectural Review Committee, as hereinafter defined, and conformity with the Architectural and Design Guidelines, and Rules and Regulations as set forth in Article VI of this Article.

f. Acceptable Range of Square Footage Size of the Home

Many of the new residential developments in second home markets now delineate either a minimum or a maximum square footage (or both) for the size of the conditioned space of the home. Note that this is the "conditioned" or "heated" living space. That definition does not include the garage or any exterior deck space, which can be substantial in mountain homes due to the amount of time people intend to spend on the porches and terraces enjoying the mountain air and the views. In recent years, the minimum square footage permitted in the covenants has trended downward to accommodate the general trend of folks downsizing their space needs. Tougher economic times have witnessed a refocusing by people on what they really need as opposed to what they might want…and what they truly need is almost always significantly less than what they may want.

The stipulation of an allowable minimum home size is obviously intended to preclude a buyer from designing and constructing a home that is so small that it detracts from the quality, market price point and perceived character of the community. The typical minimum might be in the sixteen hundred to eighteen hundred square foot range, though highly amenitized communities that cater to a wealthier clientele can certainly exceed that range. It may not be as readily apparent why a set of covenants would limit a home size to a maximum square footage, but developers do have a concern about the construction of ostentatious "McMansions" that can overwhelm not only the homesite but the entire community as well, by engendering a sense of ill will and disharmony within an otherwise cohesive community.

The critical issue here is for the buyer to be aware that such restrictions may exist within a community and to be sure that the home that one intends to build is compatible with the minimum and maximum parameters, as articulated in the covenants. You will note that in the particular example of covenant language below, a maximum height of thirty-five feet for the home is mandated, as is the requirement for a minimum two-car garage. Again, if you're not prepared to conform to the requirements in the covenants for design that can affect both what you want and how much you want to pay for what you want, then you may need to look elsewhere; alternatively, if you're in love with the community and the homesite, try to have the conceptual design of your home approved in advance of the purchase and have explicit approval of that design included as part of the purchase agreement preconditions to closing.

Square Footage, Garage and Height Requirements

Unless otherwise provided in a Supplemental Declaration, all residential Dwellings constructed on the Lots shall have a minimum of one thousand six hundred (1,600) square feet of **Heated Living Space**.[2] *Each Dwelling shall have, as a minimum, a 2-car garage,*

---

[2] "Heated Living Space" is defined as being the enclosed and covered areas within the Dwelling, exclusive of garages, carports, porches, terraces, balconies, decks, patios, courtyard, greenhouses, atriums, storage areas, attics and basements; and a minimum of one thousand (1,000) square feet of such conditioned space shall be required on the first floor alone (excluding all other floors).

unless otherwise provided in the Governing Documents, including the Architectural and Design Guidelines, and shall not exceed thirty-five feet (35') in height as measured from ground elevation. Even though there is no maximum square footage requirement set forth in this Article, approval by the Architectural Review Committee as hereinafter defined, may be conditioned upon a determination, made in its sole discretion or pursuant to design criteria, that the Dwelling or accessory structure will not crowd the Lot and not be aesthetically out of character with the Lot's surroundings.

g. **Restrictions on Tree Removal**

This language can be a real source of argument in a community that truly enforces the written word of the covenants. Typical language will state that any property owner may remove any trees on his or her property that are eight inches or less in diameter (typically measured about four or five feet above the ground) without an approval from the HOA. The removal of trees larger than this must have written approval from the HOA. The potential for conflict typically doesn't arise from the tree removal that is required to build the home and the various site elements; clearly, once the location of the house has been approved, trees that fall within the "construction zone" area of the homesite must be completely cleared. The problem arises when the property owner desires to open up the view away from the house to the long-range mountain vistas that give the property much of its perceived value. A responsible developer is often put in the position of balancing two competing efforts: 1) to retain as much of the natural beauty as possible by limiting tree and habitat removal; and 2) improving the values and increasing the sales volume of the development by, among other things, allowing long-range views to be established through the removal of the very habitat one would prefer to leave in place.

There is frankly very little that one can do in advance of purchasing a homesite to receive approval to remove *specific* trees that exceed the mandated diameter, unless the developer simply doesn't care about the enforcement of this language. This is because there is no way that one can definitively determine where and to what extent the views need to be opened up until the construction of the home is complete and the primary view corridors are established. Developers understand the value of the spectacular long-range vistas that draw so many second homebuyers to the area. In most instances, they will be willing to work with you to minimize the obstruction of the view corridors while retaining the character and integrity of the community. Your concern at the purchasing stage is to understand what the language says about the issue of tree removal and to understand how this might affect the views that you anticipate having once you build your dream home there. If the overriding basis for the decision to purchase a particular homesite was the potential views that the property would have, it would seem quite a shame if you were unable to appreciate those views when the time comes to live there. Here is a reasonably standard paragraph that you can expect in the covenants that addresses this issue:

Trees

No Owner, other than Declarant, shall be entitled to cut, remove, or mutilate any tree, shrub, bush or other vegetation having a trunk diameter of eight (8) inches or more at a point of four and one-half (4 ½) feet above ground level, (or other significant vegetation as des-

ignated from time to time by the ARC) without obtaining the prior approval of the ARC; provided, however, that dead or diseased trees which are inspected and certified as dead or diseased by the ARC or its representatives, as well as other dead or diseased shrubs, bushes or other vegetation, shall be cut and removed promptly by the Owner thereof. Nothing herein shall be construed so as to limit any applicable law or ordinance.

1. **Greenway Restrictions**

For those of you who value the presence of water on your property—streams, creeks, and other wetlands—you should be aware that if the developer has properly permitted the community through the appropriate environmental channels, there will be restrictions on what you can and cannot do within specific buffer areas that abut these water courses. The Army Corps of Engineers (ACOE) and the Department of Environment and Natural Resources (DENR) have regulatory authority over these elements, and rightly so. These permitting and regulatory agencies are charged with the task of keeping these waters (and the larger bodies of water into which they feed) as clean as possible by protecting them from the activities, particularly development activities, that have the greatest chance of polluting them.

The ACOE and the DENR have created specific language that they require developers to adopt in their covenants, the purpose of which is to restrict the types of activities and construction that are allowed to take place within a certain buffered (protected) distance from the water course, typically thirty feet from the bank on each side of a stream. This means, for instance, that you should not plan on building the exterior decks of your home to within ten feet of that babbling brook to maximize the tranquility of the peaceful sounds that it affords. You will be able to enjoy it...just not so up close and personal. If you honestly have a respect for the environment and habitat around you, you'll view these restrictions as a win/win for you and the environment and an asset to the larger community.

In the below example, excerpted from a set of real covenants governing a local community, you can see that an entire article was devoted to the subject, which underscores the seriousness with which the ACOE, DENR, and environmental causes in general hold these requirements. In this particular instance, the developer does not have the right to negotiate anything less restrictive or less protective on behalf of the environmental agencies. The best that the developer can do is make an inquiry on your behalf for an interpretation of the language and advise you accordingly.

Preserved Greenway Restrictions

A. *Purpose & Declaration*

At the time of the recording of this Declaration, Declarant is the sole owner in fee simple of the certain "Preserved Greenway" (the "Greenway") being approximately ten (10) acres, more particularly described on the Plat. The purpose of restricting the Greenway is to maintain wetland and/or riparian resources and other natural values of the Greenway, and prevent the use or development of the Greenway for any purpose or in any manner that would conflict with the maintenance of the Greenway in its natural condition. Declarant hereby unconditionally and irrevocably declares that the Greenway shall be held and subject to the restrictions, covenants and conditions as set out herein, to run with the subject real property and be binding on all parties that have or shall have any right, title, or interest in said property. This covenant is to run with the land and shall be binding on all parties and all persons claiming under Declarant, including the Association as the intended successor in interest of the property making up the Greenway.

B) *Prohibited & Restricted Activities*
1. *Generally*
Any activity on, or use of, the Greenway inconsistent with the purposes of this Section is prohibited. The Greenway shall be maintained in its natural, scenic, and open condition and restricted from any development or use that would impair or interfere with the conservation purposes of this Section.
2. *Disturbance of Natural Features*
Any change, disturbance, alteration or impairment of the natural features of the Greenway or any introduction of non-native plants and/or animal species is prohibited.
3. *Construction*
There shall be no constructing or placing of any building, mobile home, asphalt or concrete pavement, billboard or other advertising display, antenna, utility pole, tower, conduit, line, pier, landing, dock or any other temporary or permanent structure or facility on or above the Greenway. Pedestrian bridges, picnic areas and other low impact recreational features are permitted in the sole discretion of Declarant during the Declarant Control Period and thereafter the Association.

4. *Industrial, Commercial & Residential Use*
   Industrial, residential and/or commercial activities, including any right of passage for such purposes are prohibited.
5. *Agricultural, Grazing & Horticultural Use*
   Agricultural, grazing, animal husbandry, and horticultural use of the Greenway are prohibited.
6. *Vegetation*
   There shall be no removal, burning, destruction, harming, cutting or mowing of trees, shrubs, or other vegetation on the Greenway. The removal of dead vegetation, invasive species and poisonous, harmful or dangerous vegetation is permitted in the sole discretion of Declarant during the Declarant Control Period and thereafter the Association.
7. *Roads & Trails*
   There shall be no construction of roads for vehicular purposes on the Greenway. Declarant during the Declarant Control Period and thereafter the Association shall be permitted to include hiking trails on the Greenway.
8. *Signage*
   No signs shall be permitted on or over the Greenway, except the posting of no trespassing signs, signs identifying the conservation values of the Greenway, signs giving directions or proscribing rules and regulations for the use of the Greenway and/or signs identifying Declarant or the Association as the owner of the Greenway.
9. *Dumping or Storage*
   Dumping or storage of soil, trash, ashes, garbage, waste, abandoned vehicles, appliances, machinery or hazardous substances, or toxic or hazardous waste, or any placement of underground or aboveground storage tanks or other materials on the Greenway is prohibited.

10. *Excavation, Dredging or Mineral Use*

    There shall be no grading, filling, excavation, dredging, mining or drilling; no removal of topsoil, sand, gravel, rock, peat, minerals or other materials, and no change in the topography of the land in any manner on the Greenway, except to restore natural topography or drainage patterns, in the sole discretion of Declarant during the Declarant Control Period and thereafter the Association.

11. *Water Quality & Drainage Pattern*

    There shall be no diking, draining, dredging, channeling, filling, leveling, pumping, impounding or related activities, or altering or tampering with water control structures or devices, or disruption or alteration of the restored, enhanced, or created drainage patterns. In addition, diverting or causing or permitting the diversion of surface or underground water into, within or out of the easement area by any means, removal of wetlands, polluting or discharging into waters, springs, seeps, or wetlands, or use of pesticide or biocides is prohibited.

12. *Development Rights*

    No development rights that have been encumbered or extinguished by this Section shall be transferred pursuant to a transferable development rights scheme or cluster development arrangement or otherwise.

13. *Vehicles*

    The operation of mechanized vehicles, including, but not limited to, motorcycles, dirt bikes, all-terrain vehicles, cars and trucks is prohibited.

14. *Other Prohibitions*

    Any other use of, or activity on, the Greenway which is or may become inconsistent with the purposes of this grant, the preservation of the Greenway substantially in its natural condition, or the protection of its environmental systems, is prohibited.

15. Wetland Mitigation Compliance

   In accordance with the requirements of the U.S. Army Corps of Engineers pertaining to preserving wetland mitigation property, the following language shall apply to and take precedence over any contrary language in this Declaration:

   "The areas shown on any recorded Plat as wetland conservation areas shall be maintained in perpetuity in their natural or mitigated condition. No person or entity shall perform any of the following activities on such wetland conservation area:
   a. fill, grade, excavate or perform any other land disturbing activities
   b. cut, mow, burn, remove, or harm any vegetation
   c. construct or place any roads, trails, walkways, buildings, mobile homes, signs, utility poles or towers, or any other permanent or temporary structures
   d. drain or otherwise disrupt or alter the hydrology or drainage ways of the conservation area
   e. dump or store soil, trash, or other waste
   f. graze or water animals, or use for any agricultural or horticultural purpose

   This covenant is intended to ensure continued compliance with the mitigation condition of a Clean Water Act authorization issued by the United States of America, U.S. Army Corps of Engineers, Wilmington District, Action ID, and therefore may be enforced by the United States of America. This covenant is to run with the land, and shall be binding on the Owners, and all parties claiming under it."

   This language cannot be amended without the express written consent of the U.S. Army Corps of Engineers, Wilmington District.

C. *Enforcement & Remedies*

This covenant is to run with the land and shall be binding on all parties and all persons claiming under Declarant.

_____

D. *Public Access*

This Section does not convey to the public the right to enter the Greenway for any purpose whatsoever.

i. **Street Disclosure Statement**

This disclosure is mandated in many areas now and exists as a statewide general statute in some instances, because it can have a significant impact on the HOA budget and the privacy (or lack thereof) of the community to which it applies. (Please see Chapter Four on infrastructure concerns for a more detailed discussion of the public vs. private impacts.) If the roads are public, the cost and the obligation to maintain them are borne by the Department of Transportation. If the roadways are designated as private, those same costs and responsibilities are the obligation of the HOA. Most buyers interested in a gated community value the privacy and extra level of security that a gated community affords and understand that if the community is gated, by definition, the roads will be private, if they don't allow access to the general public. Unfortunately, these buyers don't always make the mental leap that "private" implies the roads' upkeep by the HOA; therefore, the intent of this language is to make that point crystal clear to the consumer. Here is some standard language that, in this case, references a general statute of the state of North Carolina and is an acceptable form of disclosure for this issue.

Roads; Street Disclosure Statement

*As of the recording of this Declaration, Declarant is in the early stages of developing the Community. At this early stage, Declarant intends that the roadways within the Community shall be privately maintained and not intended to be developed for takeover by the North Carolina Department of Transportation (the "**DOT**") or any other Governmental Entity. As private roads, the roadways within Sunset Falls at Bald Creek shall be constructed by Declarant to the minimum standards required by Haywood County which may include approved variances from such specifications. The schedule and completion of the construction and the design of said roads shall be within the sole discretion of Declarant. As private roads, the maintenance of same shall be borne, through Member Assessments as provided in Article X, by the Association or a Neighborhood Association as directed in writing by Declarant. This disclosure is given in accordance with N.C. Gen. Stat. §136-102.6. Notwithstanding the above, Declarant reserves the right to designate or re-designate any street within the Community as dedicated for public use and offer same for maintenance by a Governmental Entity. In that event, Declarant shall certify at the time of acceptance by the applicable Governmental Entity that the right of way and design of the street in question has been approved by said entity and that the street has been or will be constructed to such Governmental Entity's standards.*

j. **The Operating Budget of the HOA**

A final disclosure that you should request from the developer as an exhibit to the covenants is the budget for the HOA. If the community is still under construction and in its infancy stage, from the standpoint of infrastructure and amenity completion, the budget will be an educated guess at best, because many of the components of the development are not far enough along to even obtain bids for their maintenance. If a developer cannot yet define the total scope of the specifications for maintenance, it is obviously difficult to arrive at a real budget. That isn't to say that a close approximation isn't attainable. It depends on the developer's experience and database of historical costs of maintaining a similar community or the developer's success at engaging a community management firm that does have that experience to assist with the budgeting process.

If the community is mature, with all of the infrastructure and amenities completed, the budget should be quite accurate, barring some unforeseen emergency or natural disaster that impacts the community's common areas, amenities, or infrastructure. Get a copy of the budget from the developer before you close on the homesite. Read it. Understand it. Give it to your accountant. Ask questions. Most HOA budgets are relatively straightforward. A line-by-line analysis of them is not part of the intent of this book. Simply stated, the most important thing for you to review is what the monthly, quarterly, or annual (depending on how often they bill their clients) charge is per homesite. Can you afford it? That's great if you can. Now let's ask some other questions.

If the community is indeed a mature one, and the infrastructure and any amenities have been in place for at least five to ten years, it is reasonable to assume that the facilities are showing at least some traces of wear and tear. A responsible developer (or board of directors of the HOA) will budget for what are known as reserves, that is, for items of future replacement that can be costly. For example, suppose there is a clubhouse that has a roof that is ten years old.

A reasonable estimate of the shelf life of a roof is perhaps twenty years, which means that the roof may need to be replaced in ten more years. There is one scenario, albeit a painful one for the homeowners, where the roof is replaced in year twenty, and every homeowner at that moment in time is assessed his or her fair share of that roof replacement cost, with what is known as a special assessment. The alternative scenario, and one which is much more palatable and equitable, is that the HOA has been reserving funds to address this inevitable expense for twenty years, essentially putting in its piggy bank each year one-twentieth of the projected cost to replace the roof in year twenty. The point here is that you should take notice, when you are touring the community, of the general state of the facilities that the POA is required to maintain, and if you have some concerns, check the HOA budget to see if it includes reserves to replace those elements that are subject to a fixed shelf life. One of the most unpleasant surprises is to be hit with a special assessment for the replacement of a very costly element of the amenities, soon after you have purchased your property. You end up footing a very large bill when your responsibility should have only been for a fraction of it, had they properly reserved for the expense in the past.

In addition to the above, I would confirm that the association is covered from an insurance perspective. I would confirm that the HOA has a line item for snow and ice removal if the community is in a climate where that may be of concern. And finally, I would confirm that an expense line item is allocated for year-end accounting professional fees, to be sure that the HOA is operating pursuant to acceptable accounting guidelines and that if the developer is still managing the association, he or she is paying a fair share of the total budget.

(See Exhibit 3.2 for a typical HOA budget for a small community with modest amenities in the Blue Ridge Mountains.)

Everything You Need To Know About Buying Mountain Property

Operating Budget Projections

	Annual Total	Notes
Ordinary Income/Expense		
Income		
Membership dues	47,380.00	53 lots @ $120.12/mo.
Miscellaneous Income	0.00	
Total Income	47,380.00	
Expense		
Administrative Expenses		
Bank Charges	180.00	Standard monthly bank account fees. May not be applicable depending on bank.
Insurance	6,000.00	Property, liability, ($7,500) Directors & Officers ($2,500)
Management Fees	4,800.00	
Miscellaneous Administrative	0.00	
Office Supplies	240.00	
Postage and Delivery	240.00	
Printing and Reproduction	240.00	
Professional Fees	2,500.00	Annual tax prep and audit, plus contingency for legal fees
Telephone	720.00	$60/mo for 3 low-use lines - one for the pool area emergency phone, one for the pool card access system, and one for the gate at the main entrance.
Taxes & Corp. fees	55.00	$20/year to file corporate annual report, no property taxes for non-profit HOA, $35/yr. franchise fee for State of NC
Total Administrative Expenses	14,975.00	
Common Area Expenses	0.00	
Clubhouse Maintenance	600.00	
Fitness Equip. Maintenance	285.00	
Sauna Maintenance	240.00	
HVAC Maint.	1,200.00	Standard quarterly equipment service, filter changes, routine PM.
Basketball Courts	0.00	
Holiday Decorations	500.00	Holiday décor at main entrance and at club building
Janitorial Service Clubhouse	3,750.00	Clubhouse cleaning every other week during non-swim season, weekly Memorial Day to Labor Day (approx. $125/cleaning)
Janitorial Supplies	600.00	Toilet paper, paper towels, cleaning supplies, etc.
Landscaping Contract	9,600.00	Full service contract for common areas, bi-annual roadside mowing
Landscaping - Other	0.00	Contingency for tree removal, plant replacements, etc.
Pest Control	1,200.00	Pest control and termite contract renewal for club building
Trail maintenance	0.00	Mulch or other treatment as may be needed to maintain the trail system.
Greenway FF&E	0.00	
Bridge Maintenance	600.00	
Road Maintenance	1,200.00	
Signs	120.00	
Snow/Ice Removal	200.00	Contingency for spreading ice-melt around club entrances and entry gate
Swimming Pool Maintenance	2,500.00	Opening in spring, cleaning, chemical maintenance, winterization
Pool Chemicals	500.00	
Pool Fence & Gate	120.00	
Pool Furniture	120.00	Cleaning and storing pool furniture each fall, setting up each spring
Utilities		
Electric - Clubhouse	2,100.00	
Electric - Entrance sign/landscape	240.00	
Electric - Gate	480.00	
Electric - Pool	600.00	
Water - Clubhouse & Pool	1,650.00	Water only - septic sewer.
Propane - Clubhouse & Pool	4,000.00	Assumes propane use for pool heater, indoor fireplace, water heater, kitchen range, and heat pump w/gas backup for club (2500 to 3000 gal usage/yr at Mar. 08 prices)
Total Common Area Expenses	32,405.00	
Total Expense	47,380.00	

Exhibit 3.2: Property owner's association budget

5. **The Architectural Design Guidelines**

Almost every new residential community that is subject to a set of covenants, conditions, and restrictions is also subject to a set of architectural design guidelines (ADG). The interpretation and enforcement of those guidelines is the primary function of the design review board (DRB) (often referred to as the architectural review committee as well), which is typically comprised of the developer and/or resident members of the HOA Board as well as architects and landscape architects who have a detailed understanding of the community and the architectural theme and program that defines the aesthetics of the community. The purpose of the guidelines is typically described as follows:

- to encourage excellent, diverse, yet compatible home designs that reinforce the sense of neighborhood
- to provide direction to homesite owners, architects, landscape architects, contractors and other members of the design team
- to create a framework for consistency of architectural design while allowing room for individual creativity and expression

Consistent with the purpose of the covenants, the ADGs are intended to protect the value of your property, in this case through the guidance, direction, and specifications of the site design elements and the exterior architectural finishes, colors, and details of the home. (The interior of the home is of no real concern to the architectural and aesthetic themes and controls with which the ADG's are concerned. The elements of the interiors of homes are private in nature and not within view of anyone but the families who reside in them.) The goal is *not* to remove the design independence and creativity of your architect. The language within the ADGs is meant to steer and guide, not to mandate and dictate. For instance, the language of many ADGs will articulate the architectural styles that are acceptable: American Lodge, American Craftsman, Adirondack, etc. Some architectural detail sketches may actually be provided to more clearly depict the styles that are acceptable for the community, but the intent is not to remove your architect's individuality from the equation. In the same manner, the exterior finish materials that the ADGs allow are typically referenced generally: wood siding, stone veneer, natural logs, etc., as opposed to calling out the actual species of wood, stone, or logs.

Today's custom residential architect is intimately familiar with ADGs and with how to operate and design within the parameters of the language and direction provided by them. Part of his or her job will be to coach you through the design process to ensure that what you want to achieve with the design falls within the acceptable style and materials outlined in the guidelines. There are, as a rule, four classic stages of design that define the architectural process: 1) conceptual, 2) schematics, 3) design development, and 4) construction documents. The stages allow for step-by-step confirmation from the DRB (if necessary) that the design falls within the intent of the guidelines, to ultimately allow for a smooth and uneventful final approval by the board.

Why is it important to review the detail of the ADGs now, when you may have no plans to build for perhaps five years? Because you want to be sure at the time that you purchase your homesite that the style of your dream home is generally consistent with the ADGs, and because many ADGs preclude the use of certain materials or styles altogether that you may have planned on using, which would be an awfully unpleasant discovery to make five years later. For instance, it is not uncommon to see kit log cabins completely excluded from the permissible home types; brick and stucco are both very commonly excluded building materials in the mountains, except perhaps at crawl spaces and as an accent material; barrel tile and other Mediterranean-style roofing materials are also frequently impermissible; and in the higher-end communities, a product known as Hardy Plank, a very commonly used siding product, is typically not permitted.

One provision of a set of ADGs that you should be aware of is any fees that are associated with the architectural review process. Architects and landscape architects rarely provide their services to the developer and HOA for free, so there is usually a schedule of plan review fees that are associated with the various steps in the process. If you are fortunate enough to have a developer and/or an HOA with members who have the skills to review plan submissions, the fees may be waived. Finally, it is not unusual for the ADGs to stipulate a refundable deposit required of the homeowner upon the issuance of a building permit for the home. This is to cover potential damage to the roads and other common areas resulting from the construction of your home. As a homeowner responsible for these potential repair costs, you should make your builder keenly aware of the issue and provide language in your contract with the builder that he or she will be fully responsible for the cost of any such repair and deposit holdbacks.

To briefly summarize, architectural design guidelines provide the vehicle by which the developer and the HOA can help to ensure the "curb appeal" quality of the community. The site planning, architecture, and landscape architecture of each home is held to a standard of style, quality, and cohesiveness that protects the aesthetic integrity of the community, while allowing enough diversity to accentuate the individuality of each home. You should view these documents as "protective" and not "restrictive" and should appreciate them for the purpose they intend to serve. Real estate appraisers place a higher value on homes within communities that are subject to these protections for a reason, and the cooperation that each property owner affords to the community will only serve to solidify those values.

6. The Property Report (if Required) Pursuant to the "Interstate Land Sales Full Disclosure Act" Administered by the Department of Housing and Urban Development (HUD)

If there is one thing that every consumer can rely on, it is that the real estate development industry will never have a shortage of unscrupulous developers. Historically, they have had the uncanny ability to ruin the environment for all developers due to the increase in onerous regulation that inevitably follows in the wake of their destruction. It isn't that regulation, in and of itself, is necessarily a bad thing. It is more so an unfortunate but necessary thing, an across-the-board enactment of burdensome and expensive governmental red tape, the costs of which are inevitably absorbed by the consumer in the price of the product (real estate) that is the subject of the regulation.

In 1968, the Interstate Land Sales Full Disclosure Act (ILSA) was enacted by Congress to facilitate regulation of interstate land sales in order to protect consumers from fraud and abuse in the sale of land. The legislation was a direct result of the classic land sales schemes invented by devious developers to take advantage of unaware, out-of-state buyers. Those who were caught up in the schemes relied on the smoke and mirrors of sleazy sales and marketing pitches, only to find out later that they owned a lovely parcel in the middle of the Everglades with no water, sewer, power, or roads…and no way to recoup their investments.

ILSA, with several exceptions, requires the developer of residential subdivisions of one hundred or more lots to register the development with the United States Department of Housing and Urban Development. The document that is produced from that process, known as a property report, is intended to disclose a significant amount of information about the development that you, as a potential purchaser, would not otherwise have available to you. It is a stipulation of the law that you be given a copy of the property report before executing any contract or purchase agreement. The information is factual in nature, and you should be aware that HUD has not judged the merits or value of the property and is not issuing an opinion one way or the other about the relative worth or quality of the development. HUD is simply requiring the developer to disclose pertinent facts regarding the property in an effort to protect you from purchasing an asset that you might not have otherwise purchased without the information. The law also provides you with the added protection of a seven-day rescission period (a period of time that you can legally cancel the contract), if you were provided the property report in advance of signing a contract as required, and a two-year period during which you may cancel the contract if you were not provided the property report before signing a contract.

The problem is that there are numerous residential subdivisions in the mountains that include fewer than one hundred lots and which are therefore exempt from the HUD requirement, which is one of the many reasons that I wrote this book. Without such a document as the property report, you are put into the position of having to rely on the developer's sales staff to provide you with the information, much of which is verbal and may be subject to omissions, misinformation, disinformation, exaggerations, half-truths and otherwise. If there is something that is important to you that you cannot verify on your own, have it put into writing as part of the contractual agreement to purchase the property.

Below is a fairly typical table of contents that might be included in a property report. Most of the topics are fairly self-explanatory, and where they are not, I have elaborated on many of them in other parts of this chapter or in other chapters in the book.

a. Risks of Buying Land
b. General Information
c. Title to the Property and Land Use
   i. Method of Sale
   ii. Encumbrances, Mortgages, and Liens
   iii. Recording the Contract and Deed
   iv. Payments
   v. Restrictions on the Use of Your Lot
   vi. Plats, Zoning, Surveying, Permits, and Environment

d. Roads

   i. Access to the Subdivision
   ii. Access within the Subdivision

e. Utilities

   i. Water
   ii. Sewer
   iii. Electricity
   iv. Telephone Service
   v. Fuel and Other Energy Sources

f. Financial Information
g. Local Services
    i. Fire Protection
    ii. Police Protection
    iii. Schools
    iv. Hospitals
    v. Physicians and Dentists
    vi. Shopping Facilities
    vii. Mail Service
    viii. Public Transportation
    ix. Air Service
h. Recreational Facilities
i. Subdivision Characteristics and Climate
    i. General Topography
    ii. Water Coverage
    iii. Drainage and Fill
    iv. Flood Plain
    v. Flooding and Soil Erosion
    vi. Nuisances
    vii. Hazards
    viii. Climate
    ix. Occupancy

j. Additional Information

    i. Property Owner's Association
    ii. Taxes
    iii. Resale or Exchange Program
    iv. Unusual Situations

       v. Equal Opportunity in Lot Sales
      vi. Lot Listing
 k. Cost Sheet

 l. Receipt, Agent Certification, and Cancellation Pages

7. The Purchase Contract

The question posed at the beginning of this chapter referred to documentation to obtain "prior to signing a purchase agreement." The agreement itself is, of course, a key element of the paper trail, so I would be remiss if I didn't include it as part of the discussion. Using North Carolina as an example, the State's Bar Association and the North Carolina Association of Realtors have jointly approved a Standard Form 12-T, the "Offer to Purchase and Contract – Vacant Lot/Land." (See Exhibit 3.3 in the Appendix at the end of this chapter.)

If you are buying a homesite that is a resale, that is, buying the lot from an individual as opposed to a developer, this form will likely be the contract that is used, subject to the changes and revisions that inevitably occur from time to time. The problem is that most buyers in new communities are dealing with developers, who rarely, if ever, utilize this form because they prefer a document that more accurately reflects the specific conditions of their developments and frankly, they prefer a simpler agreement that is written to favor their interests to a greater degree than does Form 12-T.

Many of the topics and issues that are woven throughout the language of Form T-12 are already covered throughout other sections of this chapter and in other chapters in the book. The most important piece of additional advice that I can give you is not to neglect the opportunity—the mandate, I should say—to engage your own attorney to advise you regarding the terms and conditions of whatever contract form is used. A good developer should make it a point to establish an initial contact and working relationship with a local attorney, apart from the developer's legal counsel, to represent the interests of the development's buyers. This gives the buyers a sense of confidence that they have the undivided attention of and a fiduciary relationship with a local attorney to protect their interests. There is the added benefit that the attorney, through processing repeated closings, becomes intimately familiar with all of the specific documents that pertain to that development; the results are efficient, well-organized, and well-managed closings that rarely suffer delays and that keep all parties relaxed and secure that the transaction is under control. In the event that the developer has not established this practice or you are purchasing the property from an individual, seek out a local attorney on your own who concentrates on handling real estate closings in the area. The expenses incurred for legal representation are a pittance compared to the potential for negative impacts that can result from a lack of a focused legal review of all documents by an attorney who is working on your behalf. (Note that I do not recommend using an attorney from your home town. I have never found that the personal familiarity one may have with a known and trusted attorney from out-of-state overrides that attorney's lack of familiarity with North Carolina real estate law and with customary practices in the area.)

8. Geotechnical Exploration

Geotechnical exploration work is done for a variety of engineering and design purposes. In the case of the homesite buyer, the purpose of the investigation is to evaluate the suitability of the soils and subgrade conditions for the structural support of the intended residence. It is also of value in arriving at the appropriate design for the foundation system of the home. The work typically involves the excavation of test pits within the proposed foundation area of the future home. Various tests are conducted, both in situ and in the lab, to confirm the structural integrity of the soils.

I don't know of any developers that actually perform geotechnical exploration on individual homesites; nor would I expect them to. In most cases, they have already performed a significant degree of subsurface investigation in order to obtain the soils evaluations for drain field design from the Health Department (as discussed earlier) and to obtain approvals for their road and amenities construction. Doing the same for each individual homesite is cost prohibitive, and since the developer has no idea of the exact location on each lot where a buyer intends to build a future home, locating test pits appropriately is next to impossible. That doesn't mean, however, that the individual buyers shouldn't have the exploration done on their own, with a contract provision that makes it clear that the good faith deposit and closing of the transaction is conditioned upon an acceptable outcome of the geotechnical testing. On occasion, one will find soils that are comprised of elements that are unsound for the support of a home, or void spaces and/or significant cracks and fissures in subsurface rock formations that can suggest the potential for landslide activity, etc. The geotechnical exploration serves as a relatively inexpensive insurance policy against future failures such as settlement cracks, water intrusion, etc. (See Exhibit 3.4 in the Appendix at the end of this chapter.)

9. Flood Plain Maps

The question of whether or not a given tract of land or homesite is in a designated flood plain is one of the more common ones I hear from interested buyers, perhaps because many of them come from lowland and coastal areas where the issue of flooding is more prevalent. That is not to say that the mountains don't have their share of issues. In 2004, when the remnants of Hurricanes Frances and Ivan passed through Asheville, dumping tremendous quantities of rain over extended periods of time, there certainly were many areas along the major rivers that were under water for a time and sustained substantial damage. Most rural mountain communities are situated well above any flood plain concerns. However, the prospect of damage from storm events in these communities is not an issue of flooding *per se*; it is more so the potential for damage from storm water drainage patterns and erosion as the accumulation and concentration of rainwater travels along new pathways that have been created by the infrastructure development process and the construction of new homes. Though building departments require that erosion control measures and proper drainage be incorporated into all development activities, sometimes these newly directed drainage pathways haven't been naturally tested by a significant storm event. There is nothing like nature to expose the degree to which well-intentioned drainage design and reality depart from one another.

Envision for a moment a newly developed mountain community of some one hundred homesites nestled throughout three hundred acres of moderate to challenging topography. Imagine that all of the roadways and associated infrastructure have been permitted and completed pursuant to a well-designed master plan and civil engineering drawings that include the appropriate management of the flow of storm water. Slopes, grades, drainage ditches, culvert pipes, and erosion control methods are all successfully utilized and coordinated to direct and manage the precipitation. Now, subsequent to the completion of this work, imagine that there will now be one hundred individual homesite buyers who eventually become one hundred individual homebuilders who modify the slopes, grades, and drainage flows through each one of the one hundred properties that are interspersed throughout the original three hundred-acre storm drainage design. Each home becomes an impervious barrier that storm water not only cannot penetrate but also must travel around. Do you think there might be the potential for storm water to be successfully shed from one homeowner's property at the expense of another's? You bet there is. No matter how diligent the architects and building departments might be in trying to insert each of one hundred puzzle pieces into the equation, there are bound to be some exceptions. These unintended storm water drainage exceptions pose the real threat of water damage to other homesites, rather than the threat of flooding in the conventional sense of that term.

Having noted the above, flood zone maps (see Illustration 3.3) and flood insurance rate maps are available online through the Federal Emergency Management Agency (FEMA). Rest assured that if you are financing your acquisition, your lender will confirm that you have property insurance, and in turn, your insurer will be well-informed regarding the location of your property and the flood risk, if any, associated with it.

Do Your Due Diligence—Part II

Illustration 3.3: Flood zone map

Some notes on seeking advice

I have suggested in this chapter and in the previous Chapter Two that you should consider engaging various design consultants and contractors to assist you in your due diligence efforts. All of these endeavors should be completed prior to the good faith deposits on a land purchase "going hard" and an eventual closing. A land surveyor, a geotechnical engineer, a site planning firm, a general contractor, a site work contractor, a well-drilling firm, and a septic system contractor have all been mentioned as useful resources on whom to rely for valuable feedback on the viability and feasibility of a specific land parcel for your intended use. If you are looking for a homesite within a new community, where developer sales are still active and comprise the bulk of the real estate transactions, I would not hesitate to request assistance from the developer in obtaining referrals for these firms. Consultants and contractors who have already provided services to the development are bound to have a learning curve that has leveled off some time ago. Engaging them is a smart move because of their history with the development, which will inevitably translate to more competitive pricing, simply because they already have at their disposal all of the baseline information that pertains to the development. Their familiarity with the development means that you won't have to pay for the learning curve for which others would charge. The risk of the unknown is eliminated, as are the costs that others might charge for that risk.

In addition, the consultants and contractors that work for the developer *should* have a predisposition to service the development's clientele—you, the buyer—in a manner that engenders the trust and confidence of the buyer. If a developer has any reservations about referring you to the consultants and contractors whom have been used thus far in the development of the neighborhood, I would interpret that as a red flag that should give you caution about even considering buying property there. There are only three reasons that a developer might have for an unwillingness to provide those referrals: 1) the developer owes the contractor money and the contractor won't service the project until it has been paid; 2) the contractor did shoddy work, which is certainly a good reason not to recommend him or her, but now you have to be concerned about the effect of that shoddy work on those portions of the community where the contractor was involved; and 3) the developer has something to hide, of which the contractor is aware, and the developer would prefer that you engage another contractor who is unaware of the issue.

In summary, the only individual who is going to look out for your interests to the degree necessary to ensure that the potential risks associated with your land purchase have been minimized is *you*. Lawyers can, to a degree, provide the necessary protections and defenses to the written word. They can assist by safeguarding your interests through their knowledge of the documentation that properly validates your intentions and understandings of the transaction. However, many of the issues are not legal in nature at all but practical issues of "individual choice," of which only you can determine the adequacy. Topography and its impact on design, covenant language, rules and regulations, design guidelines, etc., all impact practical lifestyle choices upon which only you can decide.

Not all of the documentation described in this chapter is necessarily available upon request. For example, as noted, the property may be exempt from the ILSA requirements; a handful of developers may not have recorded a set of covenants, though that is exceedingly rare these days; and a topographic survey may not be available, though almost all counties have now completed countywide aerial topographic surveys that are not only available to developers but also to the general public as well. The point is for you to make every effort to obtain the information that is available and to know that, although a responsible developer should assist you in that effort as part of an ethical obligation to you as a buyer, in the end, you need to rely on yourself to obtain what is not made readily available to you.

Appendix to Chapter Three

Everything You Need To Know About Buying Mountain Property

Exhibit 3.1: soil/site evaluation report

Do Your Due Diligence—Part II

CHAMBERS SOIL CONSULTING, INC.

Date: 3/8/08
County: Haywood
Lot Number: 25

Soil/Site Evaluation

Owner/Agent: Michael Posey
Proposed Facilities: 3-Bedroom House
Location: Sunset Falls Subdivision Lot 25, off of James Chapel Road

Water Supply: Private Well(s) ___ Community Well(s) __x__ Municipal ___
Evaluation Method: Auger Boring ___ Pit __x__ Cut ___

Profile #	Landscape Position	Slope %	Horizon	Depth Inches	Texture	Structure	Consistence	Mineralogy	Mottle Color	Matrix Color	Other Profile Factors
Pit 25-1	Linear Convex Sideslope	44%	A	0-5	SL	Gr	VFr	ss, sp SE			Wetness Condition
			Bw	5-24	SL-SCL	Wk / SBK	VFr	, sp SE		10YR 4/6	Soil Depth: 24"/34"
			CB	24-28	SL	M-B	Fr	, sp SE		variegated	Restrictive Horizon
			C	28-44	LS	M	Fr-Fi	NE		variegated	Profile Classification: PS
											LTAR: 0.6, 8" LDP
Pit 25-2	Linear Convex Sideslope	46%	A	0-5	SL	Gr	VFr	, sp SE			Wetness Condition
			Bw	5-20	SL	Wk / SBK	VFr	, sp SE		10YR 5/6	Soil Depth: 20"/33"
			CB	20-24	SL	M-B	Fr	, sp SE		variegated	Restrictive Horizon
			C	24-46	LS	M	Fr	NE		variegated	Profile Classification: PS
											LTAR: 0.6, 8" LDP
Pit 25-3	Linear Convex Sideslope	46%	A	0-4	SL	Gr	VFr	, sp SE			Wetness Condition
			Bw	4-20	SL	Wk / SBK	VFr	, sp SE		10YR 5/8	Soil Depth: 26"/35"
			BC	20-26	SL	M-B	Fr	, sp SE		variegated	Restrictive Horizon
			CB	26-38	SL	M-B	Fr	, sp SE		variegated	Profile Classification: PS
			C	38-44	LS	M	Fr	NE		variegated	LTAR: 0.6, 8" – 10" LDP
Pit 25-4	Linear Concave Sideslope	44%	A	0-6	SL	Gr	VFr	ss, sp SE			Wetness Condition
			Bw	6-28	SCL	Wk / SBK	Fr	NF		10YR 5/6	Soil Depth: 28"/32"
			C	28-36	LS	M	Fr	-		variegated	Restrictive Horizon
			Cr	36-39	-	-	VFi				Profile Classification: PS
											LTAR: 0.6, 8" LDP
Pit 25-5	Linear Concave Headslope	43%	A	0-5	SL	Gr	VFr	ss, sp SE			Wetness Condition
			Bw	5-20	SCL	Wk m SBK	Fr	ss, sp SE		10YR 4/6	Soil Depth: 28"/34"
			BC	20-28	SCL	Wk / SBK	Fr	, sp SE		10YR 5/6	Restrictive Horizon
			CB	28-40	SL	B-M	Fr			variegated	Profile Classification: PS
											LTAR: 0.6, 8" LDP

Comments: PS= provisionally suitable, U=Unsuitable, rcld= reclassified as provisionally suitable for modified or alternative systems. 8" LDP= 8-inch large diameter pipe drainfield. LPP= Low Pressure Pipe system. Drip irr. = drip irrigation system (engineered systems). ESD= effective soil depth including usable saprolite

105

Everything You Need To Know About Buying Mountain Property

Chambers Soil Consulting, Inc.

System Proposal [2]

Owner:	Michael Posey			Phone:	(828) 545-8200
Property:	Sunset Falls Subdivision, Lot 25	Address:	James Chapel Road	County:	Haywood
	Initial system			**Reserve area**	
Type:	8-inch large diameter pipe		Type:	8-inch large diameter pipe	
Facilities:	3-Bedroom House		Facilities:	3-Bedroom House	
Design Flow:	360 gal/day		Design Flow:	360 gal/day	
LTAR:	0.5 gallons/day/ft^2		LTAR:	0.5 gallons/day/ft^2	
Trench depth*:	16-inches (lower sidewall)		Trench depth*:	16-inches (lower sidewall)	
Trench width:	10-inches		Trench width:	10-inches	
On-center spacing:	6.0-feet minimum		On-center spacing:	6.0-feet minimum	
Notes:	Approximately 360 linear feet required for initial system. Lines are flagged on contour on the site.		Notes:	Approximately 360 linear feet required for reserve system. Lines are flagged on contour on the site.	

Line #	Length (ft.)	Flag color
1	75	Blue
2	110	White
3	110	Orange
4	100	Blue
5	100	White
6	100	Orange
7	80	Blue
8	70	White
745' avail.		Lines flagged 8ft or greater o.c.

---

[2] Individual system proposals are subject to County Environmental Health Department review and approval. The location of the propose facilities may be subject to restrictive use areas.

Exhibit 3.3: Offer to purchase and contract - vacant lot/land, state of North Carolina (This form is the property of the North Carolina Association of Realtors (NCAR) and is reprinted here with the permission of NCAR)

OFFER TO PURCHASE AND CONTRACT - VACANT LOT/LAND
[Consult "Guidelines" (form 12G) for guidance in completing this form]

NOTE: This contract is intended for unimproved real property that Buyer will purchase only for personal use and does not have immediate plans to subdivide. It should not be used to sell property that is being subdivided unless the property has been platted, properly approved and recorded with the register of deeds as of the date of the contract. If Seller is Buyer's builder and the sale involves the construction of a new single family dwelling prior to closing, use the standard Offer to Purchase and Contract—New Construction (Form 800-T) or, if the construction is completed, use the Offer to Purchase and Contract (Form 2-T) with the New Construction Addendum (Form 2A3-T).

For valuable consideration, the receipt and legal sufficiency of which are hereby acknowledged, Buyer offers to purchase and Seller upon acceptance agrees to sell and convey the Property on the terms and conditions of this Offer To Purchase and Contract and any addendum or modification made in accordance with its terms (together the "Contract").

1. **TERMS AND DEFINITIONS**: The terms listed below shall have the respective meaning given them as set forth adjacent to each term.

   (a) "**Seller**": _____

   (b) "**Buyer**": _____

   (c) "**Property**": The Property shall include all that real estate described below together with all appurtenances thereto including the improvements located thereon. **NOTE:** If the Property will include a manufactured (mobile) home(s), Buyer and Seller should consider including the Manufactured (Mobile) Home provision in the Additional Provisions Addendum (Standard Form 2A11-T) with this offer.
   Street Address: _____
   City: _____ Zip: _____
   County: _____, North Carolina
   (**NOTE:** Governmental authority over taxes, zoning, school districts, utilities and mail delivery may differ from address shown.)

   Legal Description: (Complete *ALL* applicable)
   Plat Reference: Lot/Unit _____, Block/Section _____, Subdivision/Condominium _____
   _____, as shown on Plat Book/Slide _____ at Page(s) _____
   The PIN/PID or other identification number of the Property is: _____
   Other description: _____
   Some or all of the Property may be described in Deed Book _____ at Page _____

   (d) "**Purchase Price**":
   $ _____ paid in U.S. Dollars upon the following terms:
   $ _____ BY DUE DILIGENCE FEE made payable to Seller by the Effective Date
   $ _____ BY INITIAL EARNEST MONEY DEPOSIT made payable to Escrow Agent named in Paragraph 1(f) ☐ with this offer OR ☐ delivered within five (5) days of the Effective Date of this Contract by ☐ cash ☐ personal check ☐ official bank check ☐ wire transfer
   $ _____ BY (ADDITIONAL) EARNEST MONEY DEPOSIT made payable to Escrow Agent named in Paragraph 1(f) by cash or immediately available funds such as official bank check or wire transfer to be delivered to Escrow Agent no later than _____, TIME BEING OF THE ESSENCE with regard to said date.
   $ _____ BY ASSUMPTION of the unpaid principal balance and all obligations of Seller on the existing loan(s) secured by a deed of trust on the Property in accordance with the attached Loan Assumption Addendum (Standard Form 2A6-T).
   $ _____ BY SELLER FINANCING in accordance with the attached Seller Financing Addendum (Standard Form 2A5-T).
   $ _____ BALANCE of the Purchase Price in cash at Settlement (some or all of which may be paid with the proceeds of a new loan)

   Should Buyer fail to deliver either the Due Diligence Fee or any Initial Earnest Money Deposit by their due dates, or should any check or other funds paid by Buyer be dishonored, for any reason, by the institution upon which the payment is drawn, Buyer shall

This form jointly approved by:
North Carolina Bar Association
North Carolina Association of REALTORS®, Inc.

STANDARD FORM 12-T
Revised 7/2012
© 7/2012

Buyer initials _____ Seller initials _____

Everything You Need To Know About Buying Mountain Property

have one (1) banking day after written notice to deliver good funds to the payee. In the event Buyer does not timely deliver good funds, Seller shall have the right to terminate this Contract upon written notice to Buyer.

(e) **"Earnest Money Deposit"**: The Initial Earnest Money Deposit, the Additional Earnest Money Deposit and any other earnest monies paid in connection with this transaction, hereinafter collectively referred to as "Earnest Money Deposit", shall be deposited and held in escrow by Escrow Agent until Closing, at which time it will be credited to Buyer, or until this Contract is otherwise terminated. In the event: (1) this offer is not accepted; or (2) a condition of any resulting contract is not satisfied, then the Earnest Money Deposit shall be refunded to Buyer. In the event of breach of this Contract by Seller, the Earnest Money Deposit shall be refunded to Buyer upon Buyer's request, but such return shall not affect any other remedies available to Buyer for such breach. In the event of breach of this Contract by Buyer, the Earnest Money Deposit shall be paid to Seller upon Seller's request as liquidated damages and as Seller's sole and exclusive remedy for such breach, but without limiting Seller's rights under Paragraphs 2(c) and 2(d) for damage to the Property or Seller's right to retain the Due Diligence Fee. It is acknowledged by the parties that payment of the Earnest Money Deposit to Seller in the event of a breach of this Contract by Buyer is compensatory and not punitive, such amount being a reasonable estimation of the actual loss that Seller would incur as a result of such breach. The payment of the Earnest Money Deposit to Seller shall not constitute a penalty or forfeiture but actual compensation for Seller's anticipated loss, both parties acknowledging the difficulty determining Seller's actual damages for such breach. If legal proceedings are brought by Buyer or Seller against the other to recover the Earnest Money Deposit, the prevailing party in the proceeding shall be entitled to recover from the non-prevailing party reasonable attorney fees and court costs incurred in connection with the proceeding.

(f) **"Escrow Agent"** (insert name): _____

NOTE: In the event of a dispute between Seller and Buyer over the disposition of the Earnest Money Deposit held in escrow, a licensed real estate broker ("Broker") is required by state law (and Escrow Agent, if not a Broker, hereby agrees) to retain the Earnest Money Deposit in the Escrow Agent's trust or escrow account until Escrow Agent has obtained a written release from the parties consenting to its disposition or until disbursement is ordered by a court of competent jurisdiction. Alternatively, if a Broker or an attorney licensed to practice law in North Carolina ("Attorney") is holding the Earnest Money Deposit, the Broker or Attorney may deposit the disputed monies with the appropriate clerk of court in accordance with the provisions of N.C.G.S. §93A-12.

THE PARTIES AGREE THAT A REAL ESTATE BROKERAGE FIRM ACTING AS ESCROW AGENT MAY PLACE THE EARNEST MONEY DEPOSIT IN AN INTEREST BEARING TRUST ACCOUNT AND THAT ANY INTEREST EARNED THEREON SHALL BE DISBURSED TO THE ESCROW AGENT MONTHLY IN CONSIDERATION OF THE EXPENSES INCURRED BY MAINTAINING SUCH ACCOUNT AND RECORDS ASSOCIATED THEREWITH.

(g) **"Effective Date"**: The date that: (1) the last one of Buyer and Seller has signed or initialed this offer or the final counteroffer, if any, and (2) such signing or initialing is communicated to the party making the offer or counteroffer, as the case may be.

(h) **"Due Diligence"**: Buyer's opportunity during the Due Diligence Period to investigate the Property and the transaction contemplated by this Contract, including but not necessarily limited to the matters described in Paragraph 2 below, to decide whether Buyer, in Buyer's sole discretion, will proceed with or terminate the transaction.

(i) **"Due Diligence Fee"**: A negotiated amount, if any, paid by Buyer to Seller with this Contract for Buyer's right to conduct Due Diligence during the Due Diligence Period. It shall be the property of Seller upon the Effective Date and shall be a credit to Buyer at Closing. The Due Diligence Fee shall be non-refundable except in the event of a material breach of this Contract by Seller, or if this Contract is terminated under Paragraph 6(l) or Paragraph 9, or as otherwise provided in any addendum hereto. Buyer and Seller each expressly waive any right that they may have to deny the right to conduct Due Diligence or to assert any defense as to the enforceability of this Contract based on the absence or alleged insufficiency of any Due Diligence Fee, it being the intent of the parties to create a legally binding contract for the purchase and sale of the Property without regard to the existence or amount of any Due Diligence Fee.

(j) **"Due Diligence Period"**: The period beginning on the Effective Date and extending through 5:00 p.m. on _____ ***TIME BEING OF THE ESSENCE*** with regard to said date.

(k) **"Settlement"**: The proper execution and delivery to the closing attorney of all documents necessary to complete the transaction contemplated by this Contract, including the deed, settlement statement, deed of trust and other loan or conveyance documents, and the closing attorney's receipt of all funds necessary to complete such transaction.

(l) **"Settlement Date"**: The parties agree that Settlement will take place on _____
_____ (the "Settlement Date"), unless otherwise agreed in writing, at a time and place designated by Buyer.

(m) **"Closing"**: The completion of the legal process which results in the transfer of title to the Property from Seller to Buyer, which includes the following steps: (1) the Settlement (defined above); (2) the completion of a satisfactory title update to the Property following the Settlement; (3) the closing attorney's receipt of authorization to disburse all necessary funds; and (4) recordation in the appropriate county registry of the deed(s) and deed(s) of trust, if any, which shall take place as soon as reasonably possible for the closing attorney after Settlement. Upon Closing, the proceeds of sale shall be disbursed by the closing attorney in accordance with the settlement statement and the provisions of Chapter 45A of the North Carolina General Statutes. If the title update should reveal unexpected liens, encumbrances or other title defects, or if the closing attorney is not authorized to disburse all necessary funds, then the Closing shall be suspended and the Settlement deemed delayed under Paragraph 13 (Delay in Settlement/Closing).

WARNING: The North Carolina State Bar has determined that the performance of most acts and services required for a closing constitutes the practice of law and must be performed only by an attorney licensed to practice law in North Carolina. State law prohibits unlicensed individuals or firms from rendering legal services or advice. Although non-attorney settlement agents may perform limited services in connection with a closing, they may not perform all the acts and services required to complete a closing. A closing involves significant legal issues that should be handled by an attorney. Accordingly it is the position of the North Carolina Bar Association and the North Carolina Association of REALTORS® that all buyers should hire an attorney licensed in North Carolina to perform a closing.

(n) **"Special Assessments"**: A charge against the Property by a governmental authority in addition to ad valorem taxes and recurring governmental service fees levied with such taxes, or by an owners' association in addition to any regular assessment (dues), either of which may be a lien against the Property. A Special Assessment may be either proposed or confirmed.

"Proposed Special Assessment": A Special Assessment that is under formal consideration but which has not been approved prior to Settlement.

"Confirmed Special Assessment": A Special Assessment that has been approved prior to Settlement whether or not it is fully payable at time of Settlement.

2. **BUYER'S DUE DILIGENCE PROCESS**:
   (a) **Loan**: During the Due Diligence Period, Buyer, at Buyer's expense, shall be entitled to pursue qualification for and approval of the Loan if any.

   (NOTE: Buyer is advised to consult with Buyer's lender prior to signing this offer to assure that the Due Diligence Period allows sufficient time for the appraisal to be completed and for Buyer's lender to provide Buyer sufficient information to decide whether to proceed with or terminate the transaction since the Loan is not a condition of the Contract.)

   (b) **Property Investigation**: During the Due Diligence Period, Buyer or Buyer's agents or representatives, at Buyer's expense, shall be entitled to conduct all desired tests, surveys, appraisals, investigations, examinations and inspections of the Property as Buyer deems appropriate, including but NOT limited to the following:
   (i) **Soil, Utilities And Environmental**: Reports to determine whether the soil is suitable for Buyer's intended use and whether there is any environmental contamination, law, rule or regulation that may prohibit, restrict or limit Buyer's intended use.
   (ii) **Septic/Sewer System**: Any applicable investigation(s) to determine: (1) the condition of an existing sewage system, (2) the costs and expenses to install a sewage system approved by an existing Improvement Permit, (3) the availability and expense to connect to a public or community sewer system, and/or (4) whether an Improvement Permit or written evaluation may be obtained from the County Health Department for a suitable ground absorption sewage system.
   (iii) **Water**: Any applicable investigation(s) to determine: (1) the condition of an existing private drinking water well, (2) the costs and expenses to install a private drinking water well approved by an existing Construction Permit, (3) the availability, costs and expenses to connect to a public or community water system, or a shared private well, and/or (4) whether a Construction Permit may be obtained from the County Health Department for a private drinking water well.
   (iv) **Review of Documents**: Review of Documents: Review of the Declaration of Restrictive Covenants, Bylaws, Articles of Incorporation, Rules and Regulations, and other governing documents of any applicable owners' association and/or subdivision. If the Property is subject to regulation by an owners' association, it is recommended that Buyer review the completed Owners' Association And Addendum (Standard Form 2A12-T) provided by Seller prior to signing this offer.
   (v) **Appraisals**: An appraisal of the Property.

Page 3 of 9

Buyer initials _____ Seller initials _____

STANDARD FORM 12-T
Revised 7/2012
© 7/2012

Everything You Need To Know About Buying Mountain Property

(vi) **Survey**: A survey to determine whether the property is suitable for Buyer's intended use and the location of easements, setbacks, property boundaries and other issues which may or may not constitute title defects.

(vii) **Zoning and Governmental Regulation**: Investigation of current or proposed zoning or other governmental regulation that may affect Buyer's intended use of the Property, adjacent land uses, planned or proposed road construction, and school attendance zones.

(viii) **Flood Hazard**: Investigation of potential flood hazards on the Property, and/or any requirement to purchase flood insurance in order to obtain the Loan.

(c) **Buyer's Obligation to Repair Damage**: Buyer shall, at Buyer's expense, promptly repair any damage to the Property resulting from any activities of Buyer and Buyer's agents and contractors, but Buyer shall not be responsible for any damage caused by accepted practices applicable to any N.C. licensed professional performing reasonable appraisals, tests, surveys, examinations and inspections of the Property. This repair obligation shall survive any termination of this Contract.

(d) **Indemnity**: Buyer will indemnify and hold Seller harmless from all loss, damage, claims, suits or costs, which shall arise out of any contract, agreement, or injury to any person or property as a result of any activities of Buyer and Buyer's agents and contractors relating to the Property except for any loss, damage, claim, suit or cost arising out of pre-existing conditions of the Property and/or out of Seller's negligence or willful acts or omissions. This indemnity shall survive this Contract and any termination hereof.

(e) **Buyer's Right to Terminate**: Buyer shall have the right to terminate this Contract for any reason or no reason, by delivering to Seller written notice of termination (the "Termination Notice") during the Due Diligence Period (or any agreed-upon written extension of the Due Diligence Period), *TIME BEING OF THE ESSENCE*. If Buyer timely delivers the Termination Notice, this Contract shall be terminated and the Earnest Money Deposit shall be refunded to Buyer.

WARNING: If Buyer is not satisfied with the results or progress of Buyer's Due Diligence, Buyer should terminate this Contract, *prior to the expiration of the Due Diligence Period*, unless Buyer can obtain a written extension from Seller. SELLER IS NOT OBLIGATED TO GRANT AN EXTENSION. Although Buyer may continue to investigate the Property following the expiration of the Due Diligence Period, Buyer's failure to deliver a Termination Notice to Seller prior to the expiration of the Due Diligence Period shall constitute a waiver by Buyer of any right to terminate this Contract based on any matter relating to Buyer's Due Diligence. Provided however, following the Due Diligence Period, Buyer may still exercise a right to terminate if Seller fails to materially comply with any of Seller's obligations under paragraph 6 of this Contract or for any other reason permitted under the terms of this Contract or North Carolina law.

(f) **CLOSING SHALL CONSTITUTE ACCEPTANCE OF THE PROPERTY IN ITS THEN EXISTING CONDITION UNLESS PROVISION IS OTHERWISE MADE IN WRITING.**

3. **BUYER REPRESENTATIONS**:
   (a) **Loan**: Buyer ❏ does ❏ does not have to obtain a new loan in order to purchase the Property. If Buyer is obtaining a new loan, Buyer intends to obtain a loan as follows: ❏ Conventional ❏ Other: _____ loan at a ❏ Fixed Rate ❏ Adjustable Rate in the principal amount of _____ for a term of _____ year(s), at an initial interest rate not to exceed _____ % per annum (the "Loan").

   NOTE: Buyer's obligations under this Contract are not conditioned upon obtaining or closing any loan. If Buyer represents that Buyer does not have to obtain a new loan in order to purchase the Property, Seller is advised, prior to signing this offer, to obtain documentation from Buyer which demonstrates that Buyer will be able to close on the Property without the necessity of obtaining a new loan.

   (b) **Other Property**: Buyer ❏ does ❏ does not have to sell or lease other real property in order to qualify for a new loan or to complete purchase. (**NOTE**: If Buyer does have to sell, Buyer and Seller should consider including a Contingent Sale Addendum (Standard Form 2A2-T) with this offer.)

   (c) **Performance of Buyer's Financial Obligations**: To the best of Buyer's knowledge, there are no other circumstances or conditions existing as of the date of this offer that would prohibit Buyer from performing Buyer's financial obligations in accordance with this Contract, except as may be specifically set forth herein.

4. **BUYER OBLIGATIONS**:
   (a) **Owners' Association Fees/Charges**: Buyer shall pay any fees required for confirming account payment information on owners' association dues or assessments for payment or proration and any charge made by the owners' association in connection

Page 4 of 9

STANDARD FORM 12-T
Revised 7/2012
© 7/2012

Buyer initials _____ _____   Seller initials _____ _____

with the disposition of the Property to Buyer, including any transfer and/or document fee imposed by the owners' association. Buyer shall not be responsible for fees incurred by Seller in completing the Owners' Association Disclosure and Addendum For Properties Exempt from Residential Property Disclosure Statement (Standard Form 2A12-T).

(b) **Responsibility for Proposed Special Assessments**: Buyer shall take title subject to all Proposed Special Assessments.

(c) **Responsibility for Certain Costs**: Buyer shall be responsible for all costs with respect to any loan obtained by Buyer, appraisal, title search, title insurance, recording the deed and for preparation and recording of all instruments required to secure the balance of the Purchase Price unpaid at Settlement.

5. **SELLER REPRESENTATIONS**:
   (a) **Ownership**: Seller represents that Seller:
   ❏ has owned the Property for at least one year.
   ❏ has owned the Property for less than one year.
   ❏ does not yet own the Property.

   (b) **Assessments**: To the best of Seller's knowledge there are no Proposed Special Assessments except as follows (Insert "None" or the identification of such assessments, if any):_____.

   Seller warrants that there are no Confirmed Special Assessments except as follows (Insert "None" or the identification of such assessments, if any):_____.

   (c) **Owners' Association(s) and Dues**: To best of Seller's knowledge, ownership of the Property ❏ subjects ❏ does not subject Buyer to regulation by one or more owners' association(s) and governing documents, which impose various mandatory covenants, conditions and restrictions upon the Property and Buyer's enjoyment thereof, including but not limited to obligations to pay regular assessments (dues) and Special Assessments. If there is an owners' association, then an Owners' Association Disclosure and Addendum For Properties Exempt from Residential Property Disclosure Statement (Standard Form 2A12-T) shall be completed by Seller, at Seller's expense, and must be attached as an addendum to this Contract.

   (d) **Sewage System Permit**: (❏ Applicable ❏ Not Applicable) Seller warrants that the sewage system described in the Improvement Permit attached hereto has been installed, which representation survives Closing, but makes no further representations as to the system.

   (e) **Private Drinking Water Well Permit**: (❏ Applicable ❏ Not Applicable) Seller warrants that a private drinking water well has been installed, which representation survives Closing, but makes no further representations as to the well. (If well installed after July 1, 2008, attach Improvement Permit hereto.)

6. **SELLER OBLIGATIONS**:
   (a) **Evidence of Title**: Seller agrees to use best efforts to deliver to Buyer as soon as reasonably possible after the Effective Date, copies of all title information in possession of or available to Seller, including but not limited to: title insurance policies, attorney's opinions on title, surveys, covenants, deeds, notes and deeds of trust, leases, and easements relating to the Property. Seller authorizes: (1) any attorney presently or previously representing Seller to release and disclose any title insurance policy in such attorney's file to Buyer and both Buyer's and Seller's agents and attorneys; and (2) the Property's title insurer or its agent to release and disclose all materials in the Property's title insurer's (or title insurer's agent's) file to Buyer and both Buyer's and Seller's agents and attorneys.

   (b) **Access to Property/Walk-Through Inspection**: Seller shall provide reasonable access to the Property (including working, existing utilities) through the earlier of Closing or possession by Buyer, including, but not limited to, allowing the Buyer an opportunity to conduct a final walk-through inspection of the Property. To the extent applicable, Seller shall also be responsible for timely clearing that portion of the Property required by the County to perform tests, inspections and/or evaluations to determine the suitability of the Property for a sewage system and/or private drinking water well.

   (c) **Removal of Seller's Property**: Seller shall remove, by the date possession is made available to Buyer, all personal property which is not a part of the purchase and all garbage and debris from the Property.

   (d) **Affidavit and Indemnification Agreement**: Seller shall furnish at Settlement an affidavit and indemnification agreement in form satisfactory to Buyer and Buyer's title insurer, if any, executed by Seller and any person or entity who has performed or furnished labor, services, materials or rental equipment as described in N.C.G.S. §44A-8 to the Property within 120 days prior to

Page 5 of 9

STANDARD FORM 12-T
Revised 7/2012
© 7/2012

Buyer initials _____ _____   Seller initials _____ _____

the date of Settlement verifying that each such person or entity has been paid in full and agreeing to indemnify Buyer, Buyer's lender(s) and Buyer's title insurer against all loss from any cause or claim arising therefrom.

(e) **Payment and Satisfaction of Liens**: All deeds of trust, deferred ad valorem taxes, liens and other charges against the Property, not assumed by Buyer, must be paid and satisfied by Seller prior to or at Settlement such that cancellation may be promptly obtained following Closing. Seller shall remain obligated to obtain any such cancellations following Closing.

(f) **Title, Legal Access**: Seller shall execute and deliver a GENERAL WARRANTY DEED for the Property at Settlement unless otherwise stated herein, which shall convey fee simple marketable and insurable title, free of all encumbrances and defects which would be revealed by a current and accurate survey of the Property; except: ad valorem taxes for the current year (prorated through the date of Settlement); utility easements and unviolated restrictive covenants that do not materially affect the value of the Property; and such other encumbrances as may be assumed or specifically approved by Buyer in writing. The Property must have legal access to a public right of way. NOTE: Buyer's failure to terminate this Contract prior to the expiration of the Due Diligence Period as a result of any encumbrance or defect that is or would have been revealed by a title examination of the Property or a current and accurate survey shall not relieve Seller of any obligation under this subparagraph.

NOTE: If any sale of the Property may be a "short sale," consideration should be given to attaching a Short Sale Addendum (Standard Form 2A14-T) as an addendum to this Contract.

(g) **Deed, Excise Taxes**: Seller shall pay for preparation of a deed and all other documents necessary to perform Seller's obligations under this Contract, and for state and county excise taxes required by law. The deed is to be made to: _____.

(h) **Agreement to Pay Buyer Expenses**: Seller shall pay at Settlement $_____ toward any of Buyer's expenses associated with the purchase of the Property, less any portion disapproved by Buyer's lender.

NOTE: Examples of Buyer's expenses associated with the purchase of the Property include, but are not limited to, discount points, loan origination fees, appraisal fees, attorney's fees, inspection fees, and "pre-paids" (taxes, insurance, owners' association dues, etc.).

(i) **Payment of Confirmed Special Assessments**: Seller shall pay all Confirmed Special Assessments, if any, provided that the amount thereof can be reasonably determined or estimated.

(j) **Late Listing Penalties**: All property tax late listing penalties, if any, shall be paid by Seller.

(k) **Owners' Association Disclosure and Addendum For Properties Exempt from Residential Property Disclosure Statement** (Standard Form 2A12-T): If applicable, Seller shall provide the completed Owners' Association Disclosure and Addendum For Properties Exempt from Residential Property Disclosure Statement to Buyer on or before the Effective Date.

(l) **Seller's Failure to Comply or Breach**: If Seller fails to materially comply with any of Seller's obligations under this Paragraph 6 or Seller materially breaches this Contract, and Buyer elects to terminate this Contract as a result of such failure or breach, then the Earnest Money Deposit and the Due Diligence Fee shall be refunded to Buyer and Seller shall reimburse to Buyer the reasonable costs actually incurred by Buyer in connection with Buyer's Due Diligence without affecting any other remedies. If legal proceedings are brought by Buyer against the Seller to recover the Earnest Money Deposit, the Due Diligence Fee and/or the reasonable costs actually incurred by Buyer in connection with Buyer's Due Diligence, the prevailing party in the proceeding shall be entitled to recover from the non-prevailing party reasonable attorney fees and court costs incurred in connection with the proceeding.

7. **PRORATIONS AND ADJUSTMENTS**: Unless otherwise provided, the following items shall be prorated through the date of Settlement and either adjusted between the parties or paid at Settlement:
   (a) **Taxes on Real Property**: Ad valorem taxes and recurring governmental service fees levied with such taxes on real property shall be prorated on a calendar year basis;
   (b) **Rents**: Rents, if any, for the Property;
   (c) **Dues**: Owners' association regular assessments (dues) and other like charges.

8. **CONDITION OF PROPERTY AT CLOSING**: Buyer's obligation to complete the transaction contemplated by this Contract shall be contingent upon the Property being in substantially the same or better condition at Closing as on the date of this offer, reasonable wear and tear excepted.

Do Your Due Diligence—Part II

9. **RISK OF LOSS**: The risk of loss or damage by fire or other casualty prior to Closing shall be upon Seller. If the improvements on the Property are destroyed or materially damaged prior to Closing, Buyer may terminate this Contract by written notice delivered to Seller or Seller's agent and the Earnest Money Deposit and any Due Diligence Fee shall be refunded to Buyer. In the event Buyer does NOT elect to terminate this Contract, Buyer shall be entitled to receive, in addition to the Property, any of Seller's insurance proceeds payable on account of the damage or destruction applicable to the Property being purchased. Seller is advised not to cancel existing insurance on the Property until after confirming recordation of the deed.

10. **DELAY IN SETTLEMENT/CLOSING**: Absent agreement to the contrary in this Contract or any subsequent modification thereto, if a party is unable to complete Settlement by the Settlement Date but intends to complete the transaction and is acting in good faith and with reasonable diligence to proceed to Settlement ("Delaying Party"), and if the other party is ready, willing and able to complete Settlement on the Settlement Date ("Non-Delaying Party") then the Delaying Party shall give as much notice as possible to the Non-Delaying Party and closing attorney and shall be entitled to a delay in Settlement. If the parties fail to complete Settlement and Closing within fourteen (14) days of the Settlement Date, or to further extend the Settlement Date by written agreement, then the Delaying Party shall be in breach and the Non-Delaying Party may terminate this Contract and shall be entitled to enforce any remedies available to such party under this Contract for the breach.

11. **POSSESSION**: Unless otherwise provided herein, possession shall be delivered at Closing as defined in Paragraph 1(m). No alterations, excavations, tree or vegetation removal or other such activities may be done before possession is delivered.

12. **OTHER PROVISIONS AND CONDITIONS**: CHECK ALL STANDARD ADDENDA THAT MAY BE A PART OF THIS CONTRACT, IF ANY, AND ATTACH HERETO. ITEMIZE ALL OTHER ADDENDA TO THIS CONTRACT, IF ANY, AND ATTACH HERETO.

NOTE: UNDER NORTH CAROLINA LAW, REAL ESTATE BROKERS ARE NOT PERMITTED TO DRAFT CONDITIONS OR CONTINGENCIES TO THIS CONTRACT.

- ❏ Additional Provisions Addendum (Form 2A11-T)
- ❏ Back-Up Contract Addendum (Form 2A1-T)
- ❏ Contingent Sale Addendum (Form 2A2-T)
- ❏ Loan Assumption Addendum (Form 2A6-T)
- ❏ Owners' Association Disclosure And Addendum For Properties Exempt from Residential Property Disclosure Statement (Form 2A12-T)
- ❏ Seller Financing Addendum (Form 2A5-T)
- ❏ Short Sale Addendum (Form 2A14-T)

❏ OTHER: _____

13. **ASSIGNMENTS**: This Contract may not be assigned without the written consent of all parties except in connection with a tax-deferred exchange, but if assigned by agreement, then this Contract shall be binding on the assignee and assignee's heirs and successors.

14. **TAX-DEFERRED EXCHANGE**: In the event Buyer or Seller desires to effect a tax-deferred exchange in connection with the conveyance of the Property, Buyer and Seller agree to cooperate in effecting such exchange; provided, however, that the exchanging party shall be responsible for all additional costs associated with such exchange, and provided further, that a non-exchanging party shall not assume any additional liability with respect to such tax-deferred exchange. Buyer and Seller shall execute such additional documents, including assignment of this Contract in connection therewith, at no cost to the non-exchanging party, as shall be required to give effect to this provision.

15. **PARTIES**: This Contract shall be binding upon and shall inure to the benefit of Buyer and Seller and their respective heirs, successors and assigns. As used herein, words in the singular include the plural and the masculine includes the feminine and neuter genders, as appropriate.

16. **SURVIVAL**: If any provision herein contained which by its nature and effect is required to be observed, kept or performed after the Closing, it shall survive the Closing and remain binding upon and for the benefit of the parties hereto until fully observed, kept or performed.

Buyer initials _____ _____   Seller initials _____ _____

STANDARD FORM 12-T
Revised 7/2012
© 7/2012

17. **ENTIRE AGREEMENT**: This Contract contains the entire agreement of the parties and there are no representations, inducements or other provisions other than those expressed herein. All changes, additions or deletions hereto must be in writing and signed by all parties. Nothing contained herein shall alter any agreement between a REALTOR® or broker and Seller or Buyer as contained in any listing agreement, buyer agency agreement, or any other agency agreement between them.

18. **NOTICE**: Any notice or communication to be given to a party herein may be given to the party or to such party's agent. Any written notice or communication in connection with the transaction contemplated by this Contract may be given to a party or a party's agent by sending or transmitting it to any mailing address, e-mail address or fax number set forth in the "Notice Information" section below. Seller and Buyer agree that the "Notice Information" and "Escrow Acknowledgment" sections below shall not constitute a material part of this Contract, and that the addition or modification of any information therein shall not constitute a rejection of an offer or the creation of a counteroffer.

19. **EXECUTION**: This Contract may be signed in multiple originals or counterparts, all of which together constitute one and the same instrument, and the parties adopt as their seals the word "SEAL" beside their signatures below.

20. **COMPUTATION OF DAYS**: Unless otherwise provided, for purposes of this Contract, the term "days" shall mean consecutive calendar days, including Saturdays, Sundays, and holidays, whether federal, state, local or religious. For the purposes of calculating days, the count of "days" shall begin on the day following the day upon which any act or notice as provided in this Contract was required to be performed or made.

THE NORTH CAROLINA ASSOCIATION OF REALTORS®, INC. AND THE NORTH CAROLINA BAR ASSOCIATION MAKE NO REPRESENTATION AS TO THE LEGAL VALIDITY OR ADEQUACY OF ANY PROVISION OF THIS FORM IN ANY SPECIFIC TRANSACTION. IF YOU DO NOT UNDERSTAND THIS FORM OR FEEL THAT IT DOES NOT PROVIDE FOR YOUR LEGAL NEEDS, YOU SHOULD CONSULT A NORTH CAROLINA REAL ESTATE ATTORNEY BEFORE YOU SIGN IT.

This offer shall become a binding contract on the Effective Date.

Date: _____

Buyer _____ (SEAL)

Date: _____

Buyer _____ (SEAL)

Date: _____

Buyer _____ (SEAL)

Date: _____

Seller _____ (SEAL)

Date: _____

Seller _____ (SEAL)

Date: _____

Seller _____ (SEAL)

STANDARD FORM 12-T
Revised 7/2012
© 7/2012

Do Your Due Diligence—Part II

NOTICE INFORMATION

(**NOTE**: INSERT THE ADDRESS AND/OR ELECTRONIC DELIVERY ADDRESS EACH PARTY AND AGENT APPROVES FOR THE RECEIPT OF ANY NOTICE CONTEMPLATED BY THIS CONTRACT. INSERT "N/A" FOR ANY WHICH ARE NOT APPROVED.)

BUYER NOTICE ADDRESS:

Mailing Address: _____

Buyer Fax#: _____
Buyer E-mail: _____

SELLING AGENT NOTICE ADDRESS:

Firm Name: _____
Acting as ☐ Buyer's Agent ☐ Seller's (sub)Agent ☐ Dual Agent
Mailing Address: _____

Individual Selling Agent: _____
☐ Acting as a Designated Dual Agent (check only if applicable)
License #: _____
Selling Agent Phone#: _____
Selling Agent Fax#: _____
Selling Agent E-mail: _____

SELLER NOTICE ADDRESS:

Mailing Address: _____

Seller Fax#: _____
Seller E-mail: _____

LISTING AGENT NOTICE ADDRESS:

Firm Name: _____
Acting as ☐ Seller's Agent ☐ Dual Agent
Mailing Address: _____

Individual Listing Agent: _____
☐ Acting as a Designated Dual Agent (check only if applicable)
License #: _____
Listing Agent Phone#: _____
Listing Agent Fax#: _____
Listing Agent E-mail: _____

ESCROW ACKNOWLEDGMENT OF INITIAL EARNEST MONEY DEPOSIT

Property: _____

Seller: _____

Buyer: _____

Escrow Agent acknowledges receipt of the Initial Earnest Money Deposit and agrees to hold and disburse the same in accordance with the terms hereof.

Date _____ Firm: _____

By: _____
(Signature)

_____
(Print name)

Exhibit 3.4: Example geotechnical report

Report of Geotechnical Exploration
Proposed Residence, Lot 30 Sunset Falls at Bald Creek
Clyde, North Carolina

June 1, 2012
BLE Project No. J12-7825-04

AUTHORIZATION

A geotechnical exploration report for the proposed Residence for Lot 30 at Sunset Falls at Bald Creek in Clyde, North Carolina was performed generally as described in Bunnell-Lammons Engineering (BLE) Proposal No. P12-0292 dated May 22, 2012. The exploration was authorized by your signature on our proposal acceptance sheet dated May 22, 2012.

SCOPE OF EXPLORATION

This report presents the findings of the geotechnical exploration performed for the proposed Residence at Lot 30 in Sunset Falls at Bald Creek in Clyde, North Carolina (reference Figure 1). The intent of this exploration was to evaluate the subsurface soil and ground water conditions at the site and provide detailed geotechnical recommendations for design of the foundations and floor slab and associated project elements. We have also included a discussion of slopes, secondary design considerations and provided geotechnical-related construction recommendations.

PROJECT INFORMATION

The following project information was provided to us in a request for proposal (RFP) e-mail dated May 18, 2012 and subsequent telephone and e-mail correspondence. Our Mr. Will Gentry, P.E. visited the site on May 18 and May 23, 2012. We were provided with a site plan prepared by LandDesign showing Lot 30, the proposed location of house, driveway and septic field. However, the owner stated "the driveway is roughly accurate, although it won't go as far to the east as shown on the site plan. The house will be a little further south than what is shown; probably halfway between what is shown and the southern property line."

The site consists of typical wooded mountainous property in Clyde, North Carolina. Based on a review of the topographic information shown on the Site Plan and our observations during the geotechnical exploration for the subject property the overall site slopes downward from north to south at an inclination of about 2.4H:1V to 3H:1V (Horizontal : Vertical) or about 42 to 33 percent average slope.

The exact footprint, number of stories and type of construction and finished floor elevations are unknown at this time. We have not been provided with the proposed structural loading for the new residence. However, for the purpose of this proposal we have assumed that maximum individual column (if applicable) and continuous wall loads will not exceed 75 kips and 3 kips per linear foot, respectively.

FIELD EXPLORATION

The site was explored by excavating six test pits with a mini-excavator at the approximate locations shown on the attached Test Pit Location Plan (reference Figure 2). The test pits were excavated to depths ranging from 8 to 10 feet deep. The test pit locations were located in the field by our Mr. Will Gentry, P.E. by referencing the provided site plan and the survey pin (rebar) that marks the southwest corner of lot. Test Pit tables that summarize the conditions encountered at each location are presented later in this report. The test

Do Your Due Diligence—Part II

Report of Geotechnical Exploration
Proposed   Residence, Lot 30 – Sunset Falls at Bald Creek
Clyde, North Carolina

June 1, 2012
BLE Project No. J12-7825-04

pit locations shown in Figure 2 should be considered approximate. A description of our field procedures is also included in the Appendix.

LABORATORY TESTING

Natural Moisture Content

The natural moisture content of a bulk sample of the silty sand residual soil from TP-6 (1 to 2 feet) and TP-6 (5 to 10 feet) was determined in accordance with ASTM D 2216. The moisture content of the soil is the ratio, expressed as a percentage, of the weight of water in a given mass of soil to the weight of the soil particles. The results are presented in the table below.

Percent Finer than No. 200 Sieve

A percent finer than a No. 200 Sieve test was performed on a bulk sample of the silty sand residual soil from TP-6 (1 to 2 feet) and TP-6 (5 to 10 feet) to determine the fines (silt and clay) content of these materials. After initial drying, the sample was washed over a U. S. Standard No. 200 sieve to remove the fines (particles finer than a No. 200 mesh sieve). This test was performed in a manner similar to that described by ASTM D 1140. The results are presented in the table below.

LABORATORY TEST RESULTS				
Test Pit No.	Depth	Percent Finer than No. 200 Sieve	Moisture Content	USCS Soil Classification
	(feet)	(%)	(%)	
TP-6	1-2	48.0	24.4	SM
TP-6	5-10	27.4	20.1	SM

Everything You Need To Know About Buying Mountain Property

Report of Geotechnical Exploration
Proposed Residence, Lot 30 – Sunset Falls at Bald Creek
Clyde, North Carolina

June 1, 2012
BLE Project No. J12-7825-04

Moisture Density Relationship

One bulk sample of the silty sand residual soil from TP-6 (5 to 10 feet) was collected and transported to the laboratory for compaction testing. A standard Proctor compaction test (ASTM D 698) was performed on the sample to determine compaction characteristics, including the maximum dry density and optimum moisture content. Test results are presented on the attached Compaction Test sheets in the Appendix.

SITE GEOLOGY

The project site is located in the Blue Ridge Physiographic Province. The bedrock in this region is a complex crystalline formation that has been faulted and contorted by past tectonic movements. The rock has weathered to residual soils which form the mantle for the hillsides and hilltops. The typical residual soil profile in areas not disturbed by erosion or the activities of man consists of clayey soils near the surface where weathering is more advanced, underlain by sandy silts and silty sands. There may be colluvial (old landslide) material on the slopes.

The boundary between soil and rock is not sharply defined, and there often is a transitional zone, termed "partially weathered rock," overlying the parent bedrock. Partially weathered rock is defined, for engineering purposes, as residual material with standard penetration resistances in excess of 100 blows per foot (bpf). Weathering is facilitated by fractures, joints, and the presence of less resistant rock types. Consequently, the profile of the partially weathered rock and hard rock is quite irregular and erratic, even over short horizontal distances. Also, it is not unusual to find lenses and boulders of hard rock and/or zones of partially weathered rock within the soil mantle well above the general bedrock level.

SUBSURFACE SOIL CONDITIONS

The surficial conditions of the site consisted of approximately 4 to 6 inches of topsoil and root mat. Below the topsoil, the subsurface conditions generally consisted of 8 to 10 feet of firm or better, moist, reddish-brown, tan or white, silty sand residual soil. Partially weathered rock (PWR) was encountered at a depth of 8 feet in Test Pit No. 1. The PWR encountered caused refusal to the bucket of the mini-excavator.

Dynamic cone penetrometer (DCP) testing was performed in some of the test pits to quantify the consistency of the soils. DCP tests consist of driving a metal probe rod into the ground and observing the effort (i.e., the number of blows from a 15-pound weight dropped 20 inches) needed for three successive 1¾-inch penetrations. The reported blow count is the average of the last two increments. Observed blow counts from our DCP testing varied between 12 to more than 25 blows per increment indicating soils with a firm or better consistency/relative density.

Do Your Due Diligence—Part II

Report of Geotechnical Exploration
Proposed　　　Residence, Lot 30 – Sunset Falls at Bold Creek
Clyde, North Carolina

June 1, 2012
BLE Project No. J12-7825-04

The subsurface conditions encountered at each test pit location are as follows:

Table 1 – Log for Test Pit No. 1 (TP-1)

Depth (feet)	DCP Blow Count	Material Description
Surface	Not tested	4 to 6 inches of Topsoil
1	Not tested	Firm or better, reddish-brown and tan, moist,
2	25+	silty SAND (residual)
3	Not tested	Firm or better, tan or tan and white, moist,
4	Not tested	silty SAND (residual)
5	25+	
6		
7		
8		Ground water not encountered
Mini-excavator refusal encountered at 8 feet		

Table 2 – Log for Test Pit No. 2 (TP-2)

Depth (feet)	DCP Blow Count	Material Description
Surface	Not tested	4 to 6 inches of Topsoil
1	Not tested	Firm or better, reddish-brown and tan, moist,
2	Not tested	silty SAND (residual)
3	Not tested	Firm or better, tan or tan and white, moist,
4	Not tested	silty SAND (residual)
5	Not tested	
6	Not tested	
7	Not tested	
8	Not tested	
9	Not tested	
10	Not tested	Ground water not encountered.
Test pit terminated at 10 feet.		

Everything You Need To Know About Buying Mountain Property

Report of Geotechnical Exploration
Proposed Residence, Lot 30 – Sunset Falls at Bald Creek
Clyde, North Carolina

June 1, 2012
BLE Project No. J12-7825-04

Table 5 – Log for Test Pit No. 5 (TP-5)

Depth (feet)	DCP Blow Count	Material Description
Surface	Not tested	4 to 6 inches of Topsoil
1	Not tested	Firm or better, reddish-brown and tan, moist, silty SAND (residual)
2	12	
3	Not tested	
4	25+	
5	Not tested	Firm or better, tan or tan and white, moist, silty SAND (residual)
6	Not tested	
7	Not tested	
8	Not tested	
9	Not tested	
10	Not tested	No ground water encountered
Test pit terminated at 10 feet		

Table 6 – Log for Test Pit No. 6 (TP-6)

Depth (feet)	DCP Blow Count	Material Description
Surface	Not tested	4 to 6 inches of Topsoil
1	Not tested	Firm or better, reddish-brown and tan, moist, silty SAND (residual)
2	Not tested	
3	Not tested	
4	Not tested	
5	Not tested	
6	Not tested	Firm or better, tan or tan and white, moist, silty SAND (residual)
7	Not tested	
8	Not tested	
9	Not tested	
10	Not tested	No ground water encountered
Test pit terminated at 10 feet		

Report of Geotechnical Exploration
Proposed Residence, Lot 30 – Sunset Falls at Bald Creek
Clyde, North Carolina

June 1, 2012
BLE Project No. J12-7825-04

Shallow Foundations

Based on the test pit data and our experience with similar soil conditions, the existing residual soils are suitable for shallow foundation support of the proposed construction. Satisfactory performance of the shallow foundations is subject to the criteria and site preparation recommendations contained in this report.

Foundations bearing in the residual soils may be sized for an allowable bearing pressure of 3,000 pounds per square foot (psf). Foundations bearing on new engineered fill used to raise site grades or replace unsuitable soils that are placed on suitable soils and compacted to at least 95 percent of the standard Proctor maximum dry density, as recommended later in this report, may also be sized for an allowable bearing pressure of 3,000 psf. Compacted fill should be limited to backfill of undercut areas and not to raise site grades which could cause instability of the natural slopes. If new fill slopes are required for site development, we recommend that BLE review and analyze the proposed construction.

We recommend that the minimum widths for individual column and continuous wall footings be 24 and 18 inches, respectively. The minimum widths will provide a margin of safety against a local or punching shear failure of the foundation soils. Footings should bear at least 30 inches below final grade to provide frost protection and protective embedment. Also, footings **must** bear at least 5 feet horizontally from a slope face. This includes footings bearing near the crest of a slope or within the slope itself. This will result in the footing bearing deeper than the minimum frost embedment depth to allow for the 5-foot horizontal separation from a slope face. We recommend that masonry walls be provided with periodic movement joints to accommodate some possible differential settlement.

Exposure to the environment may weaken the soils at the footing bearing level if the foundation excavations remain open for long periods of time. Therefore, we recommend that once each footing excavation is extended to final grade, the footing be constructed as soon as possible to minimize the potential damage to bearing soils. The foundation bearing area should be level or benched and free of loose soil, ponded water and debris. Foundation concrete should not be placed on soils that have been disturbed by seepage. If the bearing soils are softened by surface water intrusion or exposure, the softened soils must be removed from the foundation excavation bottom prior to placement of concrete. If the excavation must remain open overnight or if rainfall becomes imminent while the bearing soils are exposed, we recommend that a 2 to 4-inch thick "mud-mat" of "lean" (2,000 psi) concrete be placed on the bearing soils for protection before the placement of reinforcing steel.

To verify that the soils encountered in footing excavations are similar to those encountered in the test pits, we recommend that foundation excavations be examined. Part of this examination should include checking the bearing soils with a dynamic cone penetrometer performed by an experienced engineering technician working under the direction of the geotechnical engineer. Foundation excavations near the natural slope should also be observed by the geotechnical engineer for evidence of conditions that could cause slope instability. New compacted fill used to support foundations should be tested as recommended in this report.

Everything You Need To Know About Buying Mountain Property

Report of Geotechnical Exploration
Proposed   Residence, Lot 30 – Sunset Falls at Bald Creek
Clyde, North Carolina

June 1, 2012
BLE Project No. J12-7825-04

Pending the results of the examination, it may be necessary to overexcavate some of the existing soils below foundations. Soft, wet soils should be overexcavated and replaced with compacted engineered fill, crushed stone or No. 57 stone. The width of the overexcavation should be equal to the width of the footing plus the depth of the overexcavation below the bearing level. It is not expected that undercutting of unsuitable soils will be required beneath all footings but it will likely be required beneath some of the footings.

Based on the estimated foundation loads, settlement of foundations on hard rock or the partially weathered rock should be negligible. Settlement of the foundations supported on firm and better residual soils is estimated to be 1-inch or less. Differential settlement between footings supported on residual soil should be expected to be about ½-inch or less.

Lateral Earth Pressure

Retaining walls if used on this project must be capable of resisting the lateral earth pressures that will be imposed on them. Walls which will be permitted to rotate at the top, such as retaining walls not part of the structure, may be designed to resist the active earth pressure. The active earth pressure coefficient is designated as Ka. Typically, a top rotation of about 1 inch per 10 feet height of wall is sufficient to develop active pressure conditions in soils similar to those encountered at the site.

Walls which will be prevented from rotating such as basement walls braced against the upper floor level should be designed to resist the at-rest lateral earth pressure. The at-rest earth pressure coefficient is designated as Ko.

The passive earth pressure may be considered as the pressure exerted on the side of a foundation which aids in resisting sliding of the foundation. The passive earth pressure coefficient is designated as Kp. Friction resistance along the base of the foundation may also be used to resist sliding. The coefficient of frictional resistance is designated as fs.

The following table provides a summary of the recommended earth pressure coefficients to be used in design. Also included are the associated frictional resistance values and soil unit weights to be used in the design. These values are based on our experience and testing of reasonably similar soils on other projects. The values presented in the following table assume the ground surface is level.

Sloping backfill (or sloping soil surfaces in front of a footing when considering passive resistance) will greatly influence the earth pressure coefficients. Bunnell-Lammons Engineering should be consulted concerning applicable earth pressure coefficients where sloping soil surfaces may be present.

Do Your Due Diligence—Part II

Report of Geotechnical Exploration
Proposed   Residence, Lot 30 – Sunset Falls at Bald Creek
Clyde, North Carolina

June 1, 2012
BLE Project No. J12-7825-04

Table 7 – Recommendations for Soil Properties and Lateral Earth Pressures									
Material	Unit Weight (pcf)	Material Properties		Active Earth Pressure		At-rest Earth Pressure		Passive Earth Pressure	
		Friction Angle, Φ' (degrees)	f_s	Equivalent Fluid Pressure (pcf)	K_a	Equivalent Fluid Pressure (pcf)	K_o	Equivalent Fluid Pressure (pcf)	$K_p^{(1)}$
On-site silty SAND or sandy SILT	125	30	0.4	42	0.33	63	0.50	375$^{(1)}$	3.0
Clean washed stone (No. 57)$^{(2)}$	100	40	0.6	25	0.22	35	0.36	230$^{(1)}$	4.6

(1) The passive earth pressure coefficient should be divided by a safety factor of 2 to limit the amount of lateral deformation required to mobilize the passive resistance.
(2) In order for this coefficient to be used, the soil wedge within an angle of 45 degrees from the base of the wall to about 2 feet below the exterior grade should be excavated and replaced with compacted clean washed stone.

The compacted mass unit weight of the backfill soil presented in the previous table should be used with the earth pressure coefficients to calculate lateral earth pressures. Lateral pressure arising from surcharge loading, earthquake loading, and ground water should be added to the above soil earth pressures to determine the total lateral pressures which the walls must resist. In addition, transient loads imposed on the walls by construction equipment during backfilling should be taken into consideration during design and construction. Excessively heavy grading equipment should not be allowed within about 5 feet horizontally of the walls.

Surface water should not be allowed to pond behind the walls. To reduce the potential for the infiltration of surface water into the backfill, the upper 24 inches of backfill should consist of relatively impervious soils (i.e., clayey or silty soils) as backfill. This soil should be compacted to a minimum of 95 percent of its standard Proctor maximum dry density within plus or minus three percentage points of the optimum moisture content in accordance with ASTM D 698.

We recommend that positive, unblocked gravity drainage be provided from behind the walls. A perforated, rigid conduit within free draining crushed stone backfill at the base of the wall can be used to help provide the drainage required. A layer of nonwoven geotextile filter fabric should wrap entirely around the crushed stone backfill. If drainage is not provided, the walls should be designed to accommodate hydrostatic pressures that could develop.

Everything You Need To Know About Buying Mountain Property

Report of Geotechnical Exploration
Proposed   Residence, Lot 30   Sunset Falls at Bald Creek
Clyde, North Carolina

June 1, 2012
BLE Project No. J12-7825-04

Surface Water Management

Control of surface water from paved areas and roof drainage is very important for this site. Surface water eroding slopes could cause slope instability. All structures should incorporate gutters with downspouts that are connected to a pipe system that will convey water to storm drains or offsite. Routine maintenance should include inspecting, cleaning and repairing the gutters, downspouts and other stormwater handling systems as needed to ensure they remain operable. Inspections and cleanings should be performed at least annually. If conveyance of surface water into municipal storm drains is not possible, the surface water should be directed away from the structure and maintained in a distributed flow onto the natural slope. Surface water should not be directed below the ground surface.

Grade Slabs

The grade slab may be soil supported on the existing sandy silt to silty sand residual soils or compacted engineered fill used to raise site grades or replace unsuitable soils assuming that the site is prepared in accordance with the recommendations in this report. Fill beneath grade slabs should be limited in thickness as much as possible to reduce the risk of instability. The grade slab should be jointed around columns and along footing supported walls so that the slab and foundations can settle differentially without damage. If slab thickness permits, joints containing dowels or keys may be used in the slab to permit movement between parts of the slab without cracking or sharp vertical displacements. We recommend that a modulus of subgrade reaction value of 150 psi/inch or less be used for design of grade slabs on residual soil or compacted engineered fill. Completed slabs should be protected from excessive surface moisture prior to and during periods of prolonged below-freezing temperatures to prevent subgrade freezing and resulting heave. Grade slabs should not be constructed on frozen soil.

Floor slabs supported on grade which will be carpeted, tiled, painted or receive some other covering or sealant should incorporate a vapor barrier. The vapor barrier should be installed in accordance with the manufacturer's recommendations with the following additional considerations. We recommend that a two inch thick layer of sand be placed over the vapor barrier to 1) protect the vapor barrier; and 2) dissipate moisture from the concrete slab during curing.

Secondary Design Considerations

The following items are presented for your consideration. These items are known to generally enhance performance of structural and pavement systems.

- Roof drainage should be collected by a system of gutters and downspouts and directed away from all structures. Control of surface water including roof drainage is very important to long term stability of the natural slope.
- Sidewalks should be sloped so that water drains away from the structures.
- Site grading and paving should result in positive drainage away from the structures. Water should not be allowed to pond around the structures or in such locations that would lead to

Report of Geotechnical Exploration
Proposed Residence, Lot 30 - Sunset Falls at Bald Creek
Clyde, North Carolina

June 1, 2012
BLE Project No. J12-7825-04

saturation of pavement subgrade materials. A minimum slope of approximately ¼ to ½-inch per foot should provide adequate drainage.
- Backfill for utility lines should be placed at the same density as surrounding material to minimize the potential for differential settlement.

CONSTRUCTION RECOMMENDATIONS

Clearing and Grubbing

All existing trees, brush, topsoil, vegetation, and surface soils containing organic matter or other deleterious materials should be stripped from within the proposed building area. Topsoil and organic soils may be stockpiled for later use in areas to be landscaped. Stumps and other deleterious material should be disposed of offsite or in areas of the site that will not be developed. Future construction of buildings or pavement in areas containing limbs or stumps, organic soils, burn pit residue or other deleterious materials will first require that these materials be removed.

Dewatering

The test pits did not encounter ground water within the expected construction depths. However, depending on the weather conditions at the time of construction, perched water may be encountered by excavations. The contractor should be prepared to promptly remove any surface water or ground water from the construction area. This has been done effectively on past jobs by means of gravity ditches and pumping from filtered sumps.

Subgrade Inspection

After stripping and rough excavation grading, we recommend that areas to provide support for the foundations, floor slab, engineered fill and pavement be carefully inspected for soft surficial soils by the geotechnical engineer. Any areas which are considered unsuitable should be excavated to firmer soils. The excavated areas should be backfilled in thin lifts with engineered fill.

Difficult Excavation

The firm or better silty sand residual soil should be excavatable with conventional construction equipment such as trackhoes. PWR was encountered at a depth fo 8 feet in test pit No. 1. Heavy, tracked excavating equipment with single tooth ripping tools will be required to remove PWR. The ease of excavation of PWR cannot be specifically quantified and depends on the quality of grading equipment, skill of the equipment operators and geologic structure of the material itself, such as the direction of bedding, planes of weakness and spacing between discontinuities. Excavation of the refusal material usually requires blasting to loosen and facilitate removal.

Everything You Need To Know About Buying Mountain Property

Report of Geotechnical Exploration
Proposed   Residence, Lot 30 – Sunset Falls at Bald Creek
Clyde, North Carolina

June 1, 2012
BLE Project No. J12-7825-04

Table 7 – Recommendations for Soil Properties and Lateral Earth Pressures

Material	Unit Weight (pcf)	Material Properties		Active Earth Pressure		At-rest Earth Pressure		Passive Earth Pressure	
		Friction Angle, Φ' (degrees)	f_s	Equivalent Fluid Pressure (pcf)	K_a	Equivalent Fluid Pressure (pcf)	K_o	Equivalent Fluid Pressure (pcf)	$K_p^{(1)}$
On-site silty SAND or sandy SILT	125	30	0.4	42	0.33	63	0.50	375$^{(1)}$	3.0
Clean washed stone (No. 57)$^{(2)}$	100	40	0.6	25	0.22	35	0.36	230$^{(1)}$	4.6

(1) The passive earth pressure coefficient should be divided by a safety factor of 2 to limit the amount of lateral deformation required to mobilize the passive resistance.

(2) In order for this coefficient to be used, the soil wedge within an angle of 45 degrees from the base of the wall to about 2 feet below the exterior grade should be excavated and replaced with compacted clean washed stone.

The compacted mass unit weight of the backfill soil presented in the previous table should be used with the earth pressure coefficients to calculate lateral earth pressures. Lateral pressure arising from surcharge loading, earthquake loading, and ground water should be added to the above soil earth pressures to determine the total lateral pressures which the walls must resist. In addition, transient loads imposed on the walls by construction equipment during backfilling should be taken into consideration during design and construction. Excessively heavy grading equipment should not be allowed within about 5 feet horizontally of the walls.

Surface water should not be allowed to pond behind the walls. To reduce the potential for the infiltration of surface water into the backfill, the upper 24 inches of backfill should consist of relatively impervious soils (i.e., clayey or silty soils) as backfill. This soil should be compacted to a minimum of 95 percent of its standard Proctor maximum dry density within plus or minus three percentage points of the optimum moisture content in accordance with ASTM D 698.

We recommend that positive, unblocked gravity drainage be provided from behind the walls. A perforated, rigid conduit within free draining crushed stone backfill at the base of the wall can be used to help provide the drainage required. A layer of nonwoven geotextile filter fabric should wrap entirely around the crushed stone backfill. If drainage is not provided, the walls should be designed to accommodate hydrostatic pressures that could develop.

Do Your Due Diligence—Part II

Report of Geotechnical Exploration
Proposed _____ Residence, Lot 30 – Sunset Falls at Bald Creek
Clyde, North Carolina

June 1, 2012
BLE Project No. J12-7825-04

SPECIFICATIONS REVIEW

It is recommended that Bunnell-Lammons Engineering be provided the opportunity to make a general review of the foundation and earthwork plans and specifications prepared from the recommendations presented in this report. We would then suggest any modifications so that our recommendations are properly interpreted and implemented. An additional modest fee would apply for review of plans and specifications.

LIMITATIONS

Our evaluation of foundation support conditions has been based on our understanding of the project information and data obtained in our exploration as well as our experience on similar projects. The general subsurface conditions utilized in our foundation evaluation have been based on interpolation of the subsurface data between the test pits. Subsurface conditions between the test pits may differ. If the project information is incorrect or the structure location (horizontal or vertical) and/or dimensions are changed, please contact us so that our recommendations can be reviewed. The discovery of any site or subsurface conditions during construction which deviate from the data obtained in this exploration should be reported to us for our evaluation. The assessment of site environmental conditions for presence of pollutants in the soil, rock and ground water of the site was beyond the scope of this exploration.

CHAPTER FOUR

"Where's The Beef?"

The community's infrastructure and municipal services

The Question:
What is the status of the construction of the various elements that comprise the infrastructure, and who is providing the utility and municipal services, including their maintenance, to the community?

1. Roads

Are the roads public or private? There are three primary concerns here: to what standards and specifications the roads are constructed, who will pay the cost to maintain them, and who has the right to use them.
   a) If the roads are to be private, you need to ascertain to what particular standards and specifications they have been (or will be) constructed. That information can typically be obtained from the county's Planning Department within their Subdivision Ordinances. If the roads are public, they must be built to the standards of that state's Department of Transportation

specifications, which is a positive, since these state guidelines are typically more stringent than the local jurisdiction's subdivision design requirements.

b) If the roads are private, the homeowners will be responsible for the costs to maintain them, the funds for which will be collected through their HOA dues. If the roads are public, the local town or county will be required to maintain them with the revenues generated from its tax base.

c) You may have already concluded now that items "a" and "b" are making a strong case for your vote for public roads. To the contrary; you should know that if the roads are public, that is, if they are maintained with funds collected from the tax revenues raised from the general public, then anyone has the right to use them. A developer cannot, therefore, provide to you the benefits of a gated community where access is controlled and restricted, if the roadway system is public. If you are looking for a community that can afford to you the benefits of heightened security, increased privacy, reduced traffic, and the otherwise more peaceful existence that a gated community can offer, roadways that are private will better suit your needs.

There are obviously both positives and negatives to either of the two scenarios, public vs. private roadways, and neither is right or wrong. It is a question of opinion and what you value, what is more important to you in the environment in which you wish to reside in your future home.

In some states, it is a statutory requirement that a developer provide you with a "Street Disclosure Statement" that clearly informs you of the public or private status of the community's roadway system and of the consequent financial responsibility of the maintenance of the roadways. (See Chapter Three within the section entitled "Covenants, Conditions, and Restrictions.") If you don't receive such a document from the developer and you have a strong preference for one or the other, be sure to ask the developer for written confirmation as to the roads' public/private status and be equally sure to review the HOA budget for line items that would reflect maintenance expenses for the roadways to be paid for by the HOA.

If the roadway system is to be private, and if the roads have yet to be completed, be sure to inquire regarding the developer's plans to pave them and particularly whether some streets will be paved and others will not. Many rural jurisdictions have no requirement for subdivision roads to be paved unless the steepness of the road exceeds a specified maximum allowable slope (such as 15 percent), and even then, asphalt pavement is only required in those locations where that maximum slope is exceeded. The paving of many internal subdivision roadways, the majority of which do not or should not exceed a 15 percent slope, is thus more of a marketing decision by the developer than a result of any regulatory influence.

There is nothing inherently wrong with unpaved arterial roadways, as long as the roadbed itself is properly constructed of a sufficiently compacted thickness of road rock per the local subdivision requirements. Interestingly enough, some folks actually prefer the more rustic appearance, feel, and sound (under wheel) of unpaved streets and the way their vehicles handle on the compacted rock surface in the event of snow and ice in the winter months.

In many mountain communities with difficult topography, the tightness of roadway widths and the shoulders where the utilities are often located can provide a logistical problem for the developer's construction of the infrastructure. (See Illustration 4.1.) Utility companies that provide underground power, phone, CATV, and Internet services have historically been willing to install their conduit, cabling, and equipment at an early stage in order to be easily coordinated with the installation of the roadways. These providers were willing to make substantial up-front investments in infrastructure with the assumption that the construction of housing within these developments would soon follow, allowing them to recoup their investment in a timely manner through the monthly revenues paid for the consumption of those services by the residents. However, recent trends in the world of residential real estate in the second home market found a combination of a) homesite buyers waiting a number of years before building their homes; b) investor/buyers having no plans ever to build a home; c) too many developers creating an oversupply of homesites; d) too many inexperienced developers bringing poorly constructed (and thus unmarketable) developments to the market; and finally e) the collapse of the market itself. This led to the utility providers waiting to install their infrastructure until the developer had at least one home under construction along a given street that would actually require the infrastructure. This, in turn, resulted in the developer delaying any paving operations until the utility infrastructure was installed, because the tight width of the road and shoulder right-of-way would result in the asphalt being torn up by the utility installation, if the road was paved before the utilities were installed.

Now, why did I go down this involved explanation of infrastructure development, schedules, and timing? It's because a developer may

Do Your Due Diligence—Part II

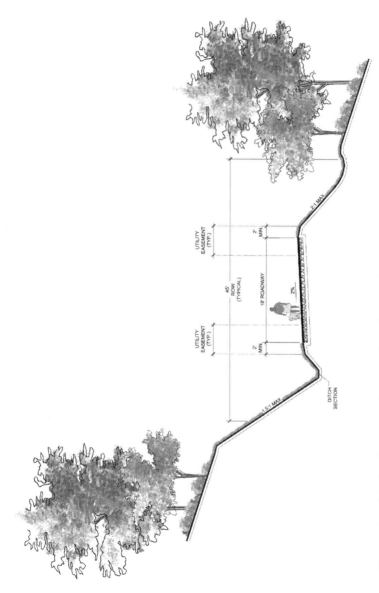

Illustration 4.1: Section view of a typical roadway, reflecting the tight width of the entire right-of-way

have a very good reason for not having paved the roads at a particular time. That is, particularly in the mountains, the developer has added pressure to tightly coordinate the installation of the utilities with the paving of the roadways.

There is another very valid reason that a developer may choose not to pave certain roadways, and that is to allow the construction operations of the homebuilding process to be completed first. Again, due to the fact that mountain topography does not allow much movement of heavy construction vehicles off of the roadways, the roadways tend to get beaten up a bit more than the subdivision roadways in coastal zones or other areas of flat to gentle topography. So it may make sense to delay paving operations in a certain area until construction of the homes in that area is nearing completion.

Finally, the topic of roadways would not be complete without a brief discussion on the subject of performance and payment bonds. Some jurisdictions will require a developer to post a performance and payment bond that essentially guarantees that a certain scope of infrastructure improvements (let's say the roadways, while we're here) will be completed to a certain standard (performance) and paid for (payment). Think of a bond as insurance for which the developer pays an insurance premium. If the work is not properly completed and paid for, the bonding company will step in and perform and pay. (It is never quite that simple, but let's keep it simple for our purposes here.) Bonding is particularly applicable when the scope of work for which the bond is required covers infrastructure that is to become the responsibility of the local jurisdiction. In other words, if the roads are to be public, and the water and sewer systems (not individual wells and septic systems) are to become an extension of a central municipal water and sewer system, the local jurisdiction is apt to require a bond to ensure that the systems are properly constructed and paid for. The local town, city, or county has no desire to take possession of substandard infrastructure, and the bond is the vehicle by which they can ensure that the developer performs his or her duties up to par.

However, here is the problem. Most rural second home developments have private roads, and the water and sewer systems consist of deep wells and septic/drain field facilities installed by each individual homeowner. The local jurisdictions are *not* assuming the ownership or maintenance of any infrastructure, so the only real reason to require a bond would be to protect you, the consumer. To date, very few governing bodies have gone down that path. It remains a "buyer beware" philosophy. The lack of a bond says nothing either positive or negative about the developer; it is simply a reflection of the policies of local legislation, reflected in the subdivision ordinances. In rare circumstances, a developer may volunteer to post a bond to ensure the completion of the infrastructure. In those instances, it is primarily a marketing benefit to a savvy and well-capitalized developer; buyers will no doubt have more confidence in making a homesite purchase in a community where the completion of the infrastructure is backed up by a bond.

2. Power

There are a number of concerns regarding power in mountain communities that are under development, which may never occur to the average buyer because the average buyer has always rented an apartment or purchased a single-family home or condominium where the existence and availability of electrical power was simply a given. You were no more concerned about power than you were about the toilet in the master bathroom or the tile on the kitchen floor. Power just was, and you weren't particularly worried that it would be anything else, unless a storm came by and knocked it out momentarily.

We need to remember that our discussion of infrastructure here is always based upon the assumption that one is buying a homesite, not a home. A homesite has no immediate need for power. In most, if not all, mountain communities where the sale of lots is the primary business model, there is no requirement that power be installed in order to legally convey a homesite. As previously noted in our discussion of roads, it is actually becoming more common for utility companies to delay the installation of their conduit, cabling, and equipment until there is a definitive need, that is, until a home is actually under construction along a given street within the community. So it is *not* necessarily unusual to *not* have power facilities installed down a particular roadway if there are no homes yet constructed along that roadway.

In most communities, there is a main arterial roadway that is considered to be the primary corridor throughout the community, off of which the various side streets originate. Power along this main arterial road should be in place prior to any sales. If it is not in place, I would be very hesitant to buy property there. On the other hand, if you are interested in buying a lot that is located down one of the secondary roads where power is not yet installed, I would be less concerned; however, I would be sure to add language in the purchase agreement that the developer agrees to have permanent power installed to your homesite prior to or contemporaneous with the receipt of your building permit, once you have decided to build your home.

If you are pursuing a loan for your lot purchase, it may very well be the policy of the lender to either require that permanent power be installed to your lot at the time of the closing or, alternatively, that the power company that is responsible for providing power to the lot that is secured by the loan provide a letter of service availability essentially makes a statement to the bank that it is the entity providing power to the development and that it will provide the necessary power facilities to the lot at the time that it is needed. This assures both you and the bank that you will not find yourself in the position of owning real estate that has no viable source of electrical power.

One final point about electric power—the providers of this utility fall into two different categories: conventional and cooperative. Conventional electrical utility firms typically do not charge developers for the initial installation of the power infrastructure, which means that for the developer, there is no issue or concern about any up-front cost; there is just an exercise of scheduling the work at an appropriate time. With cooperatives, on the other hand, or co-ops, as many refer to them, they typically *do* charge the developer for the initial installation of the underground conduit and cable and the transformers and other initial equipment. This difference in how each type of utility firm finances its activities adds an additional concern for you, the buyer, simply because if power is to be provided by an electrical cooperative, and power is not installed to your chosen lot at the time of your purchase, you have to trust that the developer will have the funds to pay for the power at the time that you will need it. Again, both you and the developer should agree on a contractual amendment to the purchase agreement that reflects the mutual understanding of when the developer shall be obligated to have the power installed to the homesite.

3. Telephone, Cable Television, Internet Access

The discussion of these three services is grouped together because, with the state of current technology, the three are often iscounted package provided by one entity. For n, all-inclusive package today might find AT&T ional land line, cell phone service, satellite tele- as DirecTV), and high-speed Internet service via DSL; or Charter Communication might provide cable TV service, high-speed Internet service, and a land-based phone line, all using the cable facilities, which might be coupled with Verizon for cell phone service.

The main point here is that developers are not required to provide any of these services by virtue of any regulatory mandate or statute. There is certainly a mandate from the general public, and the developer who casually disregards the market's mandates won't be in business for very long; however, the rural and sparsely populated nature of many developments in the mountains results in significant differences in the availability of these services from community to community. As noted previously, service providers have historically not charged residential real estate developers for the initial costs of the installation of the infrastructure, relying on the future revenue streams from the end users to provide an economically feasible model. That is changing, particularly in the second home market, where a minimally acceptable quantity of end users to provide that timely revenue stream is by no means guaranteed.

Homesite buyers need to ask the developer specific questions about specific services. Have the landlines been installed for phone service? Do those facilities include high-speed Internet capability? Is there underground CATV, or is satellite-based premium TV the only option? Which cell phone carriers have the best reception on the mountain? Are satellite-based Internet services available and affordable? Are cell tower-based Internet services available and affordable?

There is no shortage of second home buyers who intend to continue their later life careers, whether they are continuations of the old or experiments with the new, by operating out of a home office which they have designed into their new retreats in the mountains. Connectivity is of paramount importance, so don't leave these stones unturned; don't leave these questions unasked. Technology is in a constant state of change, usually for the better, from the standpoint of the quality of the service. What is written herein may be passé five years from now, but the questions remain the same. Make sure that the available technology allows you to function and operate effectively and efficiently, because I guarantee you that the longer you stay in the mountains, away from the hustle and bustle of your previous life, the longer you will do just that...*stay*...and you will be sorely disappointed if the infrastructure that you assumed was there at the time you purchased your homesite is not there then nor there when you build your home.

A last note that may seem inconsequential to some but may not be to others: many people have decided to do without their landlines altogether, and that is fine. Where it may not be fine is if, like many people, your cell phone, which utilizes an area code that is long distance from your second home, is your only form of telephonic contact. You should be aware that if you intend to live in a gated community in the mountains, unless you obtain a local landline or cell phone, you may not be able to take advantage of one of the security gate's most convenient capabilities. Most security gate systems have the capacity to have a visitor dial you from the gate keypad to ask for access, should the gates be closed. Typically, you can punch a button on your phone when the vendor calls you from the keypad phone, and that will open the gates to allow access. Those dialers at the keypad typically do not have long distance capability as part of the scope of the communication features. Therefore, you should know that if you want to be able to take full advantage of the gate's bells and whistles, you will most likely need to get a local landline or a local cell phone.

4. Wastewater Collection (or Septic and Drain Field) Systems

Most of the people in this country who are well-heeled enough to afford to buy second home properties probably have primary home locations in more metropolitan areas that are served by centralized municipal wastewater treatment systems. In those environments, people do not concern themselves much with what happens when they flush the toilet. A far greater emphasis is probably placed on the proper functioning of their bathrooms' exhaust fans than on any concern for where the wastewater is actually going. In the mountains, chances are that the wastewater won't be going too far, simply out to your septic tank with, eventually, portions of it dispersed into what is known as a drain field. Why is this important to know at this stage, when all you are doing is looking for a homesite and may not build for five or ten years? Because in five or ten years, you're still going to want the relative comfort of knowing that you can actually build that home that you've been dreaming of all that time and have the luxury of using the toilets for the purpose intended.

Still reading? Okay, good. This is not a very appealing or sexy subject, so let's get through it as fast as we can. In a nutshell, a septic and drain field system allows you to process your own wastewater on your own property; and believe it or not, the type of soil, the depth of the soil, the slope of the soil, the location of the house, driveway, deep well, and any other improvements that require you to disturb the earth—all have an impact on the area of your homesite that can be devoted to the drain field installation. Moreover, the maximum available size of that area can potentially restrict the number of bedrooms that you can legally have in the home.

(The scope of this discussion is not intended to cover the technical and biological issues involved in the design and functioning of septic and drain field wastewater treatment systems. It is enough to fully understand how such systems can impact the overall use of the homesite and the various components within it, such that the buyer can make an informed decision as to whether the property can satisfy his or her needs.)

The wastewater produced by your home will initially be captured by an underground septic tank, the solids from which will be pumped out periodically by a company that specializes in that lovely task. The effluent, however, the liquid portion of the contents, flows out to a drain field, which is essentially a number of parallel rows of perforated pipe, installed a few feet below the surface of the ground and encased in gravel or other permeable material that allows the effluent to flow through it and into the in situ soils. (See Photo 4.1.)

In most jurisdictions, the local health department will have approved a drain field area for each lot, the size and design of which will determine the number of bedrooms that will be allowed in the home for each respective lot. The health department will have analyzed the type and depth of the soil, the steepness of the topography of the area, and other technical parameters in order to arrive at the required lineal footage of drain field piping and the specific area in which that piping must be placed in order to properly serve the wastewater needs of the home. So, here is what is important: *have the developer provide you with the health department's written approval of the drain field authorization,*

Photo 4.1: conventional drain field installation

typically referred to as a soil/site evaluation report and improvement permit. (Refer to Exhibit 3.1 in Chapter Three.) This document should reflect, among other things, the approved location for the drain field, the type of drain field, and the maximum number of bedrooms that the home may have. If the county in which the community is located requires the health department's approval as a prerequisite for plat approval, the developer should have no problem providing you with a copy of that approval. If the county does *not* require the health department's approval of the drain field as a precedent to plat approval, then *do not purchase the lot until the developer obtains this approval and you are satisfied with the size, area utilized, and the type of the approved drain field.*

You will note in the above discussion that one of the items that should be reflected in the health department's approval/evaluation is the *type* of drain field system that is approved. In flattish to gently sloping topography with well-percolating soils, health departments will typically specify what are known as conventional systems, which comprise perforated piping with some form of filtering material around the pipes. These systems are fed by gravity as opposed to requiring pumps, so the equipment needs are really quite simple. The material costs do not vary considerably from one conventional product line to another. Any significant differential in the overall cost will be more a function of labor and equipment impacts from topography differences, access constraints, the location and number of trees in the area, etc.

However, if the soils are not particularly deep and/or do not percolate well, and if those soil characteristics are further compromised by steep topography, the use of a conventional drain field system may not be feasible. In those instances, the health department may specify what is known as a "drip irrigation system." These systems consist of greater lengths of smaller diameter perforated piping installed just below ground level. Pumps, distribution boxes, and manifolds are utilized to regulate the flow of effluent, so that the drain field system is "dosed" on a regular basis. The additional labor, equipment, and material cost associated with the increase in the lineal footage of piping and the added costs associated with the pump and equipment can result in costs that may be more than *triple the cost of a conventional system*. Homesite buyers need to do their homework up front to ensure that they will not be surprised down the road if the local health department has mandated a drip irrigation drain field system for the homesite that they purchased.

A further note may help to clarify concerns about what may be noted as "repair areas" on the approval/evaluation form. Most jurisdictions require not only a satisfactory primary drain field area but also a "repair area." This is an area that essentially duplicates the primary area, in the event that the primary drain field becomes unusable or its functional integrity comes into question, usually due to a lack of proper maintenance by the homeowner. The designation of a repair area assures the health department that an insurance policy of sorts exists—an area that can be devoted to the construction of a new drain field—should the original drain field be compromised. It is not unusual that the repair area drain field might not have as beneficial soil conditions as the primary area, oftentimes resulting in a drip system being specified for the repair area. *Do not fret about this.* If you take good care of the original, primary septic/drain field system through proper recommended maintenance, the need for the use of the repair area should never come into play. If it comes into play at all, the chances are that it will do so perhaps fifteen to twenty years down the road. In other words, you should have no concern about the repair area when considering the *initial* construction costs of your dream home.

One final note that is important to appreciate and understand: the fact that the health department has approved a specific location for the drain field does *not* mean that this location is the only possible area in which the drain field can be located. It is not at all unusual that when the time comes to design and build the home and coordinate that home with all of the other site elements that make the home a complete and functional residence, the area approved for the drain field is tweaked, twisted, slid one way or another, or even moved in its entirety, should the lot be large enough and the soils accommodating enough to allow it. The homebuilder will need to have the revision approved by the health department, but again, as long as the site can accommodate the change, the revision to the permit should not be a problem.

Why then, you ask, does the health department even go through the initial process in the first place, if the approved area devoted to the drain field can be relocated? Because the department wants to make sure that developers are not selling homesites to the unaware consumer that have *no options whatsoever to accommodate any drain field location in any area of the property*. Has this happened in the past? You bet it has.

5. Drilled Well Systems for Domestic Water

A significant majority of the rural second home communities developed in western North Carolina and in other similar mountainous regions are not served by centrally piped municipal water systems. The source of potable water for these communities, on rare occasions, may be satisfied by a "community well" within the development that is able to take advantage of deep underground flows that are significant enough, in conjunction with large storage facilities, to provide adequate quantities of water for the entire community. More than likely, however, is the scenario where all individual lot owners are required to drill their own domestic water wells within the confines of their own properties. For most communities and the homeowners who reside within them, this is nothing out of the ordinary and nothing to fear. As is the case with sewer facilities noted earlier, buyers who originate from more heavily developed urban and suburban settings are rarely familiar with the concept of providing their own source of water. They are often surprised and confused and view the use of wells as primitive and therefore potentially associated with health risks, neither of which is true.

Wells are typically drilled from a minimum of around 125 feet to a maximum of 1,000 feet, with a typical average of perhaps 350–500 feet. Typical flows vary considerably, from as little 3 or 4 gallons per minute (gpm) to as much as 50 to 60 gpm or more. A 3- or 4-bedroom home can easily address its demand with as little as 3–5 gpm of flow, which I will explain further below.

The key for a homesite buyer is not to be saddled with a dream home land acquisition that turns out later to be a "dry lot," a homesite that is literally without water because all efforts at finding water through the well-drilling process have come up empty. There are a couple of strategies that you can employ to avoid this scenario, both of which involve negotiations with the developer at the time of the lot purchase.

    a) The absolute safest strategy is to negotiate the drilling of the well and both its depth and flow, as a contingency to closing on the homesite purchase. I have done this on numerous occasions, with excellent results for both parties, the developer and the buyer. You should stipulate that the well be drilled prior to the scheduled closing date. Part of that stipulation should be the maximum depth that you will pay for and the minimum flow in gpm that the well must produce. A fair and equitable set of parameters might be that you pay for the first five hundred feet of well depth and that the well must produce a minimum of five gpm. A maximum of five hundred feet and a minimum of five gpm is what you, as the buyer, should be anticipating as acceptable parameters, so it is only fair that you should be responsible for the costs to achieve the same. This, then, predicates the closing on a fair expense that you pay for establishing an acceptable source of water, and it puts the onus on the developer to pay the costs for any additional depth exceeding five hundred feet. More importantly, if the well comes up dry no matter how deep it is drilled, the added contractual language to the purchase agreement should make it clear that all costs associated with the drilling of a *dry well* shall be borne by the developer and that you have the option *not* to close on the lot, and any and all good faith deposit monies shall be returned to you. You should bear in mind that the developer is going to want to be sure that your good faith deposit is at least six thousand dollars in order to make sure that if you were to walk from the deal (in spite of the fact that the well-drilling *was successful*), there would be enough of a deposit to pay the well driller. This is a fair stance for the developer to take.

b) A second alternative that may be offered by the developer and which is preferable to the developer (but not to you) is to have the developer agree to buy back the lot, should you discover it to be a dry lot, when the time comes to build your home and drill the well. I do not recommend this, because it assumes the future existence and financial health of the developer, perhaps years down the road, and it is a far less conservative approach than strategy #1. Many developers might prefer this approach because it requires no upfront cash flow on their part and puts off to the future the possibility of a buyback scenario.

From a budgeting perspective, a well driller should charge approximately $8–$10 per lineal foot (l.f.) of drilled well depth plus costs associated with the casing and grout. The casing is a plastic pipe (about $8/l.f.) or steel pipe (about $15/l.f.) that extends down only to the bedrock to help eliminate the infiltration of surface water into the well. Plastic casing is used probably in as much as 95 percent of the installations. The average casing depth is perhaps fifty feet but could be as shallow as twenty feet (the code minimum) or as deep as two hundred feet. The cylindrical walls of the well below the bottom of the casing are solid granite. Grout fills the annular space between the casing and the earth for the top twenty feet of the well. The average grout cost is around $200, but it will vary from well to well. So from an initial expense standpoint, if strategy #1 is pursued, you may have a typical, average exposure of some $5,600, which would account for a well depth of five hundred feet, plus average plastic casing and grout costs. All of my clients who have chosen to pursue Option #1 have been happy to incur this expense at the time that they closed on the homesite, even though they had not intended to build for a few years. It provided them with the peace of mind that an adequate, potable water supply was indeed available, and they would have been incurring this expense in the future, anyway, if they did not incur it now.

You should note that this is not the final expense for your well, to make it functional. It represents only the expense associated with the portion of the well work that must be done in order to establish the depth and the flow—critical to your confidence that a water source is indeed available and adequate to serve your future needs—giving you the confidence to close on the homesite purchase. When you build the home, you will have additional costs for the pump, electrical work, and piping to get the water into the plumbing fixtures of your home. In addition, if the flow is somewhat borderline (say 2–3 gpm), to allow a healthy, constant flow of water at all times, you may also find it necessary to install a storage tank and an additional pump for this tank. This will allow water to be continually pumped from the well into the storage tank, even during the times that you are not actually using any water, giving you a constant source of stored water that will offset the relatively low flow within the well itself.

6. **LP (Liquefied Petroleum) Gas**

Consistent with the lack of a centralized source of water and sewer is the lack of a municipal system of piped gas that extends to most rural communities. Homeowners in these communities have no less of a desire for the efficiency of gas, particularly for cooking, heating, clothes drying, and hot water usage. The solution for these developments is underground LP gas storage tanks that are the responsibility of each individual homeowner. The tanks are readily available and typically range in size from 250-gallon to 1,000-gallon, depending on the size of the home and the number of gas appliances creating the demand. The most common size is a 500-gallon tank. The tanks can usually either be leased or purchased. There is no great concern here for you as the future homeowner at the lot purchasing stage, other than to understand that the location of the tank will need to be coordinated with all of the other site elements and that there will be a future cost associated with your own tank that you would not normally anticipate with a centrally sourced, underground, municipal gas system that would require no tank.

7. Trash Collection

Many rural communities are located in areas where county waste removal services and private trash haulers cannot service them efficiently. Many of the counties provide solid waste and recycling centers that are conveniently located throughout their jurisdictions for use by the local residents. In these instances, the removal of trash can be handled in one of three ways: by the homeowner directly, by the homeowner indirectly via a small trucking firm that provides that service to individuals, or lastly, by a trucking firm that the community HOA has engaged on behalf of all the property owners. Again, as with item #6 above, this is not a huge deal maker or breaker in the decision-making process at the time of a homesite purchase. It is, however, one more item to add to the list of "stuff I didn't know," so that you may plan for it accordingly, both logistically and financially.

8. Postal Service and Courier Deliveries

In the rural developments in which I have been involved, the Postal Service is generally in favor of a centralized facility, preferably as close to the entrance of the development as possible. This allows the carrier to deliver the mail to all of the residents in one location, where it can be handled in a timely and efficient way. The low density of these communities, coupled with topography that is more challenging than is found in more suburban and urban neighborhoods, makes delivery to each individual home impractical and cost-ineffective for the Postal Service, which is already having tremendous difficulties making ends meet in the digital age of increasing electronic communication.

On the other hand, courier services such as Fedex and UPS continue to deliver to one's doorstep in even the most rural of communities. The only exception to this is when there are unsafe roadway conditions following significant snow and/or ice storms that make it impossible for their vehicles to navigate the roadways until snow clearing, salt spreading, and deicing operations can be completed.

9. **Snow and Ice Removal**

This issue is briefly mentioned in Chapter Three, where I touch on it within the discussion of the HOA budget. It bears further discussion here, because many of you come from areas in the south that have no winter weather to speak of; hence the question of who removes the snow and ice from the roadways would never enter your minds. Most of the roadways within these communities and developments are private. That means that no local town or county will provide any snow clearing equipment or salt spreading services to the roadway system within the community. Add to this the fact that the slope for at least some portion of the roadways will inevitably fall between a fairly steep 15 and 20 percent, and then combine these two issues with a 10-inch to 15-inch snowstorm with extended sub-freezing temperatures, and you've got a recipe for staying home for a number of days. Developers who still control the management of their community's HOA and who still own a significant portion of the homesites may very well *not budget for or have any agreement with* a contractor to provide this service. If you have ever been through a hurricane, the sentiment of that developer and HOA is no different: be prepared to stay home for a few days before the world gets back to normal. However, it doesn't need to be that way. Every responsibly managed HOA should have a contract with a firm who is retained specifically for the HOA's development to respond with snow and ice clearing manpower, equipment, and materials as soon as the snow has stopped and those in the firm have taken care of their own families. Emergencies, accidents, and health-related issues do not wait on winter weather. If no one can get in or out, the risk that an emergency will go unattended is very real indeed.

An additional benefit to living within a community that has made clear and definitive plans to address winter weather is the opportunity for the homeowners to piggyback on that contract and have their own driveways cleared and salted at the same time. The incremental cost to the homeowner is typically very affordable, as the equipment, materials, and personnel are already there to perform clearing operations on all of the common area roadways. Adding driveways to the scope of work can be done very efficiently and extends the mitigation of safety concerns to the entire community or at least to those additional homeowners who choose to participate. Alternatively, you can purchase your own four-wheeling ATV with blade attachment and furnish your own supply of bagged salt to maintain a clear driveway throughout the winter months. Many prefer this alternative of controlling their own destinies and alleviating the discomfort of having to rely on others.

The source, cost, scope, and level of residential services that are provided to many of the most popular second home regions of the country may be significantly different from those with which you are familiar in your primary home community. The design of the homesite and the home itself and both the construction budget and the ongoing operating budget to maintain the home are all affected by the way in which services are provided to the community and its residents. Before you buy a homesite, it is imperative that you understand how the infrastructure is designed and how those services are delivered to the community and its residents. To ignore those details is an oversight that can leave you feeling disillusioned with your choice when it is too late to consider other alternatives.

CHAPTER FIVE

Outside Influences

External variables that can impact the homesite purchasing decision and the quality of life inside the community

**The Question:
What factors and elements that exist outside of the community should I be concerned with that might affect my property acquisition evaluation and decision?**

There are really three "zones of concern" that you should thoroughly study as part of your property purchase decision. In expanding order of magnitude, they are:

1. The specific homesite that you wish to purchase (covered in Chapters Two and Three)
2. The development or community in which that homesite is situated (covered in Chapters Three and Four)
3. The area—town, county, region—in which that community is located (covered here in Chapter Five)

This chapter is concerned with the last and largest of the three components, the impacts on your quality of life that can be found outside of the community proper. As I have stated throughout this book, it is not my intention to elaborate on the obvious, but rather, it is to help you conceptualize and understand the various impacts to the property buying decision that are not readily apparent to those unfamiliar with the territory. In this chapter, I have not covered in any detail such things as proximity to shopping, schools, health care facilities, recreational opportunities, etc., because more than likely, you already have in mind the standard list of these facilities and outlets that are important to you. (Please see the last section in this chapter entitled "Other Considerations.") Further, there are numerous resources from which you can gather such information with a few keystrokes at your computer or with a stop at the local chamber of commerce or visitor's center. My goal throughout this book is to hopefully provide useful information that answers the questions that you may have never considered in your search for the perfect property and that you might have a hard time finding on the Internet.

It is tempting to assume that, when contemplating various off-property influences, distance from the community is inversely proportional to their impact, that is, that the greater the distance, the less the impact. That is not necessarily true, and as the very first element we will discuss illustrates, sometimes the opposite is true.

Fire Protection Facilities

Once again, this is an item that falls into the category of "I didn't even know that this was a question." The issue to which I refer here is not simply that one needs to maintain property insurance coverage and that part of that coverage must include a premium for protection against the peril (risk) of fire; the concern is how far away the closest fire protection facility is located and the degree to which that distance impacts the premiums that you will be paying for that protection. Clearly, if you are only purchasing the homesite as a first step, the premiums will be negligible until you actually build your home; however, once you have constructed the home, the amount of those premiums will be significantly influenced by the time it takes for the closest fire protection facility to dispatch personnel and firefighting equipment to your place of residence.

Those of you whose primary home is located within an urban or even suburban setting don't even consider this factor when purchasing property, because the fire protection facilities and resources are evenly spread throughout such populations to readily and safely address fire-related emergencies. In rural areas, however, the manpower and equipment are limited, resulting in fewer fire stations and firefighting resources to cover greater distances and radii of service for each fire department, many of which are volunteer in their makeup. Though volunteer firefighters are every bit as well-trained and certified as their full-time counterparts, the personnel and hours of coverage are measurably reduced; they have limitations on their resources, apparatus, and equipment; and finally, they are usually less experienced, simply because there are fewer emergencies to deal with in the smaller rural communities.

Keep in mind that the great majority of these rural mountain communities are not served by a municipal, underground, pressurized water supply system. This means that there are no fire hydrants and no sources of a limitless water supply to which the fire trucks can connect their hoses in order to contend with out-of-control residential blazes. Firefighting in these areas is typically a joint operation of various volunteer fire departments that pool their resources of firemen, trucks, water tanker trucks, equipment, and apparatus in order to capitalize on the benefits of cooperative efforts. These coordinated response efforts by multiple fire departments are governed by what are known as "mutual aid agreements," wherein the fire departments within a particular region are "joined at the hip" by multiparty consents to respond to emergencies in a fashion that maximizes the effectiveness of their resources in order to minimize the loss of life and property.

What does all of this mean for you? There is an agency called the Insurance Services Office whose business it is to provide ratings for the fire safety resources in a particular area. Those ratings correspond to risk levels, which in turn correspond to premium levels that insurance underwriters will charge you to insure your home against the risk of fire. When pursuing insurance quotes, I would strongly recommend that you deal with a local insurance firm that understands the immediate environment to discuss your insurance needs for your home. It can certainly be the same company with whom you may have insurance at your primary home, but you should engage a representative from the firm's local insurance branch who is fully immersed in and familiar with the parameters for underwriting risk in the area. You should discuss with that agent or broker, in advance of your decision to buy property, what premiums might be expected *at that location* for the size and cost of the home you intend to build, including an estimated allocation for its furniture and contents. You may be enamored with the property of your dreams, but the very things that make it so attractive—its privacy and seclusion—are what can also result in significantly higher insurance premiums due to the greater distance to the closest fire station and the resulting increase in time it will take to reach the home in the event of a fire. In an emergency, every minute counts, and every additional minute of travel equates to a higher premium for the protection against property loss. An expensive home with pricey furnishings that is located at forty-five hundred feet in elevation and is situated some forty-five minutes in travel time from the closest volunteer fire department is going to command an equally pricey premium to protect the home against the peril of fire.

One final note to consider, regarding insurance, is not so much a consideration of the question of "where" but "how often," as in how often you will be using the residence. Some insurers have become skittish about second homes and vacation homes, in particular due to the less than permanent and continuous use of the homes. The risks for intrusions and burglaries are obviously increased when the home is unoccupied, as is the damage from natural disasters (flooding, hail storms, wind, etc.) and equipment/construction failures (bursting pipes, roof leaks, hot water heater failures, etc.) that are allowed to go undetected for extended periods of time. Burglar and fire alarms can reduce premiums, as can a contract with a concierge service that monitors the home for you during your absences; however, from an insurer's perspective, the use of the home as the owner's primary residence is likely one of the most important factors in the reduction of incidents and claims.

Current and Future Land Use of Abutting Properties

The current use of properties that abut the community or land in which you have an interest is really not a mystery and can be solved by simply observing what is there. On the other hand, one of the most frequently asked questions by potential buyers is how and when the adjacent, abutting properties *will eventually be utilized* if they have not already been developed. Frankly, there is simply no definitive answer to that question unless the property in which you have an interest is abutting national or state forests, the buffer zones of the Blue Ridge

Parkway, lands subject to permanent conservation easements, or other similarly conserved and protected lands. Short of those examples, if someone does purport to give you a guarantee of how adjacent properties will be developed in the future, I would walk away from that discussion just as quickly as your feet will take you. No developer or property owner can guarantee you anything about the future use of abutting properties that the developer does not own...period.

On the other hand, from a practical perspective, for every mile that you travel into the countryside, away from the farthest extensions of centralized, municipal sewer systems, the chances that abutting properties will be utilized for anything but farming and low-density residential use become less and less. Residential homesites that are subject to providing septic/drain field systems for wastewater collection, by definition, are usually sized from one to three acres at a minimum, simply to accommodate the space needs of a drain field to serve the home. In addition, the moderate to steep slope topography that is typical of the rural areas simply doesn't lend itself to the practical needs of commercial uses and high density residential development.

So although no one can guarantee you what the future holds for the development of adjacent properties, the simple facts of the lack of a municipal sewer utility system and the moderate to difficult topography that dominates the landscape in mountainous regions should provide a degree of confidence that neighboring properties will not be developed in a manner that will negatively impact your quality of life in the foreseeable future.

Rivers and Power Company Lakes

Rivers and lakes that either border or fall within the boundaries of the community in which you might have an interest comprise a different subset of external impacts. Though you might think of them as being internal to the development, they have impacts that may originate externally (as in the case of rivers) or may have unique regulatory components that are specifically associated with the entity that controls them (in the case of lakes), namely, the power companies that created them.

The issue of water pollution is of far greater concern with rivers than with power company lakes. Rivers can travel hundreds of miles through vastly differing environments that can subject their waters to equally broad variations in the runoff that is permitted to enter their flow. Do not make the mistake of assuming that an apparently pristine and wide-flowing river is indeed pristine and unpolluted, simply because it courses through unspoiled native hardwood forests in the vicinity of the land you are looking to purchase. If purchasing a river property is important to you, take the time to find out what industry is located *upstream* from the acreage that has captured your attention.

I'll give you one classic example that illustrates the topic at hand, the Pigeon River, which flows from western North Carolina northwesterly to eastern Tennessee. Located in the town of Canton, North Carolina, in Haywood County, an otherwise picturesque county with sixteen mountain peaks in excess of six thousand feet in elevation, is the Blue Ridge Paper Mill, formerly owned and operated by Champion Paper. The discharge of pollutants into the Pigeon River has been well documented over many years, and although the practices of the mill have certainly changed and the runoff of pollutants has been systematically abated in recent decades, the river remains polluted north of the plant—in the direction that the river flows. If I were a buyer looking at property along the river north of the mill, all the way to eastern Tennessee, I would be more than hesitant, particularly if I were interested in fishing its banks and particularly if I wanted to eat the fish that I caught. It is interesting to note that south of the paper mill, in the opposite direction of the flow, the river is truly as clean and unspoiled as the Pisgah National Forest through which it flows. Again, river properties afford beauty, serenity, recreation, and more. Rivers are not isolated, however, and can bring with them unwanted and adverse impacts from operations that originate far from the land you may wish to purchase. Study the area, ask the right questions, and avoid the surprises.

The issues for your concern regarding mountain lakes (as opposed to rivers) are of a decidedly different nature than pollution. To provide a bit of background, a significant percentage of the large lakes in the mountainous regions of the southeast were created by the power companies to generate hydroelectric power through the installation of dams. Power is generated by the flow of immense quantities of water from a higher elevation at the top of the dam to a lower elevation at the bottom of the dam. The power and energy of the water flow turns a turbine that provides the source of the power generation. Power is then distributed along high-tension lines, ultimately to the homes and businesses in the area. Power lakes are typically quite clean and generally free of pollutants, offering a wide range of recreational opportunities.

If you are enamored with living on a substantial lake in the mountains, it will most likely be one that was created by the local power company. You should be aware that it typically has regulatory control over a variety of factors that can impact the land use and site planning of your future home there. The jurisdiction of the power company's control is referred to as the "project boundary," which is an actual surveyed boundary around the perimeter of the lake that outlines the hydroelectric project property. It may also be referred

Outside Influences

to as the "full pond elevation" or "full pond contour," which is the elevation of the top of the lake's spillway or floodgates. You should request a copy of the registered survey for any homesite that you are considering purchasing that abuts a power company lake, so that you are fully aware of the extent of the company's jurisdictional control within the property. Some of the permitting requirements and restrictions imposed by the power companies may include but are certainly not limited to:

- Required setback distances of the construction of any structures from the project boundary
- Permitting and inspection of any docks, piers, and shoreline stabilization (such as seawalls)
- Clearing or cutting trees, shrubs, or other vegetation within the project boundary, the approval for which may include the requirement to mitigate such removal with new plantings elsewhere
- The opening of "view sheds" (as in, the view from your house, through the trees, down to the lake)
- The size and type of boats and other restrictions on recreational usage

The detailed procedures and criteria that are used to regulate activities within these power company reservoirs are known as shoreline management guidelines. There is also a set of maps, known as the shoreline management plan, which shows various types and uses of the shoreline including areas protected for environmental or habitat values, areas of existing development, and areas of potential development. Both documents are available to the public, most easily by simply visiting the power company's website and downloading them. The objectives of the guidelines are clearly to protect the power company's power generation interests and to meet federal regulatory requirements. From the perspective of the property buyer, however, the guidelines are implemented in order to "protect and enhance the scenic, cultural, environmental, public safety, and public recreational values of the reservoirs." I view these documents in the same light as the covenants, conditions, and restrictions and the architectural design guidelines that we discussed in detail in Chapter Three. Though they may be restrictive, they should be viewed as protective—protective of the value of your real estate through the preservation of the environment and the recreational opportunities afforded by the preservation of the lake's ecology.

Noise Pollution: Interstate Traffic, Air Traffic Patterns, Racing Venues, and Shooting Ranges

The above four sources of unwanted and unpleasant environmental impacts are oftentimes neither anticipated nor experienced prior to the decision to purchase land in the mountains. The first, the noise from the traffic along major interstate highways and other primary arteries, may appear to be situated at a safe distance below and away from the homesite. The reality is that the season, the day of the week, the time of the day, the wind direction, atmospheric conditions, the contours and shape of the mountain, and the amount of forestation (vs. cleared, unobstructed topography) can all have a significant impact on the transmission of that noise from the interstate highway below to the homesite above. It is a decidedly different scenario than a home in flattish topography, where the distance from the traffic is pretty much inversely proportional to the perception of noise from that traffic. In the mountains, topography can actually help to reverberate the noise.

Early last spring, I was playing a round of golf on one of my favorite mountain courses on a Friday afternoon and was surprised by the clarity with which I could hear the din of traffic below. It was only along a certain hole that I heard it so clearly, but it was obvious that the homes along that hole were equally exposed to it. What was so surprising was that I had no recollection of hearing that noise during any of my past rounds played there. It then occurred to me that I had always played there on Saturdays or Sundays, when the traffic was apparently far less than that of a Friday afternoon. Further, I had always played from late spring through early fall, when the trees were still fully foliated, providing a buffer of sorts that must have further mitigated the noise. I certainly don't commit to memory the wind direction whenever I play golf, but I wondered if that, too, could have been a differentiating factor that day.

The point is that there are developments and communities nestled within the mountains that are quite often in close proximity to major interstates and thoroughfares. Homesites within these communities will run the entire gamut of the reception of that noise: from no reception whatsoever to a very clear and unfortunate recognition that appears to echo against the backdrop of the face of the mountain. If you have some concerns about the proximity of a given community and a specific homesite within that community to a major artery of traffic, do not make the mistake of visiting and touring the property just once, and certainly do not visit just on the weekend. Noting all of the various situational elements above that can impact the perception of noise, the best strategy is to tour the development at different times and on different days and to note the conditions at the time of your visit. Of all variables, the strength and direction of the wind is the most influential on decibel level. Strong winds in a particular direction can reduce and even eliminate noise just as easily as accentuate it. If the winds are prevailing in a direction that might be mitigating the effects, come back at a different time to tour again. Ask your broker or the developer's sales staff what he/she knows about the noise impacts from the traffic below. Should you have the opportunity, don't hesitate to ask others in the community who live in close proximity to the homesite.

The second potential source of noise pollution is that caused by air traffic patterns, which can also appreciably detract from the otherwise peaceful enjoyment of your future home. Rural living does not necessarily buffer you from all signs of the hustle and bustle of the world you wish to leave behind. The very fact that you have chosen a rural area means that smaller regional airports in the vicinity will be served by the second-tier "puddle jumpers" that routinely make short and therefore lower altitude connecting flights to the larger international airports. For instance, the smaller regional airports that serve eastern Tennessee, northern Georgia, and western North Carolina conduct numerous takeoffs and landings to and from the international airports in Charlotte and Atlanta. You should do your homework to ascertain where the community in which you have an interest is located in relation to the flight paths and elevations of the aircraft serving the proximate airport.

The third and fourth possible sources of noise pollution are ones that "city folk" rarely, if ever, encounter, and they are perhaps a bit more predominant in the rural south in particular, where both the NRA and NASCAR enjoy tremendous popularity. Shooting ranges and racing/speedway venues are two recreational pastimes and uses of country property that can pose significant noise pollution hardships on neighboring communities. The growth of the population in these rural areas, formally the domain of decades-old if not centuries-old farming families, has brought disparate elements into close proximity to one another, elements that do not coexist in harmony very well. Residential communities and their populations do not mix well with shooting ranges and racing ovals. Fortunately for the developers of these communities and the residents within them, local governments have been instituting noise ordinances within their zoning laws, effectively shutting down such recreational uses in some areas. Unfortunately for those who enjoy the recreational uses afforded by these facilities, the increase in the real estate tax base and the overall positive economic impact of community development far outweigh the economic benefit of allowing these venues to continue to operate. Many still do, however, because development has not encroached on them, or they have moved to a less populated environment. The planning and zoning departments within these towns are probably a good source of information as to where the local shooting ranges and racing venues are located. Alternatively, I sometimes find that the most colorful and accurate source of information is the gal behind the cash register at the local truck stop or the waitress at the café just off the interstate. They're apt to be far more knowledgeable and forthright and quite often answer much more than the question they are asked, simply because they enjoy the conversation with their customers. The local population can offer a wealth of information that you will never get from those trying to sell you something. Just don't let it slip that you're a Yankee fan.

Air Pollution

The term "air pollution" may be a bit too strong a term here. The phrase elicits visuals of pumping industrial smokestacks, smog, and eye, nose, and throat irritation, etc., which frankly are rarities in the Southern Appalachian and Smoky Mountain ranges. A paper mill is perhaps the one poster child that may fairly fit into this category, but I prefer to think of these mills, along with the following examples, as creating "odor pollution," an odor irritant as opposed to some sort of noxious, airborne particulate matter that threatens the health of your lungs and other organs. Paper mills quite often emit a strong odor—some would describe it as a rotten egg smell—and that odor is easily transported over a number of miles by the prevailing winds. That is the key: knowing the usual direction of the prevailing winds and the distance from the mill to the community in which you have an interest.

Other sources of odor pollution can include landfills, wastewater treatment facilities, and, to a lesser degree, livestock aromas, though I have to say that I find cow manure to be an almost pleasant odor, particularly when compared to the odors from a pig farm.

Visual Pollution

During a conversation I had not long ago with a local land broker while en route to see a particular tract of land, he advised that one of the more prominent negatives about the property was the "Appalachian art" along the primary access route. I assumed that he was referring to a handcrafts country boutique with goods from the local Cherokee tribe or one of the many antique stores that dot the landscape in the area. I couldn't for the life of me figure out how that could be anything but a positive. He said he would show me along the way. After awhile, we stopped on the shoulder of the road, and I saw nothing of the sort, just an old house that looked as though it had almost fallen off of its foundation. Some of the windows were broken, and one window opening was simply filled with a piece of plywood that had an illegible message spray-painted on it. The front door was intact but was half-open. There were also three rusted-out, tireless vehicles, one of them elevated on cinder blocks; a tractor that hadn't moved for probably a decade; a pile of pallets; various appliances that appeared to be providing housing for wildlife, which may have been the house pets; and a few couches and a couple of chairs that I would roughly describe as unrelated collections of wood, stuffing material, and springs, surrounding a fire pit or at least something that was once on fire. The broker looked at me and smiled. We pulled off the shoulder and back onto the road, and as we were leaving, I couldn't help but notice that the rebel flag on the front porch looked brand new—as did the satellite dish, perfectly oriented toward the southwestern sky.

Part of the joy of owning a home in the country is the simple pleasure of driving the country roads on your way to wherever and back again. Corn fields, tobacco fields, cattle grazing, old tobacco barns and silos, hay bales and balers, greenhouses, creeks, and streams and the rickety bridges that cross them…it's truly therapeutic just getting to where you are going. On occasion, a less seasoned developer will ignore the risk of purchasing property that is located at the end of a long stretch of country road that is dotted with a few homesteads of Appalachian Art décor, also known as "local color," for the uninitiated. It is unpleasant to look at, and more often than not, the inhabitants are equally unpleasant. (This is not intended to be a critical or condescending narrative regarding the rural inhabitants of the area covered in this book. Quite to the contrary, I have found that the country and farming communities I have come to know are inhabited by some of the classiest people I have ever met. They are caring, thoughtful, extremely down-to-earth, willing to help their neighbors in any way they can, and surprisingly open and accepting of strangers to the area. They don't appreciate an isolated few of their neighbors using their land as a dump any more than anyone else would.)

The key here is that if you are seriously looking at a community in which to purchase property, make sure that you travel the primary, standard roadways to and from the community that will serve as the daily commuting route for those who live there. There are more than a few unscrupulous salespeople who will travel an alternate route with out-of-state buyers who don't know any better and who will unfortunately have the opportunity to enjoy the Appalachian Art a bit more than they may have wanted.

Other forms of visual pollution to avoid that are frankly no different in the mountains than where you might be living now are overhead, high-tension power lines, landfills (involving both visual and odor pollution), and interstate traffic (both visual and noise).

We have focused on various forms of pollution in this chapter that I regard, in most instances, to be "irritants to the senses" as opposed to carrying the more serious connotation of toxic discharge that can threaten one's health. We should also keep in mind that in some cases, the very issue that may be viewed as a negative impact in one sense may be viewed as an equally positive impact in another. For example, proximity to an interstate highway clearly becomes a negative at the point that the traffic comes into view or becomes audible, or both. On the other hand, once it is no longer within the realm of sight and sound, its nearness is immediately treasured for providing quick and convenient access to other destinations. Proximity to a regional airport provides an analogous dichotomy: let's be close, just not too close.

In Chapter Two, we talked at length about the site characteristics of a given homesite and in particular, the orientation of the home to capture the views. That discussion focused on the panoramas that fall within the view shed during the day. However, one aspect of mountain living that few people from the flatlands ever consider is the potential view from their terrace in the evening (perhaps those in high-rise condominiums may consider this, but not those in single-family homes). I am not talking about the moon and the stars, as awesome and bright as they may be to behold within the darkness of a country setting. I am referring to the very peaceful and beautiful landscape of twinkling lights in the nearby towns below or to the sight of the illuminated night skiing runs at the ski resort off in the distance. I find the combination of the cold winter night, a roaring fire in the outdoor fireplace or fire pit, and the view of the distant lights to be as intoxicating and satisfying as the daytime ambiance, sometimes even more so. Clearly, it is a rare occasion that you'll get a property tour at night. However, during your property search, you should have no qualms about going out on your own to see at night what you couldn't possibly appreciate or visualize during the day.

What do I really want...the small city, the quaint hometown, or the middle of nowhere?

This last topic is a bit different from the other issues in this chapter because, as an influence in your buying decision, it doesn't really have an "impact on the homesite and quality of life inside the community." Nevertheless, it has a very significant impact on your satisfaction (or lack thereof) with where you choose to live, and your perceived quality of life is very much interwoven with what anchors you to the area you will call home.

Two of the most common mistakes that I have seen buyers make in their initial second home property acquisition happen to be the exact opposite of one another. "We purchased property in Asheville, but now we really want to be a little farther out" or "We purchased property in the middle of absolutely nowhere, and now we want to be a little closer to Asheville." Perhaps these were not mistakes at all but simply what the buyers wanted at the time they purchased the property, and now that they have acclimated themselves to the area, their interests have changed.

Many buyers who have resided for the bulk of their lives in metropolitan areas find that some parts of a small city, like Asheville, already feel like the country, especially in comparison to the densely populated city living to which they have been so accustomed. It isn't until they have been living in the mountains and regularly traveling throughout the *real* countryside that they become aware that they have exchanged big city living for small city living. Some are truly happy with that exchange, but others yearn for a more rustic and quieter existence—they just didn't realize it.

On the flip side of the coin, some of the more adventurous souls come here with a burning desire to reinvent themselves in stark contrast to their previous lives and personas. They settle on some isolated acreage fifty miles from the closest town, which only includes seven different surnames in the brochure-sized phone book, and they wonder why they feel a tad lonely once they've made the permanent move.

The happy medium is what seems to be the magnet for most newcomers to the area. The wonderful aspect to so much of the Blue Ridge and Smoky Mountain region is that you can find some of the most picturesque countryside within minutes of classic, southern "main street" towns, which in turn are perhaps an hour or two at the most from the "big city." Many of the transplants to western North Carolina, for example, find that the proximity to towns such as Waynesville, Weaverville, Black Mountain, Hendersonville, Brevard, Boone, Blowing Rock, Cashiers, Highlands, etc., provides a social, day-to-day connection to a hometown environment that they can call their own. The small and larger cities, Asheville, Knoxville, Charlotte, and Atlanta, provide the shopping, entertainment, and cultural experiences that fill the need, however fleeting, for the occasional big city experience that they left behind.

One of the most productive avenues to pursue during your search for property, to really allow an area to "sink into your soul," is to rent a cabin or small cottage for at least a month (if you can afford the time to do so). One's initial perceptions of the character of an area have an interesting way of mutating to a more defined and accurate reality, over time, and the change in perception is a good thing, regardless of the direction it goes, because it is the process of acclimating oneself to a new environment that makes it clear where one's real interests lie. You may truly find that the middle of nowhere is right where you want to be, or you may be perfectly content trading one big city for a smaller big city. For most, the right place is somewhere in between, but you'll never know until you try it on for size.

Remember, the effects and influences, both positive and negative (and sometimes both), that exist outside of one's property and immediate community may have every bit as large an impact as the attributes within the property. Take the time to understand that third "zone of concern." Most sales personnel are willing to spend a great deal of time with you within the community of your interest, but it is up to you to make the effort to familiarize yourself with what lies outside of the community. Grab a map, take a ride, and find out what you can only learn by immersing yourself in the area that you plan to call home.

Other considerations

The following is simply a list of those additional concerns that may impact the "where do I want to be" decision. Most are commonsense variables that are self-explanatory but which, nevertheless, should serve well as a checklist to assist you in really nailing down where you want to be, mostly as a function of proximity to what is important to you. In some cases, I have added some notes that may not be quite so "commonsensical" or which are specific to the area.

1. Property Taxes: In those states, such as North Carolina, that have a state income tax, property taxes are generally quite a bit less than in those states without a state income tax.
2. Weather and Climate: Generally, the farther up you go in elevation, the lower the average temperature, the greater the winds, and the increased potential for not only snow, sleet, and ice but also for a slower melt of those conditions.
3. Educational Facilities
    a. Elementary Schools
    b. Middle Schools
    c. High Schools
    d. Community Colleges
    e. Colleges and Universities
4. Health and Wellness Facilities
    a. Major Hospitals
    b. Indoor Recreation, Exercise and Wellness
5. Daily Shopping/Entertainment/Special Interests

a. Food and Necessities
b. Home Improvement
c. Restaurants, Clubs, and Social Establishments
d. Arts and Cultural Venues
e. Volunteer Opportunities
6. Event Shopping
    a. (This is my term for my wife's excursions to a major mall with an entourage of girlfriends)
    b. (Special Note: Asheville has no malls that qualify as "event worthy")
7. Airports
    a. Charlotte, NC
    b. Greenville, SC
    c. Atlanta, GA
    d. Tri-Cities, TN
    e. Knoxville, TN
8. Interstates (and their relative stretches through the mountain areas)
    a. I-26 (Greenville/Spartanburg, SC, northwest to Asheville, NC, then northerly to Kingsport, TN)
    b. I-40 (Asheville, NC, westerly to Knoxville, TN, or easterly to Marion, NC, then 221 north to Boone)
    c. I-75 (Atlanta, GA, north-northwest to Chattanooga TN, then north-northeast to Knoxville, TN)
    d. I-77, then 421 (Charlotte, NC, north-northwest to Boone, NC)
    e. I-81, then I-64 (Kingsport, TN, northwest to Charlottesville, VA)

    f. I-85, then 321 (Charlotte, NC, northwest to Boone, NC)
9. Recreation: Scenic Drives, Hiking, Biking, Mountain Biking
   a. The Blue Ridge Parkway
   b. The Appalachian Trail
   c. The Mountains to Sea Trail
   d. The Art Loeb Trail
   e. The Virginia Creeper Trail
10. Recreation: Outdoor Sports
    a. Golf
    b. Tennis
    c. Lakes: Boating
    d. Rivers: Whitewater Rafting, Kayaking, Canoeing, Fly-Fishing
    e. Skiing, Snowboarding
    f. Shooting, Skeet
    g. Hunting
    h. Equestrian
11. Scenic Points of Interest
    a. Waterfalls
    b. Gorges
    c. National Forests
    d. State Parks
    e. Game Land

CHAPTER SIX

The Brokerage Community

Internet-based marketing and community information websites, land listing sites, land brokers, conventional brokers, and developer sales staff

The Question:
Do websites that provide Internet-based marketing services and claim to be good sources of information for second home communities really provide a service that is valuable and useful to the consumer? And what about real estate salespersons and brokers...can I trust that they will look after my interests and work hard on my behalf?

Let's take question number one first. The answer is, for the most part, YES.

When I first envisioned writing this chapter, I imagined that the outline or structure of it would be to enumerate the main players in the field—the most visited websites that cater to those who are beginning a search for their second home property—and then to discuss their various attributes, positives and negatives, etc. As I thought about how that might unfold, it became clear to me that the chapter would read more like an advertisement for the various analysis by which the consumer that search. So before you get too that it is important for you to under- which I have written it. I have always to evaluate the integrity and consequent have made the effort to understand what relatively new businesses, which Internet-based real ting firms are, it is probably most revealing to gauge that und anding through the lens of how these websites have developed over time. New niche enterprises in the ever-changing world of Internet technology are prone to quick spurts in their evolution. Understanding how they have evolved can provide you with insight into how they are motivated and influenced and from where they generate income and, in turn, insight into why you should (or should not) view them as reliable sources of information. It should also arm you with what I keep harping on throughout this book, that is, the questions that you need to ask in order to be a more informed consumer for one of the larger purchases you may make in your lifetime. As a point of reference, the four websites with which I am familiar and which have been used as a basis for enumerating the various business models and trends in this industry are as follows, including the year each business was founded:

- PrivateCommunities.com (1996)
- PrivateMountainCommunities.com (2005)
- SouthEastDiscovery.com (2005)
- RealEstateScorecard.com (2011)

It is estimated that some 80–95 percent of the people embarking upon their initial search for a second home property do so via the Internet. The reason is simple. If you live in, say, South Florida, you're not going to be particularly interested in buying a second home property on the beach in South Florida, where you know and understand the market and can conveniently visit and tour real estate on any given day. Your real interest will be to research and explore property in the mountains of Northern Georgia, eastern Tennessee, western North Carolina, or some other part of the country that appeals to your sense of a permanent escape from that which has become all too routine in your life. But it being more than just a little inconvenient to drive that far for regular property tours, there is an obvious initial need to narrow the field of choices through some other method, namely, the Internet.

Beginning with the founding of Private Communities (privatecommunities.com) in 1996, a number of websites (such as those noted above) have since been established that endeavor to assist you with your efforts to locate the right community for the purchase of your second home. Private Communities, which was not only the original entry in the field but which also remains quite active after sixteen years, has been very loyal to and consistent with its original business model. The company operates as an extension of the marketing efforts of the developments that are represented on the site, and the developers of these communities pay the site a marketing fee for the added exposure of their communities on the website. From your perspective as a consumer, the site essentially offers up a "catalogue" or summary list of real estate developments that allows you to familiarize yourself with a community and to "try it on for size" at the comfort of your desk, to determine whether a visit might be in order. The site provides you with a "one-stop shopping" location to browse the characteristics of numerous developments and communities. Having so much information on so many communities within the same website allows for the convenience and efficiency of "comparison shopping" at one site instead of struggling through the time-consuming task of locating each individual website of the communities in which you have an interest. Once you have browsed the site and located a community that seems to fit your parameters of interest, you can click on a link to visit the individual website of that specific community and then return to Private Communities to browse more properties. This is a fairly simplistic description of the site, and there are certainly more site features and components that have been developed through the years, which will be discussed in the website development trends below.

Over time, the business model of the subsequently established websites included an additional revenue component to complement the fees from developers, that of sales commission referral fees from the sale of a property to a client for which the website was the "procuring cause," as they say. (The referral fees are typically paid at closing, but there is no additional cost to you, the consumer, as the developer pays the full sales commission, which is typically 10 percent on vacant land and 6 percent on existing homes.) Once a potential buyer has effectively registered his or her name and contact information via the site's registration process and then has expressed an interest in a particular community, the site forwards that message of interest to the developer, thereby securing its referral fee, should the buyer eventually elect to make a purchase in that community. The buyer shouldn't have any hesitation in registering with the site, as again, the consumer pays nothing more for the property, due to the referral fee generated by the website. The developer pays the sales commissions and typically doesn't really care how that 10 percent is divided among the developer's sales staff, cooperating brokers, and referring websites. However the commission is broken down or divvied up, it still equates to 10 percent.

The evolution of the sophistication of these websites and how those advances have benefited both developers and consumers alike has been very interesting to watch unfold over the years. I have witnessed at least five trends in the continually changing and improving practices of these sites (and I predict that a sixth trend is currently emerging):

1. **The Effort to Match Buyers with a Specific Community or Group of Communities**

Private Mountain Communities (PMC) (privatemountaincommunities.com) appears to have been the first site to structure its software algorithm to allow you to find communities that are the best match for your specific interests. Think of it as the Internet dating approach to pairing you with the specific communities that best match your interests. When you enter the PMC website, you will be asked to fill out a seventeen-item survey/questionnaire. The answers to this provide the basis for PMC's software to narrow the list of prospective communities from some two hundred in western North Carolina alone to a handful, perhaps a dozen, that best match what the buyer is looking for in the way of price point, product type, amenities, location, nearby recreation, etc. This approach allows for an immediate simplification of the menu, so to speak, a logical methodology to reduce the list of possibilities to a manageable handful of communities that can be explored over a long weekend in an effort to make the first cut. This ability to instantly reduce the playing field to a more palatable sum of developments can remove quite a bit of anxiety from what may have seemed an undoable task at the outset.

2. The Effort to Qualify Developments and Be More Selective with the Communities That Are Represented on the Website

Southeast Discovery (SED) (southeastdiscovery.com) advanced the more recent "focus on the consumer" approach a step further in its business model, through diligent efforts to appraise the worthiness of communities via more detailed research and "boots on the ground" property visits. The earlier web-based models, at the time of their inception, really did not make a concerted effort to qualify or quantify the strength and viability of individual developments. Previous practices were not that much different from when the Yellow Pages would call to ask if a developer would like to list the business in the phone book. There was no Q and A about the inherent value, worthiness, or integrity of the business; if the developer wanted to be in the phone book, then the developer was in it. In the nascent stages of some of these sites, the philosophy was not much different. If you were a developer that wanted additional marketing exposure on these sites, you paid your fee and you got your exposure.

That changed with the efforts by SED, when it was founded in 2005. The folks at SED realized that if you and other buyers perceived that a site had conducted a certain level of due diligence into the communities and into the developers to whom it was granting exposure, then you would place a greater value on the site's relevance and would funnel your search for all possible communities through that site, thereby increasing the site's potential for commission-based revenues. Moreover, as word spreads about the more thorough due diligence efforts of the site and its increased firsthand knowledge of the communities and the developers for whom it is providing marketing exposure, the site's traffic increases and thus the potential for increased sales commissions. The website may lose some monthly fees from developers who didn't pass muster to be marketed on the site, but those lost revenues are more than offset by the increase in sales commissions from buyers who have come to trust the site for its integrity and its efforts to qualify the developments it recommends.

3. The Effort to a) Eliminate Any Perceived Conflict of Interest by the Elimination of Marketing Fees Paid by Developers and b) the Addition of Community Reviews by Community Residents

These two changes are grouped together because they were both instituted for the first time by a site that was very recently founded, Real Estate Scorecard (RES) (RealEstateScorecard.com). The founder of this site took the more purist "Consumer Reports" approach by eliminating any monthly or annual fee structure paid by the developers to the site for the value of the marketing exposure. RES generates its revenue from sales commissions only, preferring to do without fees from the businesses that it is "scoring," so as to avoid any question that the payment of those fees might prejudice the scores. This argument can easily be understood within the context of the Consumer Reports analogy, that is, that consumers might find there to be an obvious conflict of interest if a manufacturer of a product that the magazine was reviewing was paying a fee to the magazine. This analogy is not without its weakness, though, because these websites do indeed have different business models, and those that generate revenues from both monthly developer fees and sales commissions believe they can serve the interests of both the developer's marketing exposure and the consumer's need for information, without compromise. Moreover, each developer presumably pays the same fee (which provides for a level playing field), and the developer fees account for a very small amount of revenue in comparison to the sales commission revenue. The more applicable analogy is perhaps that of a real estate broker that practices dual agency, wherein the broker represents the interests of both parties in a transaction, as is allowed in some states, including North Carolina.

The second change—the website acting as a vehicle through which consumers can review their own communities—is a very interesting one. I have wondered if consumers will be willing to voice an honest negative opinion about such a significant investment. They would risk the adverse impact from negative reviews to the value of their own property, not to mention that of their neighbors' properties. On the other hand, if they are truly upset with their acquisition, they may feel that they have an obligation to help others avoid the same pain. It is frankly too early to tell if the complete shift to the consumer's interest is here to stay and will find success as a business model, but the latest transition is worth noting, and the consumer will ultimately make that decision.

It is important for you to realize here that the evolution of the business models and approaches by Private Communities, Private Mountain Communities, Southeast Discovery and Real Estate Scorecard shifted the emphasis of the focus from the developers and developments to the consumers. Earlier Internet-based models were focused on acting as an extension of a developer's marketing efforts. These newer models are focused on helping you and other consumers navigate your way through the flood of information and choices that were apt to overload you with far too many options to effectively qualify what you planned to purchase. The altered focus is to truly evaluate the developments and the developers who are responsible for bringing these communities through to fruition. The business model for these websites, without stating so, has been transitioning to that of a "buyer's broker," because these sites realized that the consumer viewed them as a genuinely independent source of information, that is, a sales force that was not associated with a particular development. The Consumer Reports analogy bears repeating. You can visit every car dealer in the neighborhood and spend hours listening to the sales pitch, reading their ads in newspapers and magazines, and listening to their spin on the radio, on TV, and via their websites....or you can go purchase the special edition issue of Consumer Reports on automobiles and truly get an education. Similarly, you can visit every new gated community in western North Carolina, listen to the spiel of the on-site salespeople, read their magazine, newspaper, and billboard ads, and visit their websites...or you can contact your choices among the sites mentioned herein to gather information and opinions that are not conflicted by competing interests. The sales personnel from these websites have no incentive to sell one development over another. Their goal is surely to make sales, but sales that match you to a specific community, based on a multitude of factors and commonalities between your wish list and what the development has to offer.

4. The Effort to Regularly Publish Blog Articles Concerning Related Topics of Interest

This trend is a direct result of the second trend noted above. One way for these websites to ensure that their readers and followers deepen their confidence that the sites are truly immersed in the subject about which they claim to be experts is to write—copiously—about the subject. Well-written blog articles are churned out regularly on a wide array of topics: the character of the various towns, nearby colleges and universities, festivals and gatherings, hiking and biking venues, local farmer's markets, volunteer opportunities, health facilities, "green" building technologies, fly-fishing hangouts, the best rapids to kayak, museums, restaurants, music venues, you name it, you can find a blog article on it within a site's archives. For the owners of the website, the articles serve to pique your interest in the site and, through word-of-mouth, increase the visitor traffic to the site. The articles also have a positive impact on the site's search engine optimization, which also increases the visitor traffic to the site. From your perspective as a user of the site, the articles make for very interesting reading and can easily become a significant, contributing factor to your decision-making process.

5. **The Effort to Serve as a Portal for Developers' E-Newsletters and Community Updates**

Notwithstanding that the focus of these sites has witnessed a shift of emphasis from the developer to the consumer, it would be wholly inaccurate to say that developers are somehow being ignored. In that regard, a fifth trend has grown in response to the convergence of three notable developments that strengthened the ties of developers with these web-based real estate marketing sites:

    a. the near-cataclysmic collapse of the real estate market that started somewhere in 2006/2007, resulting in severe restrictions of every developer's pro forma budgets available for marketing

b. the steady and sometimes steep growth of the databases of prospects that these websites were able to harvest
c. the excellent quality of the prospects, both 1) because the prospects that visit these sites are clearly in the market to buy real estate, and 2) due to the prospects' growing understanding of the integrity of these sites and the independence of these sites from the developments for whom they provide exposure.

In the heyday of the world of real estate during the first six years or so of the new millennium, a developer could hardly spend enough on marketing efforts. Billboards, mass direct mail campaigns of leather-bound invitations, over-the-top, six-figure grand opening events with helicopter rides, live bands, and tented and catered feasts...nothing was too much, bigger was better, and smaller was a sure sign that you just didn't have much to offer. When the market began its precipitous decline, the very first expense line item that began to shrink was the marketing budget. And it shrank to almost nothing in a matter of a few short months. Every developer needed to spend his or her dissipating allocation of marketing dollars in a manner that maximized exposure with a minimum of expense. Elaborate marketing events were history, and even simple marketing campaigns using conventional print media—ads in newspapers and magazines—were quite suddenly a luxury one had to do without. What remained, what was clearly an affordable alternative, even in this time of budgetary austerity, was the Internet.

Developers were already paying a fairly modest annual marketing fee for the exposure of their developments on these sites. What many of the developers wanted was a vehicle for communicating new and pertinent information about their communities through these websites. The sites needed to retain their independence and arm's length integrity; however, the blogging or editorial component of the sites, which we discussed above, provided a format that could marry a topic of interest to the site's readers with a developer's community. The developer is allowed to "sprinkle" some news and updates within the article to lend some specificity and application to the topic. In a best-of-both-worlds scenario, a special topic of interest to the site's users is made more "real" by illustrating its application to a community, and the community is highlighted, to the benefit and service of the developer. The articles reach the tens of thousands of prospects within the various databases, and presumably, everyone is happy with the outcome.

6. **The Evolution of the Client Relationship from Referral-Based Commissions to Buyer's Broker**

This is the sixth and last trend that seems inevitable for those firms that are locally set up to perform brokerage services or which, if not, are willing to establish partnering relationships with a local real estate brokerage firm. The issue for those Internet-based marketing firms whose business models are more consumer-based (the buyer) instead of developer-based (the seller) is that they are far more likely to establish a closer relationship and commitment with a buyer-client if they establish a contractual understanding with them via a buyer's broker agreement. Imagine for a moment that you are a buyer who is interested in starting your due diligence effort to find a property in the mountains, and you initiate that effort by logging onto your computer and visiting these sites that cater to your interests. With whom would you feel that you have established a stronger working relationship: a firm that is local to the area and which has a physical presence with local brokers who can assist you with your needs while you are in the area and with whom you have an agreement to represent you; or a firm that is located outside of the region, without a local presence and with whom you do not have a written, contractual relationship?

The above narrative regarding Internet-based real estate marketing firms should be viewed as a snapshot of these websites at a moment in time. The sites may change their focus, strategies, and goals over time. They may borrow from each other, they may expand to other markets, or they may cease to exist. Other websites will inevitably enter the marketplace, should they believe there is room for growth and innovation. It has not been my focus here to suggest that any particular website or its business model is better or worse than any other. For some folks, the approach of the Private Communities site may be the resource that you need because you prefer to come to your own conclusions about which developments are best for you and you're not interested in engaging in a brokerage relationship. Others may prefer Private Mountain Communities' approach of systematically matching buyers with a community and may prefer their local knowledge if the buyers' interests are specifically in western North Carolina, where PMC maintains an office in Asheville, with brokers who can guide prospective buyers along the way. Still others may prefer the heightened degree of investigation and evaluation for which both Southeast Discovery and Real Estate Scorecard are known.

My introduction to this chapter suggested that an appropriate way to judge the integrity, independence, and value of these websites is to understand how they have evolved in this new industry over time. The six trends that I discussed should trigger some questions, which you should feel free to ask of these websites and of any others, if you are going to engage them, trust them, and rely on them for unbiased assessments of the communities for which you develop an interest:

- How is your firm compensated? (Through developer fees? Sales commissions? Both?)
- Who writes the Community Summaries? (The website's writers or the developers of those communities?)
- Who writes your site's blog articles when specific communities are referenced? (The website's writers or the developers of those communities, or both?)
- Have the senior members of your staff personally visited the communities that you market on your site?
- What level of investigation have you done in order to recommend these communities?
- Are there measurable minimum standards that a community must equal or surpass in order to be recognized and included on your website?
- Can you recommend an owner in the community who would be willing to talk to me about the community?
- Do you have personal knowledge of the developers of the community, and can you attest to their integrity and character?

Land Listing Websites

There are a number of websites that cater to real estate brokers and individuals who simply want the added exposure of marketing their listings and properties through venues other than the Multiple Listing Services (MLS) that the boards of realtors maintain in regions throughout the country. These sites are more akin to classified ads or

Craigslist entries, where no attempt is made to qualify the or the communities in which they may be located, but ra their existence and availability is simply advertised. These sites are probably best described as nationwide listings of land for sale, used predominantly by land brokers who desire a larger global exposure that goes beyond the local MLS. Some of these sites are LandandFarm.com, LandsofAmerica.com, Loopnet.com, LandFlip.com, and LandWatch.com. If you are particularly interested in larger tracts of land that are not necessarily within a developed subdivision, these sites may be the best alternative by which initially to narrow down your interest before coming to the area to tour selected properties.

Land Brokers vs. Conventional Real Estate Brokers vs. Developer Sales Staff

Now let's address the second question posed at the beginning of this chapter, which considers the alternatives for real estate brokerage. (Note that the terms broker and salesperson are used interchangeably here.) Regardless of the initial resources that you use to arrive at the area, county, town, and eventually the communities that seem to be a good match for your interests and lifestyle, you need to make a decision about the next step in the process. There is a variety of options, and the one you choose is a function of what you are looking for. Before we can talk about what you're looking for, let's look at the available alternatives for information and representation.

- **Self Reliance**: There are those who prefer to avoid brokers and sales personnel at all costs, which is actually getting easier these days. The growth of websites that cater to self-promotion (Facebook, Twitter, LinkedIn), the marketing of personal effects and assets (eBay, Craigslist), and the valuing and selling of real estate (Zillow, Trulia, and FSBO) has given the individual a number of powerful avenues to research available real estate offerings and data without assistance from the brokerage community. These resources are in addition to the more conventional print media outlets that are usually available at no cost in newsstands, shopping venues, restaurants, and other retail outlets.

- **Conventional Real Estate Brokers/Salespersons**: By conventional, I am referring to brokers who are unaffiliated with any particular development and whose primary efforts are focused upon the general brokerage of homes as either buyers' agents, sellers' agents, or dual agents representing both sellers and buyers, which is allowed in some states.

- **Land Brokers**: These are real estate sales personnel who specialize in transactions where the land is the primary component of value, and not the home, if there is one. These tracts are typically not homesites within a planned subdivision, but rather are stand-alone parcels of land from perhaps 10–25 acres in the small range, 25–250 acres in the medium range, and 250–2,500 acres in the large range. Tracts of land that exceed 2,500 acres start to involve global, high-end brokerages with international name recognition that have the experience and the capital to put together sophisticated marketing packages and cater to a fairly exclusive clientele.

- **Developer's Sales Staff**: These are captive brokers, solely dedicated to the sale of properties within a specific community. They normally do not participate in general brokerage outside of the community. There are three typical arrangements: in one, the sales staff are actually employees of the developer; in the second, they are independent, commission-based contractors who work solely within the development; in the third, they are actually employees of an outside brokerage firm with whom the developer has contracted as a third party to handle the sales (and sometimes marketing as well) scope of responsibilities. These are perhaps "distinctions without a difference," except that independent contractors and third-party salespeople are much more inclined to try to continue to assist you with referrals outside of the community, should you make it clear that you are not interested in the one at which they are selling.

Now, let's talk about what you are looking for. There are basically two categories of land acquisitions that account for the vast majority of all such transactions: homesites within a planned community and stand-alone acreage.

Homesites within a Planned Community:

Almost all developers prefer to employ (and therefore control) their own sales staff. They want their salespeople to be solely dedicated to the marketing and sale of real estate within their communities in order to avoid the conflicts of interest that are inherent with outside brokers who may be just as happy to sell real estate outside of the developments—and who can blame them? So when it comes to a planned community that is still controlled by the developer, you are going to be dealing with the developer's sales force, whether you have engaged your own broker or not. Generally, developers will be happy to "cooperate" with all outside brokers, so there is no drawback to pursuing the purchase of developer-owned homesites with your own broker as your agent.

However, I would strongly suggest that your broker take a step back and let the developer's staff lead the way, once you are within the community for a guided tour of the available lots. The on-site sales staff are (or no doubt should be) intimately familiar with each and every homesite and should be able to answer every question that you have about the area, the community, the amenities, the covenants, the design guidelines, the POA budget, and most importantly, the attributes of each homesite. If they don't know the answers off the top of their heads or don't at least resolve to get you the answers posthaste, they probably shouldn't be working there. Your own broker can certainly advise you regarding his or her impressions of all that is discussed and disclosed, but the broker needs to take a backseat during most of the visit and the tour, to let the developer's staff do their thing.

Land brokers usually express minimal, if any, interest in representing buyers who are focused on homesites within developer-controlled planned communities, simply because they prefer to deal with larger land tracts where they are often the only brokers in the transaction. That means 10 percent of a large acreage, large dollar volume transaction as opposed to a cooperating brokerage fee of 5 percent on a small acreage, small dollar volume transaction. Do you blame them? So in the case of a homesite within a planned developer community, the options are 1) using your own agent from a general brokerage, who will work in cooperation with one of the developer's brokers or 2) going straight to the developer. The primary concern with the second alternative is to remember that you are dealing with a broker who has a responsibility to maximize the developer's interests and not yours.

Stand-Alone Acreage

I will always advise the use of a broker who specializes in raw land for your representation in these types of transactions. A possible exception might be very small tracts, say two to five acres, where the topography is comparatively tame and the setting is more suburban or urban. Other than that one scenario, I would engage a land broker for large tract acquisitions.

Conventional real estate brokers who are primarily involved in the general brokerage of single-family homes, townhouses, condominiums, etc., are rarely qualified to assist you with raw land, simply because they don't have the experience and the resulting understanding of all of the issues that have been presented in the previous four chapters of this book. Land brokers, on the other hand, by and large have a very good understanding of those issues. They are also far better equipped to deal with the logistics of showing large land tracts. Land brokers are a distinctly different breed from general brokerage agents. They wear old flannel shirts, faded blue jeans with holes in the knees, and hiking boots with different colored laces; they drive in mud-caked SUVs and carry around wooden stakes, colored surveyor's ribbon, and hundred-foot tape measures in the back of them; behind their SUVs, they pull knobby-tired ATVs on trailers, they have keys to every pasture gate in the county, and scale four rows of barbed-wire fencing with ease; they've been stung by so many bees and walked through so much poison ivy that they are now immune to both…and that's just the gals in the business.

Having said the above, by no means do I mean to denigrate the skills and knowledge of general brokerage agents. Many are astute, diligent, and honest practitioners, who excel at the art of home sales. Their strengths, however, are focused on the physical attributes of the home—the living spaces and their relationships to one another, kitchen and bath upgrades, staging your home for quicker sale, techniques and embellishments for better showings, market comparables for similar homes, home inspections and appraisals, and so on. There is much to be said for their qualifications and expertise, but those talents simply do not translate to the world of large tracts of raw land.

As a closing note to this chapter, I think it is important to recognize that there is no infallible source of either Internet-based advice or local brokerage, when it comes to the evaluation and recommendation of residential communities that serve the second/vacation/retirement home market. The websites, no doubt, provide a very valuable source of information to assist you in your search, particularly in the initial stages when you are trying to pare down what may seem like an exhausting list of communities to a manageable few. You may then choose to transition to local brokerage to take advantage of their more intimate knowledge of the market. However, once you have become comfortable with the homesite, whether it be within a gated, master planned community or a stand-alone parcel, it is up to you to do your research, to ask the tough questions, and to have the stamina and patience to obtain the right answers.

CHAPTER SEVEN

Buyer Beware!

The "One-Day-Only Sales Event"

THE QUESTION:

I keep receiving postcard advertisements and e-mail invitations about land for sale at these one-day-only sales events. I've even responded to a few of them, because I'm tempted to go see what all the excitement is about, but I haven't attended one yet. Do these property sales events provide good venues to buy land for my future dream home in the mountains?

The Perfect Storm...

To answer this question, I find it instructive to set the stage for the conditions under which such events have found a niche in which to thrive. As you read this chapter, however, please keep in mind that many of the issues discussed here are relevant to the purchase of land in the mountains of western North Carolina and similar areas, regardless of how you are going about making that purchase, whether through a broker, from an individual, from a developer, or at an event sale. I have chosen to elaborate on the issues within the context of the one-day-only sales event simply because the issues are that much more pronounced and are thus easier to use as examples within this context. In other words, you need to be aware of the importance of many of the factors enumerated herein, regardless of the venue or process through which you are making the purchase.

There are times when the confluence of specific circumstances in a given environment can give rise to a perfect storm of seemingly unrelated variables. Unfortunately, in the world of real estate development, those variables can often combine into a volatile mixture that is clearly detrimental to the consumer's interests. The variables include the following:

- An area of the country that is in high demand for relocation and in-migration
- A preponderance of uninformed buyers who originate from feeder markets that are vastly different from the market to which they are moving
- An exceptionally well-trained sales staff and an especially well-choreographed sales technique that is religiously employed at the events
- A lack of real estate development regulation
- Inexperienced and undercapitalized developers
- Unscrupulous and shady developers
- A significant delay from the time a homesite is purchased to the time when a home is actually constructed on the homesite.

1. **An area of the country that is in high demand for relocation and in-migration**

Asheville, North Carolina, in particular (and western North Carolina in general) has made so many top ten lists of positive attributes since the turn of the millennium that almost any segment of the population can find a compelling reason to consider relocation to the area. (See Exhibit 7.1 in the Appendix at the end of this chapter.) The accolades are well deserved, and until the region begins to suffer from the maladies of overpopulation, it will continue to attract those who wish to relocate to an environment that provides a wealth of lifestyle enhancements that are all but extinct in the metropolitan areas to which people have become accustomed but which they desire to abandon. This factor within the storm has the effect of creating a sense of urgency in the buying process, because there is a resulting perception that demand is exceeding supply and that "I'd better buy my piece of paradise before it's gone." The fact that some 80 percent of western North Carolina is comprised of government lands, predominantly national forests and national parks that will never be developed, certainly adds to that perception. Couple the physical beauty and attractive lifestyle of the area with the very well documented demographic growth of the baby boom generation into its retirement years, and you find a place that is in very high demand for residential real estate.

2. A preponderance of uninformed buyers who originate from feeder markets that are vastly different from the market to which they are moving

That describes, unfortunately, many of you, though I hope that after you have read this book, you won't qualify as such any longer. For those who don't know the right answers but are at least armed with the right questions, your journey may not be so difficult. For those who haven't even the foggiest notion of what the questions are, be advised that you are the dream clients for the one-day-only sales event. You can't possibly expect a sales person to give you an answer to a question that you don't ask. Frankly, you can't even depend on getting a complete answer to a question that you do ask. Let me compare two conversations, both of which I have had and heard when I have attended these events, to confirm and reconfirm the dialogue that takes place at them.

Conversation No. 1 (Typical):

<u>Uninformed Consumer:</u> "I understand that each homeowner has to take care of the sewer needs with their own septic system. Does this homesite have approvals for a septic and drain field system?

<u>Salesperson:</u> We guarantee that every lot will "perc." (as in "percolate")

<u>Uninformed Consumer:</u> "Oh great, thank you." *(I have no freakin' idea what "perc" means but it sounds technical and official, and I'm too embarrassed to ask what that means, and my wife will think I'm a moron if I do.)*

Conversation No. 2 (Atypical):

<u>Informed Consumer:</u> "I understand that each homeowner has to take care of the sewer needs with their own septic system. Does this homesite have approvals for a septic and drain field system?

<u>Salesperson:</u> We guarantee that every lot will "perc."

<u>Informed Consumer:</u> Okay, but that's not really what I asked. Where is the drain field located?

<u>Salesperson:</u> I don't know.

<u>Informed Consumer:</u> How many bedrooms is the approval for?

<u>Salesperson:</u> Umm…I'm not sure.

Informed Consumer: Where is the repair area located?

Salesperson: I don't know that either. *(What the hell is a repair area?)*

Informed Consumer: Is the drain field system a conventional system or a drip irrigation system or some other engineered system?

Salesperson: Excuse me? *(Who is this guy?)*

Informed Consumer: Okay, let's try this one: Where is the well located, because the drain fields, both the primary and repair area, need to be no less than one hundred feet away from the well, and then I need to know about the drain field locations on the adjacent lots also, to be sure that I'm one hundred feet away from them too?

Salesperson: Uuhhhh… *(Who the hell is this guy?)*

The above is just one example of a comparison of dialogue that reflects two distinctly different exchanges: what a typical buyer at one of these events might ask and the one-sentence response he or she might receive vs. the atypical series of relevant and informed questions that rarely get an answer.

There are as many as four possible reasons that the salesperson in the second scenario responds as he or she does: a) the salesperson simply doesn't know the answer because he or she didn't even know it was a question; or b) the salesperson at least knows it's a pertinent question but never bothered to get the answer in preparation for the event; or c) the salesperson knows it's a pertinent question, but the firm he or she works for will not allow him or her to answer it; or d) the person knows the answer and chooses not to provide it. Is any one of these reasons valid? Does it really matter whether it's ignorance, negligence, a company policy of deception, or a personal policy of dishonesty?

I have reiterated, ad nauseam, I suppose, the fact that most buyers in the second home markets of the mountains inevitably come from coastal or other "flatland" environments. They come from urban or suburban population centers where the highest mountain is the pitcher's mound at the local little league field. They haven't a clue what they are looking for, what they are looking at, or what questions to ask. Their home environment may consist of a concrete jungle with a few palm trees strategically scattered about the neighborhood. Now the vista includes long-range, layered blue mountains, hardwood trees of inordinate height and thickness, fall foliage that dazzles even the locals, streams, creeks, hiking trails, and maybe even a waterfall, and…well, the mesmerization on the day of the event is just about complete. How could a place this beautiful be anything but heaven? How could these sales folks be anything but shining examples of the local, down-to-earth, southern hospitality that they've read so much about? How could they possibly go wrong buying this homesite in this paradise? Well they can go wrong, and many have, and many more probably will, though I hope that is not the case.

3. **An exceptionally well-trained sales staff and an exceptionally well-choreographed sales technique that is religiously employed at these events**

I don't know exactly where or when this particular sales technique for selling land originated, nor is it clear to me in what ways the technique may have changed over the years. I thought about researching the history of the subject, which probably would have brought me close to some large land tracts bordering the Florida Everglades. For the purposes of this book, however, that story really had little relevance to what I was trying to achieve. It is enough for the reader to understand what this sales technique involves in its current evolution and to be empowered to deal with it successfully, should he or she decide to attend such events or, alternatively, to avoid them entirely and choose a different process that is built upon honest and fair disclosure, where issues that can impact a very pricey decision are openly discussed in a forthright manner.

Understand from the get-go that *the primary goal of every step of this process is to create a deep sense of urgency for you to ultimately make a purchase on the day of the event.* From the very first advertisements that you receive via direct mail pieces and e-mail campaigns to the first phone contact you initiate to request information on the property and the event, to every single ounce of communication you have during the event itself, the singular focus of the sales personnel is to create in your mind an undeniable sense of urgency. How is this accomplished? Let's start with the advertisements, which are designed to create a sense of urgency from both timing and pricing perspectives. (See Exhibits 7.2, 7.3 and 7.4).

If you've seen one of these, you've seen a hundred, because unless you choose to "unsubscribe," your e-mail will be deluged with one after another.

1. **Pricing Urgency:**

- Typically, during the recent, extreme "down market" where developers and lenders have been looking for exit strategies, the three absolute worst quality homesites are marketed at prices that would buy you a used car with high mileage. **The standard three teasers are in the neighborhood of $9,900, $14,900, and $19,900.** How can you *not* come to a sales event where you can buy your dream vacation homesite for $9,900? In this example scenario, the actual average price for all of the

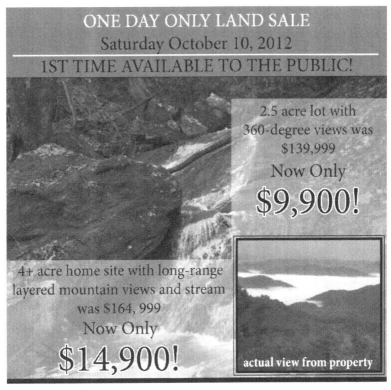

Exhibit 7.2: typical style and copy for a mass mailing or e-blast ad for one-day-only sales events

Buyer Beware!

Exhibit 7.3: typical style and copy for a mass mailing or e-blast ad for one-day-only sales events

Everything You Need To Know About Buying Mountain Property

ONE DAY ONLY
MOUNTAIN PROPERTY SALE
BANK FORECLOSURE!
Saturday August 22, 2012

Finished Infrastructure	Gated Entrance	Free and Clear Title
Private Lots	Underground Utilities	Minutes to Shops & Dining
Excellent Financing Available	Paved Roads	Blue Ridge Parkway Close By
Old-Growth Forest	General Warranty Deed	Kayaking, Canoeing & Fishing

4 acre lot with long-range layered mountain views
WAS $144,999 - NOW ONLY $8,900!

7 acre lot with river frontage
WAS $194,999 - NOW ONLY $18,900!

10+ acres, family getaway with 1,800 sf log cabin package*
ONLY $44,900!

* package is a lot and building materials package only, the cost of construction is the buyers responsibility

Exhibit 7.4: typical style and copy for a mass mailing or e-blast ad for one-day-only sales events

available homesites will probably be about $50,000–$60,000. There are only three available homesites that are actually priced per the ad, because the only purpose those three have is to entice you to come to the event. The company that sent you this ad is keenly aware that if the average prices are kept in this range, about four to five times the lowball teaser number, you'll only be a little bit pissed off, but not so pissed off that you won't still make a purchase at the higher prices. Oh, and you might think that it would be reasonable to ask for and receive the price list before the event so that you can actually study it a bit to get a jump-start on your endeavor. Good luck with that. The standard response is something like, "Our company executives will be completing the pricing exercise the night before the event, so we don't have that information available just yet." The truth? They don't ever give out the pricing before the event, because half the people wouldn't show up if they saw it. *URGENCY. When you don't have the facts, the sense of urgency stays intact. Too much information negates the urgency, particularly when such information is in direct opposition to what they want you to believe.*

- A reference in the advertisement to some previously listed price, as in **"WAS $129,900, NOW $9,900!"** Okay...six years ago, at the peak of the insane real estate market that almost put this country into a second Great Depression, the homesite was *listed* (not sold, *listed*) for $129,900. What possible relevance or bearing does that have on anything? What you're supposed to think is that if you act quickly, *you'll save $120,000 before it goes back up to $129,000, possibly as early as tomorrow!*

- **"A lot and home package for $39,900."** This one is truly remarkable for the sheer magnitude and brazenness of its disingenuousness. Yup, there's an asterisk. Turns out the price excludes one small detail—a veritable afterthought—you have to pay someone whatever they might charge to actually build it for you. I'm not kidding. The small print, if you can find it with an electron microscope, says, "Package is a land and building materials package; construction is buyer's responsibility." Have you ever, say, thought about buying a car and come across an ad that said, in the finest of fine print, "Package is a tires, frame, and engine package, assembly is buyer's responsibility"?

2. **Timing Urgency:**

- **"One-Day-Only."** Enough said. *If you don't buy a homesite that day, you will never run across this opportunity again, ever in your lifetime*...or at least not until next weekend, when we do this again at another development.
- **"Call today to reserve your appointment!"** Man, this event is in such high demand that I can't just show up and hope for a spot. I need an appointment! If I don't get an appointment, I'll miss out! I'll lose my opportunity to buy my dream, getaway homesite for $9,900, or better yet, a log cabin for $39,900 delivered in pieces. I'd be a moron to miss out on this opportunity. I'm going to call now!
- **"Properties will be sold first come, first choice."** Not only do I need an appointment, I need the earliest one.
- **"Gates open at 9:45."** Gates? This must be like a Stones concert.
- **"First time available to the general public."** I see. Before, it was only available to a private select few, which I guess would explain the slow sales pace that got it into trouble in the first

place. Now the marketing gurus of the firm have figured out that you actually have to offer it to the *general public*.

I wish my low opinions and impressions were a reflection of just how silly, insincere, and deceptive these ads are perceived by the intended audience. Sadly, the reason they keep coming into your mail and e-mail is that people continue to respond to them, regardless of their questionable integrity.

Let's also review some great examples of pointless and useless information contained within most of these ads:

- **Underground Utilities:** What would you think this means? Power? Phone? High-speed Internet access? Water and sewer? Cable TV? Gas? What it more than likely means is power and phone. Wow! Electric power and telephone are provided and… not just provided…but *underground*! What a bonus!
- **Large Useable Acreage Lots:** What exactly does the keyword in this phrase, "Useable," mean? Useable for what? The salesperson doesn't know where the drain field goes, where the well goes, where the drain fields and wells are on the adjacent homesites, or where a driveway or the building pad would be constructed, and has no knowledge of the plat that would show possible easements and other encumbrances, and on and on. For what, if anything, has anyone definitively determined that this homesite is useable? The answer is probably "nothing."
- **Towering Hardwood Trees:** Yup, we are in western North Carolina, and the property has trees on it. And that differentiates it from all other properties in the mountains in what way?
- **75-mile views:** One cannot see for seventy-five miles. Either other mountains intercept the view well before you get even

halfway to seventy-five miles, or the curvature of the earth limits the distance one can see, or both.

- **Large Private Properties:** Again, what does that mean? Virtually all second home, rural communities in the mountains are "large," I suppose, compared to urban and suburban communities, for the simple reason that you cannot locate all of the required elements of a mountain homestead (house, driveway, drain field, well, etc.) on much less than an acre, or possibly two or three acres, depending on the topography. The privacy issue is a direct result of the buffer that woods can create between you and your neighbor. So what is being differentiated here, what is special about this community that sets it apart from any other community with "large private properties"? Nothing.

- **Finished Community:** One more time now, what does that mean? The infrastructure is 100 percent completed? The amenities are 100 percent completed? The construction of homes is 100 percent completed? If you are extremely fortunate, it probably means that the infrastructure and amenities are complete, but you had better confirm that, and you had better confirm just exactly what is meant by "infrastructure."

- **Free and Clear Title, General Warranty Deed:** This is a patently ridiculous phrase to pass off as some kind of bonus benefit or added luxury. The hope is that you really have no idea what the terms "free and clear title" and "general warranty deed" mean. "But gosh, they sound so legal and technical that they must be great to have, just like a lot that 'percs.'" Going back to our analogy of the car buying experience, it would be a bit like seeing advertising language that states, "Tires are fully inflated, steering wheel included." The fact is that if you are using a lender to help finance your purchase, the lender will absolutely require that the loan closing be predicated upon the established fact of free and clear title and a transfer of the property via a general warranty deed. And even if there is no lender, your attorney will stipulate that both of these conditions must be met prior to closing.

The second step of the sales process begins at the moment that you make that first call to inquire about the specifics of the event, and it continues up until the day of the event. It is unimportant to belabor the discussion with numerous examples of how the event sales staff creates the urgency on the phone. Be assured, however, that they are tirelessly trained to categorize you, as the buyer, into a number of different "personality types" and then, based on your personality type, to gear the conversations they have with you to the kind of discussion that will push your particular hot button. They are also trained to give you as little information as they possibly can, which accomplishes two things: it prevents the possibility that some bit of that information will turn you off, and it also keeps up the "urgency pressure," as in, "You can only find out this information if you attend the event." I will provide one example, simply because it is so classic and because it underscores what is , in my opinion, the disingenuousness that is at the heart of these events. Try asking if you can come to the event and look at the lots prior to the day of the event. Here is just a sampling of the possible responses that you might hear:

- The gates will be closed at that time, and we are not authorized to provide access.
- Our liability insurance only covers us for the day of the event.

- The safety precautions won't be set up until the day of the event.
- Crews are working on the entire property, setting it up for the event, and with all the equipment there, it isn't safe.
- It isn't fair to the others to give someone the advantage of a sneak preview.

The truth is that probably none of these statements is true, or if any were, they could be easily overcome if one were simply motivated to do so. The last one is certainly valid but not true; if they really had any concerns about fairness, they wouldn't be holding such an event in the first place. The reason that you cannot attend early is because 1) more knowledge creates less urgency; 2) the potential for seeing something that you don't like and having the time to think about it is heightened; and 3) the atmosphere on a solo visit (compared to the carnival-like atmosphere on the day of the event), is not conducive to urgency.

You may receive a document during this second phase of the sales process, probably by e-mail if you have provided that information, entitled "Frequently Asked Questions." (See Exhibit 7.5)

Almost every sentence in this document is either "sales talk" or is a requirement of the law, meaning that the statement gives you nothing more than the law already gives you. Furthermore, some of the language is, in my view, plainly and purposefully deceptive. Take for example the posed question, "Do I need to find an attorney on my own if I decide to purchase?" The answer that they provide has nothing to do with the question:

"(Developer/sales entity) has obtained an attorney who is familiar with the property and region. The attorney's knowledge of the property and area will make for a smooth and timely closing. They

FREQUENTLY ASKED QUESTIONS

(Insert Subdivision/Development Name Here)

1. **Is now a good time to buy land in the mountains?**
   Without a doubt. They're not making land anymore. Right now is a perfect time to find once-in-a-lifetime deals on buildable homesites in the mountains.

2. **What can you tell me about the firm from whom I am buying the property? Is the sales staff knowledgeable and experienced?**
   Our staff is very professional and we have years of experience in the development and sale of mountain properties. Our Land Consultants are very familiar with all of the details affecting mountain property in general and the property that is the subject of this sale in particular.

3. **Is bank financing available for a homesite purchase?**
   Yes, we have lenders standing by who are intimately familiar with the property as a whole and the individual homesites. They have had each one of the available homesites appraised and have various lending programs to suit your individual needs and circumstances.

4. **What about guarantees? Will I receive a deed to the property that I purchase? Can I obtain a Title Insurance Policy?**
   You will receive a General Warranty Deed as part of the closing documentation, which will guarantee free and clear title to your property.

5. **What about a survey?**
   A Professional Land Surveyor licensed to operate in this state has completed survey maps or "plats" of all homesites, showing the various

easements and other encumbrances affecting each property and verifying deeded access to a public right-of-way for ingress and egress.

6. **Is there any minimum time frame from the date of closing that we will be required to start building our new home?**
   No, you are free to build your home whenever it is convenient, as long as you have obtained all of the necessary approvals and permits to do so.

7. **Do I need to find an attorney on my own if I decide to purchase?**
   Our firm has obtained an attorney who is familiar with the property and region. The attorney's knowledge of the property and area will make for a smooth and timely closing. They can also arrange the closing via mail which will save you considerable time and make for an easy process.

8. **Is there a requirement for a good faith deposit?**
   Yes, so be sure to bring your checkbook! We require a deposit equal to 10% of the purchase price of the homesite, which will be held in escrow by the attorney and credited to the purchase price on the day of the closing.

Exhibit 7.5: typical language that may be found in an FAQ for one-day-only sales events

can also arrange the closing via mail, which will save you considerable time and make for an easy process."

The real answer is "Yes, you should secure your own attorney, because the attorney that we use can only have a fiduciary responsibility to us and can only represent our interests, not yours." Is that what their posed answer reflects? Hardly.

The third and final step of the process is the day of the event, which is truly a masterfully choreographed and scripted affair. Depending on the marketing budget for the event, there is typically a tent, seating, food and drink, and perhaps some entertainment at the arrival area. At a prescribed moment, a caravan of some thirty, forty, maybe fifty brand new SUVs shows up in perfect procession, which is actually quite a sight to behold. If you've ever seen the president of the United States show up at a function or even just seen the president's motorcade traveling along an interstate highway on its way to one, you know what I mean. Here's what you should know:

There is a salesperson in every one of the vehicles, and the number of salespeople typically exceeds the number of lots that are available. **Urgency.** *Probably less than 5 percent of those salespeople are actually employees of the sales firm. The rest are individuals who work their real nine-to-five job in another place, another town, and perhaps another industry altogether. They have spent less than one day, the day before the event, walking the property and the lots, to familiarize themselves as best they can with the development. The shirts they have on say the name of the development. The vast majority are neither employees of the developer nor even employees of the sales and marketing firm that is conducting the event. They do not own the vehicles. They are all rentals, rented for just that weekend, for just that event. They call themselves "Land Consultants." There is no such designation of, testing for, or licensing of any such category of professional by any state real estate commission.*

The actual arrival area for the event is rarely at the property itself, a fact that is as predetermined as every other aspect of the day. The environment is about control, control by the sales staff of every controllable variable of the day. If you, the buyer, have your own car close by, you can be in control of where you go. If it is not close by, you are in the control of the salesperson who has been assigned to you. You are in that person's car, essentially that salesperson's office, until you make the decision either to buy or not to buy. Here's what you can expect during your tour.

You will typically be shown a ""site plan" of the development. (See Exhibit 7.6.) You may also be told that it is a plat. It is not a plat. A plat is an official document, recorded in the public records of the county, and is essentially a very detailed survey showing critical information regarding the lot size and dimensions, easements, and rights-of-way that impact each homesite (see Chapter Three). A site plan, on the other hand, is simply an artistic rendering of the development, and it has no legal or official standing of any kind.

You will probably be shown a summary of bullet points that may be titled something to the Effect of "Vital Information Statement." (See Exhibit 7.7.)

The information is, at best, an extremely abbreviated and limited list of disclosures that is a small tip of the iceberg of what you really need to know. More importantly, keep in mind that, *once you have provided a good faith deposit check, the only valid legal reason that you can get your good faith deposit money back is if you cannot obtain financing.* So in the case of the bullet point on the development's covenants, for example, the disclosure reads, "Purchaser acknowledges receipt of the protective covenants for (development name) and understands all items contained within." This is typically a fifty- to hundred-page document, sometimes longer. You couldn't possibly absorb the document and its implications while you're driving around

Buyer Beware!

Exhibit 7.6: example of an illustrative site plan, not to be confused with a legal plat

Contract Addendum - VITAL INFORMATION STATEMENT

(Insert Subdivision/Development Name Here)

This Vital Information Statement provides important information to prospective home site buyers regarding estimated costs, duties and responsibilities associated with the future development of this property. The data has been gathered from presumably reliable sources. Seller makes no representation or guarantee as to the accuracy of such information and therefore all information contained herein is subject to change without notice.

1. The homesite being purchased by Buyer through Seller, Lot #__, in the platted subdivision known as *Subdivision name*, located in *County and State name* has been developed pursuant to and in conformance with all local codes and ordinances having jurisdiction.

2. Buyer acknowledges receipt of a copy of the recorded Covenants, Conditions and Restrictions of the *Subdivision name* Property Owner's Association (POA), including the By-Laws, Articles of Incorporation, Rules and Regulations and any addendums thereto. Buyer acknowledges his/her understanding of all items contained therein.

3. Buyer acknowledges the receipt of the Architectural Design Guidelines and understands that the design of any future home must be in accordance with these Guidelines as well as all local building codes and ordinances having jurisdiction.

4. Buyer acknowledges and understands that various easements have been granted by the Developer that are either described in the Covenants, Conditions and Restrictions or are reflected in the survey map (recorded plat) of the Subdivision. Such easements and encumbrances serve to provide for ingress and egress to a public right-of-way and the installation and maintenance of utilities that serve the Subdivision.

5. Buyer acknowledges and understands that potable water for household usage is not provided by a central, municipal water system and that Buyer shall be completely responsible for drilling a well that must be located within the legal boundaries of the homesite to provide for an adequate water supply to serve the needs of the future home.
6. Buyer acknowledges and understands that sanitary sewer facilities are not provided by a central, municipal sewer system and that Buyer shall be completely responsible for the installation of a septic tank and drain field sewer system that must be located within the legal boundaries of the homesite to provide for adequate sewer collection and treatment to serve the needs of the future home.
7. Electrical utility service is provided by *Power Company Name.*
8. Cable Television and wide-band Internet service is provided by *Cable Company Name.*
9. Telephone and DSL Internet Access is provided by *Phone Company Name.*
10. The current property tax rate in *County Name* is __ cents per $100 of assessed value as determined by the County's Property Appraisal Office. The property taxes will be prorated as determined by the date of closing, meaning that Seller and Buyer will each pay their fair share according to their respective ownership periods.
11. The current POA dues are $__ per year and are subject to change each fiscal year. The POA Dues will be prorated as determined by the date of closing, meaning that Seller and Buyer will each pay their fair share according to their respective ownership periods.
12. Buyer acknowledges and understands that the Subdivision is a gated community and that the internal roadway system serving the Subdivision is private and that all costs to maintain the roadway system shall be borne by the *Subdivision name* POA.

13. Local contact information that may be useful:

    Building Dept: _____

    Health Dept: _____

    Erosion Control: _____

    Planning and Zoning: _____

    Property Taxes: _____

14. The contact information for the closing attorney is as follows:_____
15. Buyer acknowledges and understands that there are inherent risks involved in the purchasing of a homesite and that Seller has made no express or implied warranties as to the future value of such homesites.

CERTIFICATION BY SELLER: Seller has provided the above disclosures to the Buyer and Buyer has had adequate time to completely read and fully understand all of the disclosures.

Buyer Signature: _____ Date: _____

Buyer Signature: _____ Date: _____

Exhibit 7.7: typical language that may be found in a so-called Vital Information Statement distributed at one-day-only sales events

in an SUV trying to pick out a homesite; further, any objection you may have *after* you have provided a deposit check and actually had a chance to read the document is moot, because an objection to the language of the covenants is not a valid reason to void the contract. *Only in the case of the denial of credit by a financial institution or the seller's inability to transfer clear title will the refund of your good faith deposit be issued. No other objection by you that might arise from any additional due diligence effort subsequent to providing the good faith deposit will be a valid objection on which to cancel the purchase agreement.*

While you are being given the tour, a very effective technique is used to bolster the sense of urgency. All of the salespeople have communication radios that are all set to the same channel and all set to be heard, at a volume not only loud enough for the salesperson to hear but for anyone else in each SUV to hear, loud and clear, as they say. Because the sales activity can be extremely active at times, there is no doubt that a genuine need exists for the sales staff to communicate with one another. Otherwise, there is significant potential for the same lot to be mistakenly purchased by two people at almost the same moment. But that isn't the primary purpose of the use of radios. The intended consequence is to provide each and every customer within easy earshot of the radios a constant, real-time status of every sale, as the buyer is now part of a captive audience in every SUV. As you travel from homesite to homesite, the radio blares with:

"Please take lot #42 off the market…repeat, lot #42 has been sold."

"Please take lot #33 off the market…I repeat, lot #33 is now unavailable."

"Lot #17 is gone…please note, lot #17 has been sold."

This has the obvious effect of creating an environment where all of the buyers feel that if they don't act quickly, they'll lose out. **URGENCY.**

One last document employed in this process is certainly worthy of note: the "Contract of Sales and Purchase," as one example I have seen is entitled. (See Exhibit 7.8)

Offer to Purchase and Contract

Lot at *Subdivision Name*

Buyer Name(s), as Buyer, with an address of _____ hereby agrees to purchase and *Seller Name*, as Seller, with an address of _____ hereby agrees to sell and convey all of that plot, piece or parcel of land described herein upon the following terms and conditions:

1. **Real Property**: Located in the County of _____ in the State of _____, being known as and more particularly described as all of Lot # __ as recorded in the Plat of *Subdivision Name* in Plat Book __ Pages __ of the public records of *County Name.*

2. **Purchase Price:** The purchase price is $_____ and shall be paid as follows:

    a. An amount equal to 10% of the Purchase Price ($_____), Earnest Money Deposit, receipt of which is hereby acknowledged by Seller and which Deposit shall be immediately delivered to the closing attorney named in Paragraph 5 herein, to be deposited and held in Escrow in said attorney's Trust Account pending Closing, the sum of which will be credited to the Purchase Price at Closing. Should Buyer breach this contract, the Earnest Money Deposit shall be paid to Seller, at the Seller's request, as liquidated damages.

    b. $_____ Balance of the Purchase Price, in cash, at Closing.

3. **Conditions:**

    a. **Financing Contingency:** Buyer's obligation to purchase the property is _ / is not_ (check and initial one) contingent upon Buyer's ability to obtain purchase financing. If the Purchase is contingent upon financing, Buyer agrees as follows:

      i. Buyer must provide proof of application for the loan commitment to Seller within **three (3) business days** of the date of the final execution of this Contract (the Effective Date).

      ii. Buyer must provide to the lender all documentation required by lender in order for Buyer to obtain a loan commitment within **five (5) business days** of the Effective Date.

      iii. Buyer shall have the option to terminate this Contract and the Earnest Money Deposit shall be returned to Buyer, only if Buyer is unable to obtain financing; provided however, that in order to obtain such refund, Buyer must make a complete loan application to at least one lender from the Seller's list of approved lenders for this Subdivision. In such case, buyer shall, within **fifteen (15) calendar days** of the Effective Date, give Seller written notice, signed by the lender, of its refusal to provide financing. Failure of the buyer to identify the refusing lender within **three (3) business days** of the Effective Date, or to give notice of Buyer's inability to obtain financing within **15 Calendar days** of the Effective Date, shall be construed as a waiver of the Financing Contingency and all of the terms and conditions of this Contract shall be binding on all parties to the Contract. **TIME IS OF THE ESSENCE WITH RESPECT TO THIS FINANCING CONTINGENCY.**

b. **Title:** Title must be delivered by Seller at closing by General Warranty Deed and must be fee simple title and insurable as such by a reputable title insurance company, free of all material encumbrances except: ad valorem taxes for the current year (prorated to the day of closing), rights-of-way of record, the Declaration of Covenants, Conditions and Restrictions (CCR's) for the Subdivision and such other matters as they may appear on the recorded Plat of the Subdivision or as specifically accepted by Buyer. Buyer acknowledges receipt of the aforementioned Declaration of CCR's and Plat of the Subdivision.

c. **Inspection:** Buyer hereby acknowledges that he/she has made a personal on-the-Lot inspection of the Lot and accepts such property in its present condition. Seller represents that the lot is currently suitable for an on-site sewage system. The risk of loss or damage to the Lot prior to Closing is the responsibility of Seller.

4. **Closing Expenses:** Buyer agrees that Buyer shall pay all closing costs, including but not by way of limitation, attorney's fees, excise taxes (revenue stamps), recording fees, lender fees, title examination fees and title insurance premiums.

5. **Closing:** Closing shall take place on or before _____ at the offices of _____ located at _____. Closing may be arranged in person or by mail to accommodate the wishes of the Buyer.

6. **Addendum:** Buyer acknowledges receipt of the Contract Addendum entitled Vital Information Statement, which is hereby made a part of this Contract.

I,_____ agree to purchase the Real Property described herein on the above terms and conditions. Buyer acknowledges receipt of a copy of this Contract and understands that the terms and conditions of this Contract and the Vital Information Statement Addendum are legally binding upon the Buyer and Seller. Buyer and Seller agree that this Contract is the only Contract between them and that no other oral or written representations have been made or have been relied upon which are not a part of this Contract. **Buyer has been advised that this Contract has no Right of Rescission and** is therefore immediately binding upon the execution of the Contract by both Buyer and Seller.

Buyer: _____   Date: _____

Buyer: _____   Date: _____

Seller: _____   Date: _____

Exhibit 7.8: typical language that may be found in a contract form utilized at one-day-only sales events

Take a close look at this document, which is typically a single page in length, and compare it to Exhibit 3.3, which is the standard "Offer to Purchase and Contract – Vacant Lot/Land" used in the state of North Carolina, a document that is *nine pages* in length. Why is the document that is jointly approved by the state's Association of Realtors and the state's Bar Association nine pages long? Because it is intended to be a fair and equitable agreement that balances the risks and the protections that both parties, the seller and the buyer, deserve to be afforded in such an important transaction. Why is the contract that is used at a one-day-only sales event one page in length? There are two reasons. First, from a legal perspective, it is written entirely in the favor of the seller and is intended to give the buyer the absolute least amount of protection possible. When you want to write a document that is grossly one-sided, it doesn't take a whole lot of verbiage to accomplish that task. "Heads I win, tails you lose" are about the only words of shorter length that come to mind. Secondly, the last thing that any of these sales folks want to be guilty of doing is "confusing you with the facts." The less you have to read, the less chance that any issues or topics will arise about which you should be concerned, and believe me, if you don't bring it up, it won't be discussed. Let's just be blunt here. I know of no real estate attorney who would ever suggest that any buyer consider executing such a contract; further, I know of no real estate attorney who would suggest that you sign any contract without being given the appropriate amount of time to conduct the due diligence necessary to make an informed decision...period.

Keep in mind that the focus of this entire sales and marketing effort, in my judgment, has absolutely nothing to do with the product itself, the land. What they are selling is the "sell" itself. Every ounce of energy is devoted to the sales process, the sales technique, which is exactly why the salespeople can show up all of one day before the event and see the property and the homesites—for the first time—for a mere few hours in preparation. To put it simply, the consumer had better beware any time an enterprise puts forth such an extraordinary effort and focus on the selling technique that the quality of the product itself becomes an afterthought. The whole exercise can be reduced to the simplicity of a numbers game, and the firms that conduct these events know the numbers very, very well. The game goes something like this: "I've got X homesites to sell. I therefore need XXXXX direct mail pieces and e-mail notifications to generate XXXX phone inquiries from potential prospects, which will produce XXX customers who will say they are coming to the event and make appointments, which will result in XX people actually showing up to the event, which will result in X actual purchases." The numbers are the numbers. It is akin to actuarial science and statistics in the insurance industry. The numbers don't lie. There may be anomalies every now and then, but generally, the numbers do not lie.

Finally, I think it is important to clarify one point. This book has been written at a time that immediately followed one of the worst downturns in the real estate market that anyone can remember. Many of the examples and exhibits in this chapter have been reflective of that period of time. However, it should be noted that the downturn in the real estate market, or for that matter, whatever state the real estate market is in, has nothing to do with providing a better or worse environment or condition for the use or success of the one-day-only sales event. The only difference is that when the real estate market is strong, the developers that utilize this technique actually employ the core of their sales teams because they can afford to do so; in a bad market, the developer (if he or she still exists) or the lender (if it has foreclosed) hires the sales and marketing firm as a third-party consultant to organize and manage the event. I would argue that during a bad market, the sales and marketing firm, as a detached third party, has absolutely no financial, legal, or emotional ties or connections to the property at all, making it that much more probable that the entire process will be fraught with an even greater degree of questionable sales practices rather than honest and full disclosure.

At the risk of being redundant, permit me to sound the alarm one last time before we leave this section on the dynamics of the sales process.

- *If you ever feel that a salesperson is spending more time and effort on pressing the urgency for you to make a decision to purchase property rather than on the urgency for him or her to provide you with the needed information necessary for you to form the educated basis for making that decision to purchase,* **walk away.**
- *If you ever feel that you are being corralled and seduced into an environment where emotion is the basis of the purchasing decision, as opposed to sensible and informed logic,* **walk away.**

- *There are thousands of home sites across this region from which to choose. They were there yesterday, they are there today and they will be there tomorrow. If you ever feel that you have not had the appropriate amount of time to analyze all of the relevant specifics that may have an impact on the viability and feasibility of a given home site for your future home,* **walk away***.*

4. A lack of real estate development regulation

The regulation (or lack thereof) of this particular segment of the real estate industry provides an excellent case study for the continued, hotly contested, and often-ideological debate in this country that is sharply divided along political party lines. On the one hand, conservatives would postulate that the enactment and enforcement of burdensome regulations is a catalyst for increased costs that developers must necessarily either pass on to the consumer or make up by reducing their payrolls, or both, in order to maintain a profitable business model. Liberals would counter that a lack of regulation allows the intrusion into the marketplace of the inexperienced and/or unscrupulous developer who will usurp the opportunistic openings that a lack of regulation engenders, to his or her benefit and to the detriment of the consumer. I understand clearly both sides of the argument, and as with most ideological debates, the truth lies somewhere in the middle. My personal belief is that there is a need for some degree of regulation to protect the consumer in a given industry, when the size of a typical transaction within that industry is such that the potential loss of those funds could be disastrous for the average consumer. I also believe that regulations may not have gone far enough when the extent to which consumers remain exposed to such a catastrophic loss results in a loss of confidence in the industry. Finally, I think regulations have gone too far when the protections afforded the consumer have made the business model untenable due to the competition from alternatives available to the consumer that are not subject to such regulations .

Though I tend to have a personal bias toward fewer regulations in business, generally, it is my opinion that the regulatory atmosphere in many rural counties in the mountains remains at a level below that by which consumers should expect to be protected. Right now, in a number of counties across the region, a buyer can close on the purchase of a platted homesite that has no road, no power, no phone, no water, and no sewer. All that a developer has been required to do in these counties is to have a planner, engineer, and land surveyor draw up the plans that show the roadways that *will be built in the future*; to delineate the utility easements on those plans that *will allow for power and phone in the future*; and finally, to have those plans (known as plats) recorded in the public records of the county, and the developer is off and running with a sales team. No infrastructure may actually be constructed at all, other than unrocked and unpaved trails that may actually have been the existing logging trails from an earlier era. It is almost unfathomable to realize that, in this day and age, a handful of logging trails and a recorded plat are just about all that is needed to provide for sales tours of the property and a legal transfer of a homesite.

Some counties may require that a developer post a payment and performance bond with the county to ensure the completion of the infrastructure; however, buyers should be aware that having the infrastructure in place is immeasurably more reliable than counting on the bond, should that developer fail financially. Bonding companies can be fabulously responsive when asked to provide a bond; unfortunately, when put into the position of actually having to perform on the promise, should circumstances call on them to do so, be prepared to watch a legal case plod through a lengthy and contentious court procedure while none of the work to complete the infrastructure is initiated for years.

So—tying back to our one-day-only sale event—it is the lack of regulation that would require the completion of at least the key components of the infrastructure prior to the legal transfer (sale) of a homesite that makes it a very risky proposition for you to be given a matter of minutes (*a la* the one-day-only events) to decide on a land purchase that will most likely be one of the larger purchases of your lifetime. Why should you allow yourself to be subjected to that kind of pressure when you cannot count on the regulatory environment to remove the risk that the future infrastructure may never be constructed? What good is a piece of property in the mountains if you have no assurances that the services you will need in order to reside there happily will even be available? Perhaps framing this argument in a different manner will help to simplify the issue. When a particular industry is insufficiently regulated, the only person you can rely on to bridge that gap of assumed, built-in protections is *you, the buyer*. Taking thirty to sixty minutes to properly assess those risks (which are magnified by the lack of regulation) prior to executing a nonrefundable check with no rescission period is just not very smart.

5. Inexperienced and undercapitalized developers

This fifth item is a direct result of the fourth item that preceded it, the lack of regulation. There is one very important albeit probably unintended consequence of regulation, and that is that by necessity, a developer has to become more experienced, seasoned, and comfortably capitalized in order to survive the bureaucracy and afford its repercussions. A lack of regulation means a simpler development process, and the simpler the process, the easier it is for a novice—inexperienced and underfunded—to stumble into the development profession, if only for a short time. Unfortunately, the brief period of perceived success is long enough to do some irreversible damage to the environment, to the market in general, and to the buyers who purchased from the wrong developer, in the wrong place, at the wrong time.

Over the past ten years, I have run into more unqualified individuals passing themselves off as developers than at any previous time in my career. The almost manic atmosphere in the real estate market that peaked from approximately 2004 to 2006 no doubt had much to do with it. It was a time when even fledgling beginners could have some sustainable degree of success, in spite of themselves. Inevitably, whatever degree of success they may have had was never matched by the quality of development and construction that one would assume would have accompanied that success; and therein lies the problem with these particular properties being the subject of the one-day-only sales event.

Many inexperienced developers, almost by definition, will produce an inferior product simply because of their ignorance of what is required to avoid it. They are the very reason that county subdivision ordinances, building codes, materials testing requirements, and licensing of various trades are stipulated in the first place. What can make matters worse is that the symptoms of their inexperience—the foreshortened useful life span of the infrastructure which they have built—typically don't show up until a few years into the future, after far too many purchasers have made the mistake of buying property there.

- How do you know if the developer installed and compacted the proper thickness of road rock for a stable and structurally sound roadbed within all of the roadways?
- How do you know if the developer installed a full compacted thickness of two inches of asphalt on top of those roadways?
- How do you know the quality of the soils for adequate drain field percolation?
- How do you know the average depth of wells to access potable drinking water, and how do you know if you will get adequate flow for your domestic water needs?
- How do you know if there will be erosion control problems caused by future storm events?

The answer to these and numerous other questions is that you don't…and you don't have enough time to find out, if you're thinking about buying property at a one-day-only sales event.

About six years ago, I was consulting with a firm that fit the moniker of inexperienced developer to a tee. When I was first familiarizing myself with one of its developments, I came upon a pond within the community that I assumed was natural, or at the very least, was there when the developer had purchased the property. It turns out that the company had redirected the flow from a stream, excavated numerous yards of fill on either side of the new streambed, lined the bottom of the pond floor, and dammed the lower end of the excavation to create the pond. I asked how the firm was able to get the Department of Environment and Natural Resources and the Army Corps of Engineers to approve the work, and the firm's representatives said "Who?"

I don't think they actually tried to circumvent any agencies or the rules and regulations that those agencies have been entrusted to legislate and enforce. I don't think they had any idea who these agencies were or what their roles were in the regulatory process. I also don't think they had any clue as to the potential for harmful environmental impacts to the water quality and the cleanliness of natural bodies of water and wetlands that these laws were intended to prevent. What I do think is that inexperienced developers can unfortunately thrive, at times, in an under regulated environment and create untold problems for the unfortunate buyers within their communities as well as for the immediate environment that surrounds them. The one-day-only sales event simply expedites and compounds that process. It is no way for a consumer to buy real estate.

Finally, the issue of being undercapitalized serves as a multiplier and magnifier of all that is potentially wrong with the inexperienced developer. The most common mistake that regularly befalls the neophyte developer is an inability to correctly estimate the total costs of the development. Once the developer's acquisition and development loan is closed, it is typically like pulling teeth for the developer to get the bank to raise the loan amount. Similarly, raising new equity may be equally as difficult. That means that as the developer starts to run out of money, he or she starts to cut corners wherever possible, including corners that have a material and adverse impact on the quality and longevity of the infrastructure. The lack of regulation is certainly a contributing factor, and it is a factor of which an inexperienced and undercapitalized developer can take full advantage. This is one of the many reasons that you, as a consumer searching for that perfect property, should never put yourself in the position of acquiring an asset with such a hefty price tag within hours, if not minutes, of your initial introduction to it.

6. Unscrupulous and shady developers

I might easily have included this within the fifth item above, but I have always considered malicious intent to be far more insidious than plain ignorance. The results may be the same, but at least ignorance can be cured through experience. Duplicity and dishonesty are another matter.

Within any profession, there are those individuals that experience significant financial success as a direct result of their passion for excellence and their quest for perfection, for which they constantly strive. And then, there are those who are driven by some deep sense of insecurity, which they try to overcome by the pursuit of wealth for the sake of wealth. The process by which they achieve that wealth is irrelevant and insignificant to them. The only barometer of success is the attainment of wealth and typically, the ostentatious display of it. For developers of that ilk, any path that suits their purpose in achieving that wealth is a viable one, regardless of the impacts. The real estate development business is a complicated one, with numerous moving parts, any and all of which present opportunities to those so inclined, to gravitate to questionable business ethics and practices. Loan and mortgage fraud, appraisal fraud, shoddy infrastructure construction, the skirting of environmental and other regulatory laws and ordinances, deceptive marketing and sales practices – all of these, and more, have appeared via various schemes and practices in developments scattered throughout the region. Your job is to try to inoculate yourself against the possibility of making the wrong purchase, by taking your time, asking the right questions that have been put forth in this book, and having the patience and stamina to get the correct answers before you make your decision.

7. **A significant delay from the time a homesite is purchased to the time a home is actually constructed on the homesite**

This last piece or part of the storm is perhaps the least obvious and the most painful for the buyer because it is responsible for setting the stage for the moment at which the dream of what the buyer thought he or she purchased and the reality of what was actually purchased come into stark contrast.

Most of you live in a primary residence where you purchased a home and homesite as a total package, whether it was a single-family home, townhouse, duplex, condominium, cooperative, etc. You didn't concern yourself with the existence of the elements of infrastructure and services that were required to make the home livable. I have already enumerated in previous chapters of this book a fairly exhaustive list of concerns for you to analyze and quantify in order to be sure that a particular homesite will suit your needs. Now imagine that you don't build the home for maybe two, maybe five, perhaps ten years. What are you going to do, years later, when you discover that the lot is dry and has no water at any depth, or that the drain field can only accommodate a one-bedroom cabin though you had planned on a four-bedroom chalet, or that both neighbors have constructed drain fields that almost abut your property, leaving no place anywhere that you can drill a well that will be one hundred feet from both of their drain fields, or that you have to spend thirty thousand dollars blasting solid rock, even though the developer's salesperson told you the soils were perfect for excavating for foundations? It is years later, the developer is gone, the broker is gone—and even if they aren't, the statute of limitations has run, and you have no right to sue.

I have refrained from using specific examples throughout this book, because my goal has been to educate the consumer, which is easily and effectively accomplished without "naming names," as they say. For the purposes of this section, I'll deviate from that philosophy and refer to the almost infamous failed development known as "Grey Rock," located in the truly gorgeous Lake Lure area of western North Carolina, located about forty to forty-five minutes east of Asheville. The Grey Rock development typifies just about everything I have written about in this book that can be wrong in the world of real estate development in the mountains. It would be redundant for me simply to reword the preponderance of articles in the media that have covered this story over the years. For those that have an interest, the Asheville Citizen-Times alone carried no less than six featured articles on the development from 2005-2008. The stories ran the gamut of coverage; from the feel-good positives regarding the initial sales velocity to negatives of the well-documented environmental degradation to the sudden shut down of the development altogether.

Though I commend the local media for their efforts to follow the precipitous rise and fall of the Grey Rock development, I believe that they may have missed the real story here. Exactly how did a failure of this magnitude happen? What were the circumstances that allowed such a debacle to occur? What were the red flags that should have foreshadowed this collapse?

To me, the most interesting aspect on which to focus is the financing structure, and so a very brief discussion of how typical, second home communities are financed is warranted here.

Developers usually fund their development and construction costs through a combination of *debt*, that is, loans from one or more banks, and *equity*, essentially private money from investors. During normal market conditions, a bank may fund as much as eighty percent of the project's total hard costs, which are the costs associated with the physical (hard) land development and construction costs. The other twenty percent of the hard costs is typically funded through private equity sources. If the projects are large, these equity sources may be institutional in nature, such as insurance companies, pension funds, and real estate investment trusts. If the projects are small, "friends and family" are more apt to be the sources of equity. This is an overly simplified explanation of development financing, but it is more than adequate to serve as background for the discussion.

Now let's look at what can happen to this typical financing structure when you add the component of an insufficient regulatory environment. Put simply, consumers should be able to rely on real estate development regulations, enacted through the local government's subdivision ordinances, to ensure that the product the consumer is buying is able to be used for its intended purpose. In other words, you are buying a homesite and you should be able to rely on the assumption that the home that you eventually intend to build there will have the infrastructure necessary to make the home habitable. At a bare minimum, that should include a *completed*, deeded access (road) to a public right of way, *completed* primary electrical power, phone and internet access and *approvals* for septic and well locations (should there be no centralized water and sewer facilities). In the case of Grey Rock, *hundreds* of home sites were sold that had *none of the above*.

Now, returning to the issue of financing structure, there were two circumstances that acted as catalysts for the failure. First, the local subdivision ordinances did not require the infrastructure to be completed as a prerequisite for the Grey Rock developers to record plats in the official records of the county and thus to legally close on the sale of homesites to buyers. So what did the developer do? He chose not to borrow that money, be it debt or equity, to construct the infrastructure to make each and every homesite useable for its intended purpose. Well actually, they *did* borrow the money. *They borrowed it from you, the consumer, the home site purchaser.* That's right. You paid them the total cost for what should have been a fully developed (infrastructure completed) retail home site, except that is not what you got at the time of the purchase. They then planned to use your capital, interest free, to construct the infrastructure after the fact. *You, along with every other home site buyer, unwittingly became the de facto equity partner of the developer and you received no interest or no preferred return for the use of your money. And in the sad case of Grey Rock, you didn't even get what you gave much of the money for, the construction of the infrastructure!*

The second financing component that contributed to the mess was the local government's allowance of the use of a bond to supposedly insure the completion of the infrastructure. Performance and payment bonds, briefly discussed in chapter four, essentially serve as insurance policies that, should the developer become insolvent, are intended to cover the completion of, and payment for, the scope of work that is the subject of the bond. In the case of Grey Rock, the initial bonds that were purchased were for the completion of $41 million in infrastructure improvements. Eight years later and with the developer long gone, the county, on behalf of the development and its individual homesite owners, collected all of $15.2 million from one of the two bonding companies, barely more than a third of the original value of the two bonds.

Suffice it to say that Grey Rock serves as a microcosm of almost everything that one should be wary of in a planned residential community in the mountains. For hundreds of homesites there are no roads, no power, no phone, no infrastructure to speak of, environmental degradation and regulatory fines, no history of wells drilled, no drain fields permitted, an infrastructure bond that was tied up in legal proceedings for years, an unsavory, undercapitalized and bankrupt developer and…oh yes, lots of homesite sales…by a sales staff exceptionally proficient at the tactics, ploys and techniques that are the highlights of the one-day-only sales event. According to the records of the county in which Grey Rock is located, the development took in over $79,000,000 in sales revenues. They originally acquired the property for $12,000,000. They put in almost no infrastructure. Nobody quite knows where the money went but I don't think the founder and CEO of the now-defunct development firm is spending it right now. He'll be in jail for quite awhile, having been found guilty of the murder of his wife in 2009.

In concluding this chapter, I would like to clarify a number of points that may arise in the minds of some readers who may have a different point of view than the overly skeptical one that I have espoused in this chapter.

To those of you who may have purchased property at one of these events and have since built your home there and were able to realize or even maximize the dreams that you initially formulated for your mountain retreat, I think it is wonderful that you've achieved that result, and it is truly a benefit to the region to see the growth of new residents who have enjoyed a positive transition experience. It has not been my intent to suggest that the only result or even a majority of the results of property purchases transacted at one-day-only sales events are ones of misfortune and disappointment. However,

I want to be very clear that it seems needlessly risky to rely on luck and serendipity, which is all that can be relied on at these events, as opposed to education, investigation, analysis, and patience.

To those of you who may have purchased a homesite during this most difficult and deep housing recession and who may have benefited from "foreclosure-esque" pricing, you may ask, "The price was so cheap; how could I possibly go wrong?" To that I say, ask those who have purchased a dry lot, a lot that is so rocky that drain field areas don't exist, or a lot that has no roads, no power, and no infrastructure of any kind. There is no price that is cheap enough to purchase a lot on which a functional home cannot be built. Ask those who purchased in Grey Rock how they feel about their acquisitions.

To those developers that say, "This is a proven, successful technique that, under the right circumstances, we view as a viable alternative to other exit strategies," I say, you're right. For the developer, it is sometimes the best strategy to take, depending on his or her debt structure, access to additional equity, staying power, and stomach for additional risk. But this book is not written from the perspective of what is in the best interests of the developer. It is written from the perspective of what is in the best interests of the consumer, and from that perspective, these events pose a very risky proposition indeed. Think for a moment what the term "exit strategy" means. It used to be that developers talked about development strategies. For the past five or six years, everyone talks about an exit strategy, as in "I'm outta' here, here's the keys, don't wait up for me, don't call us, we'll call you." There is absolutely no concern on the part of the developer for the interests of the community or the individuals who purchased homesites there, once the exit has been made. The development may very well have no houses constructed. There is no community because there are no residents. The Property Owner's Association is left for the property owners to contend with, yet no one lives there to care what the community looks like.

To those developers that have utilized a variation on the one-day-only event wherein full and open disclosure is presented in an *honest and ethical process well in advance of the event*; where the event itself is really one of a "grand opening celebration," wherein a drawing or lottery format is utilized to determine who gets the first choice of homesites, I commend you. This format allows for buyers to conduct as much due diligence as they choose, leading up to the event, as the only real task left to accomplish on the day of the event is finalizing the order of their homesite preferences and putting their names into a hat and awaiting the selection process. These events epitomize the balance of full disclosure with the excitement of a gala event that incorporates a lottery selection process for the homesites.

Appendix to Chapter Seven

Exhibit 7.1: Asheville Accolades and Media Praise (reprinted here with the permission of ExploreAsheville.com)

Asheville Accolades & Media Praise: 2000-2011

Asheville has been recognized for its splendors by dozens of magazines, Web sites and publications in recent years. Accolades range from the designation by Frommer's as one of a dozen top travel destinations in the world to recognition for the Asheville area arts community, outdoor adventures, cuisine, organic and vegetarian eats, and much more.

2011

TripAdvisor.com lists Asheville as one of its "15 Destinations on the Rise." (December 2011)

Zagat.com included Firestorm Cafe & Books in a list of the "10 Coolest Independent Coffee Shops Across the US."

Condé Nast Traveler's annual Reader's Choice Awards Poll chose two Asheville properties among the best in the nation. The Grove Park Inn Resort & Spa was rated a Top U.S. Resort, and the Grand Bohemian Hotel Asheville was rated at Top U.S. Hotel.

Asheville is named "Best Place to Start a Fall Foliage Tour" by Livabiliy.com (October 2011)

The editors of *Prevention* magazine and Fitbie rank Asheville as the #5 best U.S. city for weight loss, thanks to a wide variety of options for finding farm fresh food choices. (October 2011)

Asheville comes in at #10 in TripAdvisor.com's Travelers' Choice Awards for top food and wine destinations in the U.S. (October 2011)

Good Morning America featured Asheville as one of its "Most Beautiful Places in America." (August 2011)

DogFriendly.com released its list of "Top 10 Resort Areas to Visit with your Dog" in the U.S. and named Asheville and the Blue Ridge Parkway as #2. (August 2011)

Yoga Journal magazine includes Asheville in its list of "10 Fantastically Yoga-Friendly Towns." (August 2011)

Asheville again rises to the top of *AmericanStyle* magazine's Top 25 Small City Arts Destinations, narrowly beating Santa Fe in the annual readers' poll. (May 2011)

AmericanStyle: For the second year, Asheville held the number two spot in the small cities category (population under 100,000) in the annual "Top 25 Arts Destinations" reader's poll. (April 2009)

Forbes.com: In their 11th annual ranking of the "Best Places for Business and Careers," Asheville ranked as #6 in the top metro areas category. (March 25, 2009)

D.K. Shifflet & Associates: This leading travel and tourism research company ranked Asheville as a top 10 value destination for couples in search of romance on its list of cities with the best value for the money. Asheville came in third place, beating out Nashville, San Diego, San Francisco, Myrtle Beach and Las Vegas. (February 2009)

Southern Living: Announced their "Best of the South Readers' Choice Awards" and readers of the magazine recognized these Asheville favorites:

- Best Breakfast or Brunch Restaurant – Moose Café (Placed #9 out of 10)
- Southern Favorite Restaurants – Moose Café (Placed #10 out of 10)
- Best Splurge Restaurants – The Grove Park Inn Resort & Spa (Placed #3 out of 10)
- Best Scenic View – Grandfather Mountain (Placed #2 out of 10) and Chimney Rock Park (Placed #3 out of 10)
- Best Public Gardens – Biltmore Gardens (Placed #3 out of 10)
- Best Southern City – Asheville (Placed #8 out of 10)
- Best Hotel – The Grove Park Inn Resort & Spa (Placed #1 out of 10) and the Inn on Biltmore Estate (Placed #8 out of 10)

(January 2009)

2008

Yahoo! Real Estate: Asheville was named as one of the top ten places to live. (December 2008)

National Geographic Traveler: Asheville received honors in the magazine's Fifth Annual Places Rated Survey. Asheville ranked in the top 50 globally and top 10 nationally. The city placed first among North Carolina destinations. (October 2008)

Forbes Traveler: Included Asheville Green Cottage in its list of top green hotels in America. (September 2008)

Travel+Leisure: Asheville's Grove Park Inn Resort & Spa ranked number 13 in magazine's list of Top 20 Hotel Spas. (August 2008)

Travel+Leisure: Asheville's Inn on Biltmore Estate ranked number 36 in magazine's list of Top 100 Hotels in the Continental U.S. and Canada. (August 2008)

Travel+Leisure: Asheville's Richmond Hill Inn ranked number 9 in magazine's list of Top 10 Hotels: $250 or Less. (August 2008)

AmericanStyle: Ranked Asheville number two in the small cities category (population under 100,000) in the annual "Top 25 Arts Destinations" reader's poll. (June 2008)

Where to Retire Magazine: Honored Asheville as one of its "Eight Enriching Towns for Art and Music Lovers," touting the many wonderful art studios, seasonal art walks and Bele Chere, the largest free outdoor music festival in the Southeast. (May/June 2008)

Rolling Stone: The Orange Peel music club was named one of America's best rock music venues in its "Best of Rock" issue. (April 2008)

NuWire Investor: Named Asheville one of the top 10 places to buy vacation rental homes in the U.S. (March 2008)

Condé Nast Traveler: Announced its fourteenth annual Gold List and recognized the Inn on Biltmore Estate. For the Gold List, the magazine takes its 2007 Readers' Choice Awards winners and delves deeper in the responses, rating hotels for their food, activities, service, rooms, design and location. (January 2008)

Country Home Magazine: Asheville was recognized as one of the top 25 green cities in America for their "2007 Best Green Places" rankings. (January 2008)

Southern Living: Announced their "Best of the South Readers' Choice Awards" and readers of the magazine recognized these Asheville favorites:
Best Resorts/Hotels – The Grove Park Inn Resort & Spa and Inn on Biltmore Estate
Best Mountain Destination – Asheville
Best Scenic Highway – Blue Ridge Parkway in the Asheville corridor
(January 2008)

2007

Conde Nast Traveler: The Inn on Biltmore Estate was recognized in *Conde Nast Traveler's* readers' choice awards as one of the top 100 best hotels in the world. (November 2007)

Outside Magazine: Asheville ranked as "Best Southern Town" in its "Best Towns In America" story. In each region of the country, the magazine selected the best town with a population of fewer than 100,000 people and the best city with a population of more than 100,000 people. Winners are all "smart, progressive burgs with gorgeous wilderness playgrounds,"places that "have realistic housing and job markets," according to the magazine. (August 2007)

TopRetirements.com: Asheville made the list as number one in topretirements.com's "Top 10 Most Popular Retirement Towns." (August 2007)

AmericanStyle Magazine: Ranked Asheville number five in the small cities and towns category (population under 100,000) in the annual "Top 25 Arts Destinations" reader's poll. (June 2007)

Appendix To Chapter Seven

Cities Ranked & Rated: This sourcebook for anyone looking to find the best place to live ranked Asheville as number seven among their analysis of more than 400 metro areas in the U.S. and Canada. Asheville was ranked on the following criteria: economy and jobs, cost of living, climate, education, health and healthcare, crime, transportation, leisure, arts and culture, and overall quality of life. (May 2007)

Relocate-America.com: Asheville rated number one in the Web site's annual ranking of the most popular places to live for 2007. (April 2007)

America's 100 Best Places to Retire: This guide to today's top retirement towns included Asheville as one of the best cities or towns for modern retirees. (April 2007)

VirtualTourist.com: Asheville is featured as one of the "Top 10 Up-and-Coming Travel Destinations" announced by VirtualTourist. (March 2007)

American Institute of Architects: Named Biltmore Estate on its list of Top 10 Architectural Wonders based on a public poll. Biltmore Estate is ranked among the Empire State Building, White House, Golden Gate Bridge and Chrysler Building on this prestigious list issued by the AIA.

Condé Nast Traveler: Announced its thirteenth annual Gold List and among those recognized are Inn on Biltmore Estate and Richmond Hill Inn. For the Gold List, the magazine takes its 2006 Readers' Choice Awards winners and delves deeper in the responses, rating hotels for their food, activities, service, rooms, design and location. (January 2007)

Southern Living: Announced their Best of the South Readers' Choice Awards and readers of the magazine recognized these Asheville favorites:
Resort/Hotel – The Grove Park Inn Resort & Spa
Mountain Destination – Asheville
Scenic Drive – Blue Ridge Parkway
Public Gardens – Biltmore Estate
Country Inn/ Bed & Breakfast – The Red Rock Inn, Black Mountain
(January 2007)

2006

Frommer's: Named Asheville one of twelve top travel destinations for 2007. (November 21, 2006)

Conde Nast Traveler: Named the Inn on Biltmore Estate in its "2006 Gold List: The World's Best Places to Stay." (January 2006)

Southern Living: In the 2006 Reader's Choice Awards, Asheville took first place in the best mountain destination category. The Blue Ridge Parkway also ranked first in the scenic drive category and the Grove Park Inn Resort & Spa won the best resort / hotel top spot. (February 2006)

GoVeg.com: Asheville voted first as "America's Best Vegetarian-Friendly Small City." (March 2006)

Men's Journal: Named Asheville one of the 50 best places to live in the "Singles Scene" category. (April 2006)

Forbes: In its annual ranking of "Best Places for Business and Careers," Asheville ranked #24. (May 4, 2006)

Kiplinger's Personal Finance: The magazine combed the country for cities that embody a reasonable cost of living coupled with a great quality of life. Asheville ranked seventh in the "50 Smart Cities" list. (May 8, 2006)

AmericanStyle Magazine: Ranked Asheville second in the small cities and towns category (population under 100,000) in the ninth annual "Top 25 Arts Destinations" reader's poll. (June 2006)

Southern Accents: Asheville was ranked first in the favorite mountain getaway and third in the favorite golf and spa destination in the Southern Accents Reader Travel Awards. (May/June 2006)

Cottage Living: Asheville's Albermarle Park neighborhood was chosen by Cottage Living magazine as one of the "Top Ten Cottage Communities in the U.S." (June 20, 2006)

Blue Ridge Outdoors: Saw Asheville as a Southern town leading the Green Revolution and named Asheville one of the greenest towns in the south. (July 2006)

Outside Magazine: Asheville rated the number one whitewater town in the country. (August 2006)

Designated Preserve America Community by First Lady Laura Bush: Asheville's communities and neighborhoods were designated as preserving and using their heritage resources for community economic, educational, and cultural benefit and development. (October 2006)

2005

Organic Style: Asheville was ranked seventh in a listing of the 10 Greatest Escapes in America. (July/August 2005).

Vegetarian Times: Asheville named one of 10 small towns in the article, "The 20 greenest spots in the country."

Southern Living: Readers voted Asheville the First Place winner in the "Mountain Destination" Category.

Appendix To Chapter Seven

AmericanStyle Magazine: Readers voted Asheville eighth in a poll of the Top 25 Arts Destinations, up from tenth in the 2004 poll.

RelocateAmerica.com: Named Asheville ninth in "America's Top 100 Places to Live in 2005." The nominated towns were compared against education, crime, employment and housing data for the past year.

Men's Journal: Western North Carolina attractions, Asheville's Early Girl Eatery and The Grove Park Inn Resort & Spa listed in its "12 Months of Adventure" expert's guide to the perfect trip in 2005. (February 2005)

Conde Nast Traveler: Named the Inn on Biltmore Estate to its 2005 Gold List: The World's Best Places to Stay. The Grove Park Inn Resort & Spa was named to the 2005 Gold List Reserve.

Pinnacle Living Magazine: Asheville rated one of the top 25 towns in the Southern mountains for relocation, second homes and retirement. (2005)

2004

Mountain Bike Magazine: Pisgah Forest voted one of the best trails for mountain biking. (October 2004)

USA Weekend Magazine: Asheville named one of five "Cities that are Special." (July 2004)

National Geographic Adventure: Asheville listed as one of the "10 Great Adventure Towns." (September 2004)

Men's Journal: Asheville ranked as one of "The 10 Best Fall Mountain Bike Rides" in North America. (September 2004)

Southern Living Magazine: Asheville chosen as one of the top mountain destinations in the Southeast in a Reader's Choice poll. (April 2004)

RelocateAmerica.com: Asheville came in fifth in "America's Top 100 Places to Live in 2004." The nominated towns were compared against education, crime, employment and housing data for the past year.

Where to Retire Magazine: Named Asheville one of eight great college towns. (May/June 2004)

AmericanStyle Magazine: Readers voted Asheville #10 in a poll of the Top 25 Arts Destinations, up from #18 in the previous year's poll.

Men's Journal: Nantahala Outdoor Center -- "the Harvard of paddling instruction" -- named one of the 100 Best Trips on the Planet. (April 2004)

Cities Ranked and Rated: Named Asheville the #8 rated city in America to live in 2004. Determined by a number of essential factors, including economy and jobs, cost of living, climate, education, health and health care, crime, transportation, leisure, and arts and crafts. Presented by Frommer's Travel Guides. (March 30, 2004)

Travel and Leisure: Named The Grove Park Inn Resort & Spa as one of the top 500 greatest hotels in the world. (January 2004)

Travel and Leisure: Named The Grove Park Inn Resort & Spa as one of the top resort spas in the world. (2004)

2003

Where to Retire Magazine: Asheville selected as one of eight great walking towns. (12/15/2003)

MSN Money: Named Asheville one of the top 10 towns for a second-home investment. (2003)

MSN: Asheville named one of the top five "Best Places to Retire." (2003)

AmericanStyle Magazine: Readers voted Asheville #18 in a poll of the Top 25 Arts Destinations. (2003)

Travel and Leisure: Named Grove Park Inn Resort & Spa as one the world's best golf resorts in a reader survey. (2003)

Blue Ridge Country Magazine: In the 15th Anniversary edition, Asheville was ranked in the top three in "Best Mountain Town," "Best Couples Getaway," "Best Festival," for Bele Chere, "Best Retirement Town," "Best Weekend Getaway," and "Best Shopping Overall." (August 2003)

Southern Living Magazine: Asheville chosen by a Reader's Choice poll as one of the top mountain destinations and weekend getaways in the Southeast. (May 2003)

Mountain Bike Action: Named Asheville one of the 10 best mountain bike towns. (May 2003)

National Geographic Adventure: In their Best of Adventure 2003 Issue, Asheville was named one of the top mountain biking destinations in the Southeast. Asheville "is fast becoming the Boulder of the Southeast – with better riding."

AARP Magazine: Asheville selected as one of the Top 15 Best Places to Reinvent Your Life. (May-June 2003)

Parents Magazine: In the round-up of "editors' picks," Asheville is listed among of the top destinations for family travel. (April 2003)

2002

Appendix To Chapter Seven

Self Magazine: Named Asheville the Happiest City in the United States.

New York Times: Asheville made the Harris Poll list of "Most Desirable Places to Live". (September 2002).

Hemispheres: Asheville joined a select list of 70 of the world's most visible and visited cities—the only in NC ever featured in the popular United Airlines magazine. The feature piece is titled, "Three Perfect Days in Asheville." (September 2002)

USA Weekend: Blue Ridge Parkway listed as one of noted cyclist Greg LeMond's best scenic routes to train. (August 2002)

USA Today ran two stories one week apart entitled, "Top 10 Literary Destinations" and "Historic towns that invite you to stroll." (July 2002).

National Trust for Historic Preservation: Listed Asheville among its List of America's Dozen Distinctive Destinations, describing it as "offering diverse natural, historic, and cultural experiences that preserve generations of the 'Appalachian tradition.'" (July 2002)

Men's Journal: In the Best of Summer Issue, Asheville was listed as one of the Top 50 Hot Road Trips that "will make the greatest three months of your life."

AmericanStyle Magazine: Readers voted Asheville as #13 in the list of the Top 25 Arts Destinations in America for "sharing a love for the arts and promoting cultural tourism." (Summer 2002)

Bike Magazine: In nominating 2002's premium places to live and ride, Asheville was ranked as one of America's Top Five Best Mountain Biking Towns. (June 2002)

Where to Retire Magazine: Asheville listed as one of the Best Tax Heavens in the Country. (Spring 2002)

Book Magazine: Asheville ranked 3rd in the Top 10 Great Literary Trips in the nation. (May/June 2002)

USA Today: Ranked Gold Hill Cafe in Asheville one of "10 Great Places for Caffeine and Conversation." (March 2002)

Barron's Online: Asheville listed as one of the Best Places to Retire. (March 2002)

Wallpaper Magazine Annual Round-Up Edition: Asheville ranked the #1 Urban Haven in the World—with benefits of rural life, urban sophistication and energy. (Jan./Feb. 2002)

Outside Magazine: Named Asheville one of the ten best outdoor towns.

2001

Southern Living Magazine: Asheville was chosen by Reader's Choice poll as one of the top mountain destinations and weekend getaways in the Southeast. (Fall 2001)

National Geographic Traveler: Rated Biltmore Estate in Asheville as one of America's Top 50 Places of a Lifetime. (October 2001)

MSN Home Advisor: Ranked Asheville among the Best Five Places to Retire.

Where to Retire Magazine: Asheville rated in Ten Great Towns for Retired Singles. (Summer 2001)

Employment Review: Asheville rated one of Ten Top Small Cities in America's Best Places to Live and Work.

American Style Magazine: Asheville rated eighth of the top 25 arts destinations in the USA. (Summer 2001)

Whitewater Paddling Magazine: Rated Asheville a Top 10 Whitewater Town.

Canoe and Kayak Magazine: Asheville named one of the top 10 paddle towns. (April 2001)

FamilyFun Magazine: Asheville named one of the top five Southeast cities for family vacations.

Mountain Bike Magazine: Named Asheville one of the 10 best U.S. cities for mountain bikers. (June 2001)

2000

AmericanStyle Magazine: Asheville rated sixth of the top 25 arts destinations in the USA.

Modern Maturity Magazine: Ranked Asheville the #1 place to live in the small town category of 50 Most Alive Places to Live. (May-June 2000)

Money Magazine: Asheville ranked in the top five best places to retire. (July 2000)

Southern Living Magazine: Asheville was chosen in a Reader's Choice poll as one of the top mountain destinations in the Southeast. (Fall 2000)

Expansion Management Magazine: Ranked Asheville 43rd in a Top 50 Hottest Cities list.

Rand McNally Places Rated Almanac: Ranked Asheville one of the best places to live in the United States among metropolitan areas smaller than 250,000 people, as well as one of the top five places to retire. (2000)

CHAPTER EIGHT

Conservation Easements

Property ownership, habitat preservation, and economic benefits

The Question:
I'm considering the acquisition of a large tract of land in the mountains, and I wonder what alternatives are available to me to preserve the land while still retaining ownership, so that I can bequeath the property to my children?

This is a rather specialized chapter in that it may be the most relevant to those who are considering a large land purchase, perhaps at least fifty acres and, more realistically, one hundred acres and up. Not everyone can afford such a purchase; however, if you are interested in land conservation, regardless of your financial resources, I hope that you will continue to read on, as the subject matter is most interesting for all who regard the preservation of our natural resources as a clear and present priority.

One of the primary reasons that so many families seriously consider a move to the mountains is to live amidst a more down-to-earth environment, surrounded by nature and by national forest, if one is lucky, within the wooded countryside that nurtures a quality of life previously unattainable within their former hometowns. It is not unusual that a renewed sense of environmentalism is either responsible for their initial interest in the mountains or grows from within, once they have arrived. Many who relocate and now reside here are able to realize those interests through a variety of outlets, both volunteer and otherwise, to conserve one of the area's most notable resources, its land and natural beauty.

The conservation easement, as a vehicle for private landowners to take part in the conservation and protection of our natural resources, has been around for decades, though many are unaware of its availability and how it works. It is a fabulous way for individuals to do their parts in the effort to preserve our natural habitat without straining the financial resources of land conservancies and land trusts that would otherwise have to raise an inordinate amount of funds to purchase these properties. It is difficult to arrive at a brief and concise definition of a conservation easement. Its many moving parts lend themselves more to a discussion than a definition; however, let us endeavor to have both.

A conservation easement is a voluntary agreement, a recorded, legally enforceable grant of rights, given by a private landowner to a recognized, qualified government agency, land conservancy, or land trust. The easement typically restricts those activities that would have any material and adverse impact on the preservation of the natural habitat and resources that give the land its conservation value. Clearly, any further subdividing for the purpose of development of the land that is subject to the easement is, in most cases, the primary activity that the easement language will focus on preventing. The protection of the natural eco-system— the flora, fauna, water courses, wetlands, and habitat that naturally thrive there—is the ultimate goal of the conservancies and trusts that are involved in these transactions. Now let's expand on this limited definition through a discussion of the attributes and impacts of such an easement, what it is intended to accomplish, and how it works.

A conservation easement does not affect ownership. When an easement is granted, ownership does not change hands. In that regard, it is really no different than when you grant an easement to the local power company to provide electricity to your home. The power company does not *own* the property over which the easement lies. It simply has certain rights to provide and maintain and repair the power facilities located within that easement; you, in turn, must abide by certain restrictions on the activities that you are allowed to do within that easement. However, you remain the owner of the land that is encumbered by the easement. The same holds true for conservation easements.

A conservation easement does not restrict your freedom or ability to sell your land or to pass it down to your children or other heirs. You may sell all or any portion of your property that is subject to the easement to anyone at any time; however, the easement is an "easement in perpetuity," an easement that "runs with the land," meaning that all subsequent owners must abide by all of the terms and conditions of the easement for as long as they own the property.

*A conservation easement does **not** need to cover all of the acreage of the land parcel that you own.* In fact, it is quite rare that one would grant a conservation easement over one's entire property if the intent were to reside on some portion of the property. Typically, the grantor of such an easement would carve out a small tract within the overall acreage on which to construct a personal homestead and then grant a conservation easement over the remainder of the property. A logical corollary to this is the fact that a partially developed property may indeed be compatible with a conservation easement and in fact, many developers will actually plan for a conservation easement as part of the overall master plan of their developments from their inception. This is most often done not so much because the developer is necessarily conservation-minded (though he or she may be), but rather, it is done due to one or more of the following: 1) the portion of the land being offered for conservation does not have appropriate development characteristics; 2) a proximate conservation easement actually increases the value of the developable homesites if the buyers know that portions of the green space within the development will remain undeveloped greenways in perpetuity; 3) the economic incentives and benefits in recording a conservation easement, though limited, can be attractive (explained later in this chapter).

The land subject to a conservation easement is NOT required to be accessible to the public, though the grantor may certainly agree to such a provision, should he or she so choose.

There will be a requirement for the tract that is encumbered by the easement to be monitored on an annual basis (or some other agreed-upon regular interval) for the continued compliance of the land's use with the easement restrictions. The obligation to comply is the responsibility of the easement grantor-landowner, while the requirement to monitor that compliance is the obligation of the grantee-conservancy, trust, or other government agency. It should be noted that one of the stipulations of almost all conservation easement agreements is a financial contribution by the grantor of a sum set aside to help fund the staff that is responsible for the monitoring obligation.

The language within a conservation easement is designed to be flexible and to be customized to meet the specific attributes of the land in question and the particular needs of the landowner who intends to grant the easement. This adaptability of the language that will define the restrictions and protections to which the land will be subject is one of the truly positive advantages to the approach by many of the land conservancies and land trusts that participate in these grants. They understand that every tract of land differs in the conservation value that it presents and that every owner's specific circumstances and desires for granting an easement may be equally unique and individualized. They understand that in order to successfully address those differences, the easement terms and conditions must be flexible and capable of being tailored to the personal interests, conditions, and context of the grantor. This is not to imply that the conservancies and trusts will allow the integrity of their goal—the preservation and protection of natural habitat—to be compromised. Quite to the contrary, the strategy to embrace the fact that "one size does not fit all" allows them to reach their goals more readily—to actually expand the conservation opportunities—by not restricting the acceptable language to cast-in-stone dogma and ideology. Some examples of the terms and conditions that can typically be negotiated are:

- The specific acreage that will be subject to the easement
- What can be built within the easement area
- Logging rights
- Acceptable recreational activities
- Acceptable farming activities
- A negotiated financial contribution to fund the endowment for the grantee to monitor conformance with the easement agreement

Notwithstanding the obvious ecological and environmental benefits of granting a conservation easement over one's personal property, why would anyone choose to encumber their valuable real estate holdings with a permanent covenant to, among other things, never develop it to its economically highest and best use? Though the answer to that question may be as multifaceted and as individualized as the personalities who own these large tracts, part of the answer, as you might expect, involves multiple financial incentives. These incentives involve both federal and state tax benefits that have been legislated in an effort to assist with the preservation of the country's natural resources. They fall into four basic categories:

- Federal Income Tax Deduction
- State Income Tax Credit
- Property Tax Benefit
- Estate Tax Deduction and Exclusion

Before I elaborate on each of the above, it is important to note two critical points. First, I am neither a tax attorney nor an accountant, both of whom you should contact should you wish to pursue transacting a conservation easement agreement and desire a full and detailed consultation regarding these benefits. Secondly, these incentives tend to come and go with changes in the political environment and the economy, such that any programs I might outline within this chapter may be altered or eliminated completely depending on the legislative climate at the time. My purpose in writing this section is to make you aware of the potential for these benefits, though they may differ from state to state, and the Internal Revenue Code may change in any given year.

1. Federal Income Tax Deduction

The federal income tax deduction that may be taken is equal to *the value of the donation. That value is defined as the difference in the fair market value of the land before and after the encumbrance of the easement.* This brings up an interesting scenario from a real estate development perspective. Let's say we have a raw piece of undeveloped land of five hundred acres that we wish to develop. We spend significant time, effort, and money on a land surveyor, site planning firm, civil engineer, architect, and attorney, getting a proposed master-planned community of two hundred homesites and associated amenities fully entitled, permitted, and approved—all but ready for bulldozers to start their engines. Now, having accomplished the above, does this tract of land have the same value now as the value it had when we first purchased it six months ago? Haven't we increased its value substantially, having obtained and secured the rights to develop it? We surely have. In fact, there are many real estate development firms that actually make a very healthy living *not developing land* but rather obtaining all of the development approvals required *in order to develop the land* and then selling the tract to a developer who can begin construction immediately, thereby eliminating the cost, risk, and time that the new developer would have consumed in the land acquisition and entitlement process.

I bring the above example to light to illustrate that the value of a given tract of land can be significantly impacted without ever having turned the first blade of grass with a dozer. The term "highest and best use" is a real estate term that generally refers to the most profitable use (development) of the property, taking into account all of the regulatory constraints (zoning statutes, planning ordinances, building codes, etc.) to which such development would be subject. In the example, the process by the first developer of securing various development approvals to ensure the potential to develop the land to its highest and best use clearly adds significant value to the land that could otherwise only be recognized in theory and not in practice. In calculating the federal income deduction, the value of a property before the encumbrance of the conservation easement is apt to recognize "practice" more than "theory," meaning that a greater deduction *may be* available if the property has actually obtained development approvals. (Please not that the example is not intended to suggest that one should pursue obtaining development rights and entitlements on their property as a means to an end of increasing the value of the donation. It is simply intended to demonstrate that the value of conservation easement donations is affected by a wide variety of factors, all of which will be considered as part of the valuation process.)

From August of 2006 until the end of 2011, when calculating the federal income tax deduction, the Internal Revenue Code allowed a landowner to utilize the deduction at the rate of 50 percent of adjusted gross income per year. In addition, any amount of the donation remaining after the first year was allowed to be deducted over an additional fifteen-year period (maximum) or until the full amount of the gift had been amortized, whichever came first. As an example, if you had an adjusted gross income of $100,000 per year (and let's assume that never changed) and you just donated a new conservation easement valued at $200,000, you could have deducted a maximum of $50,000 (50 percent of your adjusted gross income) for each of the next four years, or you could have spread out the deduction in any way that summed to $200,000 over a total of sixteen years (and didn't exceed $50,000 in any one year). Unfortunately, that federally enacted legislation was allowed to expire at the beginning of 2012. The current tax laws for 2012 allow the value of conservation easement donations to be deducted at the decreased rate of 30 percent (compared to 50 percent) of the landowner/donor's adjusted gross income, and any amount of the donation remaining after the first year may be carried forward for a maximum of five additional years (in lieu of the previously allowed fifteen years).

2. State Income Tax Credit

In many states, including North Carolina, their legislatures have taken the initiative to offer a dollar for dollar reduction in the amount of state income tax owed. In other words, the benefit is not a tax deduction analogous to the above federal income tax deduction wherein you deduct the conservation easement value first from your income and then apply your income tax rate to it; rather, you calculate your state income tax due first and then deduct the conservation value—dollar for dollar—from the state income tax that you owe. Under the current state tax laws, the credit is worth 25 percent of the fair market value of the donation and is capped at $250,000 for individuals and $500,000 for corporations, partnerships, and married couples. The amount of the deduction cannot exceed one's total state income tax liability for a given year (net of any other credits), and there is a maximum five-year carryover of any excess that one cannot use due to the limitations.

It should be noted that some states are now allowing state tax credits to be sold to investors on the open market. This policy has come about to address the needs of those individual landowners who may wish to donate a conservation easement but who cannot benefit in any meaningful way from the state tax credit because they do not generate enough income against which to apply the credit. A retired farmer who has significant land holdings provides a good example of this scenario. Tax benefits of a set maximum duration (five years) are only beneficial to those who, within that time frame, earn enough income to be worth sheltering. If that farmer can sell his tax credits (at an acceptable discount) to an investor who needs the tax credits, he can monetize (sell the entire value of) the credit and generate the revenue from that sale in one lump sum payment. This is a win/win/win situation, really: the farmer obtains an instant economic benefit paid in today's dollars; the investor obtains a needed tax shelter that can be amortized over one to five years; and finally and perhaps most importantly, additional natural habitat is added to the growing list of lands that are being preserved and protected for future generations to enjoy, as it should be.

3. Property Tax Benefits

This economic benefit is fairly straightforward. Clearly, a simple conclusion has been drawn in this chapter that the recording of a permanent and perpetual conservation easement over a given tract of land eliminates any possibility of developing that tract pursuant to its highest and best use. It has, therefore, at least from the perspective of the lost economic opportunity, been devalued and should logically be assessed by the county taxing authority at a lesser value than it was assessed prior to the encumbrance by the conservation easement. The resulting reduction in assessed value will, by definition, result in a reduction in property taxes once the easement is recorded.

4. Estate Tax Reductions and Exclusions

High net worth individuals are prudent to consider all of the many alternatives to ensure that as much of their estate as possible is left to their heirs and not to the government. This is particularly important if their heirs do not have the liquid financial resources to afford to pay the estate taxes upon the death of the owner. This fourth economic benefit (comprised of three components) associated with the placement of a conversation easement on one's property is intended to address this issue.

Reduction in the value of the real estate: First, as stated above in item #3, there is an obvious reduction in the economic value of a tract of land if it is made subject to a permanent conservation easement and can never be developed. Once it loses its value as a highest and best use development site, the value for estate tax purposes must necessarily be the valuation it then has as a conservation parcel. The estate tax burden is accordingly reduced to reflect the lesser value.

Estate exclusion: Secondly, the Tax Revenue Code also allows for an additional 40 percent of the value of the land to be excluded from the estate upon the death of the owner. Keep in mind that this is *in addition to* the significant reduction in value that has already occurred based on the notion of conservation value vs. development value. As an example, say we have a five hundred-acre parcel that is assessed at a value of $1,000,000 for real estate tax purposes. After the placement of a conservation easement on the property, its assessed value is reduced to $600,000. When the additional 40 percent exclusion kicks in, the value of the land for estate tax purposes is reduced by another $240,000, leaving only $360,000 of remaining value.

After death easement or post-mortem election: Thirdly, an heir may choose to encumber the property with a conservation easement subsequent to the death of the owner (but before filing the estate tax return) and, in such cases, may still take advantage of the above two benefits.

If all of this sounds as though it could be quite complicated, I suppose that it can be; however, the land trusts and conservancies, whose business it is to increase the acreage of protected tracts of land for the preservation of natural habitat, are happy to assist their clients in that endeavor. Additionally, there are firms that have found a niche providing consulting services to individuals who wish to pursue the conservation of their properties but are intimidated by the perceived complexity of doing so. The consultant can act as a broker, of sorts—managing the individual parties that may need to be involved to bring the process through to a successful conclusion for both the owner and the conservancy. These services may include the management and direction, on behalf of the owner, of some or all of the following parties:

- **The qualified land trust or land conservancy** selected to be the grantee (beneficiary) of the easement, including assistance with the selection of that party, which is based upon the best fit of the attributes and location of the land with the interests and goals of the grantee. (Please see Exhibit 8.1 in the Appendix at the end of this chapter, the 2011 directory of twenty-four individual land trusts currently operating within the State of North Carolina.)
- **The land surveyor** who will provide an accurate and up-to-date boundary survey of the property to serve as the legal document that defines the exact lands that are to be subject to and governed by the conservation easement. Additional special purpose surveys may also be required such as surveys that locate wetland areas, identify areas of protected species of flora, and delineate centerlines of creeks and streams, etc.

- **The planning and design firm** that specializes in the overall site planning of a real estate development concept that would provide the owner with an accurate basis for understanding the value of the development potential that would be sacrificed in favor of a conservation easement.
- **The Department of Environment and Natural Resources (DENR)**, the state agency that is responsible for approving that a particular property will actually qualify for conservation purposes and whether or not state tax credits may be available to the grantor. In the eyes of the DENR, in order for a tract of land to qualify as viable acreage for conservation easement purposes, the easement must be all of the following:

    a. permanent/perpetual;
    b. granted to a qualified government agency or nonprofit land trust or land conservancy;
    c. serving a valid "conservation purpose," (which may be broadly defined as the protection and preservation of natural habitat including but not limited to timber, flora, fauna, clean waters, wetlands, watershed areas, scenic views, and endangered species).

- **The tax lawyer or certified public accountant** who specializes in understanding the Internal Revenue Tax Code language and rules applicable to conservation easements. This is critical to maximizing the tax incentives and benefits while steering clear of any practices that may be frowned upon and thus questioned by the IRS and state taxing authorities.
- **The appraiser** who is qualified in conservation easement valuations to accurately assess the value of the land with and

without a conservation easement, the difference being the value upon which tax benefits that may accrue to the owner will be based.
- **The miscellaneous environmental consultants**, such as naturalists, biologists, and wetland consultants, who may need to work in conjunction with the DENR and the grantee to assess the property's environmental and ecological value to the preservation of the area's natural habitat.
- **The lender,** that is, if a lender holds a mortgage on the property. The lender must be willing to subordinate its loan to the conservation easement, meaning he or she must acquiesce to the resulting diminution of the property's value, since it is typically the value of the property that provides the security for the loan. In other words, the lender will always want to be sure that the value of the collateral (the land) that secures the loan comfortably exceeds the loan balance at any given time. If the encumbrance by a conservation easement renders the property less valuable than the outstanding loan balance, the lender may pursue various alternatives such as requiring that the owner offer additional collateral (other assets or properties) to properly secure the loan or to pay the loan down so that it conforms to the lender's underwriting standards for such loans. (Note that the lender also has the legal right simply not to allow a conservation easement to be placed on the property if the owner is unable to address the reduction in collateral value issue.)

Finally, as noted previously, a very interesting niche business has recently developed wherein a firm may not only specialize in orchestrating the above players and consultants but also can actually provide a pool of investment capital that is waiting in the wings to purchase the state tax credits in those states where such transactions are permitted. This allows an owner to immediately monetize a future stream of tax benefits into a current payment (at a discount in order to attract investors). This alternative has even become a palatable "exit strategy" in recent years for developers, in response to the significant and steep downturn in the real estate market since 2006 and 2007.

Conservation easements may not be available to the average landowner, simply because the size of one's tract may not be substantial enough to attract conservation interests and/or the preservation value may not be significant enough to qualify. Even if these two elements were satisfactory, the fact is that many individuals do not have the financial resources and/or the environmental sensitivity to forego the economic opportunity either to develop the land themselves or sell the land to others for development purposes. Notwithstanding those facts, I have included this chapter in the book because I think (or at least hope) that land conservation should be of interest to all. I also wanted to bring into focus the extent to which both federal and state governments, in conjunction with environmental preservationists, have made a concerted effort to incentivize individual landowners to preserve and protect the natural habitat of the areas in this country that remain so rich in natural beauty and resources.

Appendix to Chapter Eight

Everything You Need To Know About Buying Mountain Property

Exhibit 8.1: land trusts operating in the state of North Carolina

North Carolina's local land trusts work in communities across the state to preserve land and water quality, protect public health and quality of life for North Carolina families, and strengthen the economy. Land trusts conserve the places that make each community and region in North Carolina special.

Through partnerships with landowners, communities, and public agencies, land trusts work to preserve the heritage of North Carolina's most beloved places through voluntary conservation options. Land trusts save places that are critical to clean drinking water, wildlife habitat, healthy food from family farms, recreation, and tourism each day.

Use this directory to find out more about your local land trust and how to help *save the places you love*.

North Carolina land trusts are members of the Land Trust Alliance, a national association of conservation groups. The land trusts in this directory have adopted the Alliance's standards and practices to ensure the long-term protection of North Carolina's most valued lands. To learn more about the Alliance and its standards and practices, visit www.lta.org.

As of February 2011, nine NC land trusts have earned accreditation from the Land Trust Accreditation Commission, an independent program of the Land Trust Alliance; they are noted with asterisks in the table of contents. Other NC land trusts are in the process of applying for accreditation.

LAND TRUST ALLIANCE (SOUTHEAST PROGRAM)
Mission: To save the places people love by strengthening land conservation across America.
PO Box 35555 • Raleigh, NC 27636
919-515-0760
southeast@lta.org

TABLE OF CONTENTS

MAP NUMBER		PAGE NUMBER
1	Black Family Land Trust	2
2	Blue Ridge Rural Land Trust	2
3	Carolina Mountain Land Conservancy*	2
4	Catawba Lands Conservancy*	3
5	Conservation Trust for North Carolina*	3
6	Davidson Lands Conservancy	3
7	Eno River Association*	4
8	Foothills Conservancy of North Carolina*	4
9	Highlands-Cashiers Land Trust	4
10	Land Trust for the Little Tennessee*	5
11	LandTrust for Central North Carolina	5
12	Lumber River Conservancy	5
13	National Committee for the New River*	6
14	North Carolina Coastal Land Trust	6
15	North Carolina Rail-Trails	6
16	Northeast New Hanover Conservancy	7
17	Pacolet Area Conservancy	7
18	Piedmont Land Conservancy*	7
19	Sandhills Area Land Trust	8
20	Smith Island Land Trust *A subsidiary of Bald Head Island Conservancy*	8
21	Southern Appalachian Highlands Conservancy*	8
22	Tar River Land Conservancy	9
23	Triangle Greenways Council	9
24	Triangle Land Conservancy	9

*Accredited (see description at left)
SEE BACK COVER FOR INDEX BY COUNTIES SERVED.

2011 North Carolina Land Trust Directory • 1

Appendix To Chapter Eight

BLACK FAMILY LAND TRUST

Ensuring, Protecting, Preserving

MISSION STATEMENT: The mission of the Black Family Land Trust is to provide educational, technical and financial services to ensure, protect, and preserve African American land ownership.

ADDRESS:
Street: 400 W. Main St. Durham, NC 27701
Mailing: PO Box 2087 Durham, NC 27702
PHONE: 919-682-5969
FAX: 919-688-5596
EMAIL: ebonie@bflt.org
WEB: www.bflt.org
ESTABLISHED: 2005
BOARD MEMBERS: 5

STAFF: 2
GEOGRAPHIC AREA: North Carolina and South Carolina, Alabama, Georgia, Mississippi and Virginia.
CONTACTS:
× Savonala "Savi" Horne, Board Chair
• Ebonie Alexander, Executive Director
• Dannette Sharpley, North Carolina Project Manager

CUMULATIVE LAND PROTECTION TOTALS: Protected 34 acres in two places. Placed 34 acres under conservation agreements.

BLUE RIDGE CONSERVANCY

BLUE RIDGE CONSERVANCY
SAVING THE PLACES YOU LOVE

MISSION STATEMENT: To protect the natural resources of northwestern North Carolina by conserving land with significant agricultural, ecological, cultural, recreational or scenic value.

ADDRESS: PO Box 568 Boone, NC 28607
PHONE: 828-264-2511
FAX: 828-355-9423
EMAIL: info@blueridgeconservancy.org
WEB: www.blueridgeconservancy.org
ESTABLISHED: 1995 (High Country Conservancy), 1997 (Blue Ridge Rural Land Trust) Merged 2010.
BOARD MEMBERS: 18
STAFF: 5
GEOGRAPHIC AREA: Alleghany, Ashe, Avery, Mitchell, Watauga, Wilkes, Yancey
CONTACTS:
• Walter Clark, Executive Director

• Eric Hiegl, Co-Deputy Director for Land Protection
• Zachary Lesch-Huie, Communications Director
• Joe Potts, Co-Deputy Director for Land Protection
• Maria Whaley, Operations Director

CUMULATIVE LAND PROTECTION TOTALS: Protected 15,873 acres in 163 places. Own fee simple title to 439 acres; transferred fee simple title to governments on 3,513 acres. Placed 11,921 acres under conservation agreements.

2010 LAND PROTECTION TOTALS: Protected 1,180 acres in 10 places. Transferred fee simple title to governments on 907 acres. Placed 273 acres under conservation agreements.

CAROLINA MOUNTAIN LAND CONSERVANCY

CMLC
CAROLINA MOUNTAIN LAND CONSERVANCY

MISSION STATEMENT: Carolina Mountain Land Conservancy partners with landowners and organizations to protect land and water resources vital to our natural heritage and quality of life. As an effective nonprofit organization dedicated to saving the places you love, CMLC works to permanently conserve and actively care for an ever-growing regional network of locally and nationally significant farm, forest, park and natural lands.

ADDRESS: 847 Case St. Hendersonville, NC 28792
PHONE: 828-697-5777
FAX: 828-697-2602
EMAIL: info@carolinamountain.org
WEB: www.carolinamountain.org
ESTABLISHED: 1994
BOARD MEMBERS: 19
STAFF: 9 F/T, 3 P/T
GEOGRAPHIC AREA: Henderson, Transylvania, and parts of Buncombe, Jackson and Rutherford counties
CONTACTS:
• Kieran Roe, Executive Director
• Rick Merrill, President
• Aimee McGinley, Membership/Development Coordinator
• Amy Stout, Project Conserve Program Director
• Bonnie Millar, Stewardship Director

• Kristin Harkey, Development Director
• Mary Ann Hailey, Administrative/IT Coordinator
• Heather Sains, Finance Director
• Tom Fanslow, Land Protection Director
• Julianne Johnson, Volunteer Coordinator
• Rebekah Robinson, Land Program Coordinator
• Julie Brockman, Stewardship Coordinator
• Lisa Fancher, Finance Associate

CUMULATIVE LAND PROTECTION TOTALS: Protected 22,179 acres in 101 places. Own fee simple title to 3,072 acres; conveyed fee simple title to governments on 2,180 acres. Own 8,032 acres under conservation agreements; transferred conservation agreements to governments on 1,117 acres.

2010 LAND PROTECTION TOTALS: Protected 911 acres in three places. Own fee simple title to 786 acres. Placed 10 acres under conservation agreements; transferred conservation agreements to governments on 115 acres.

Everything You Need To Know About Buying Mountain Property

CATAWBA LANDS CONSERVANCY

MISSION STATEMENT: Catawba Lands Conservancy's mission is to save land and connect lives to nature.

ADDRESS: 105 W. Morehead St. Charlotte, NC 28202
PHONE: 704-342-3330
FAX: 704-342-3340
EMAIL: heike@catawbalands.org
WEB: www.catawbalands.org
ESTABLISHED: 1991
BOARD MEMBERS: 20
STAFF: 14
GEOGRAPHIC AREA: Catawba, Gaston, Lincoln, Mecklenburg, Iredell and Union counties. Lead agency for the Carolina Thread Trail in Anson, Cabarrus, Catawba, Cleveland, Gaston, Iredell, Lincoln, Mecklenburg, Rowan, Stanly and Union counties in North Carolina and Cherokee, Chester, Lancaster and York counties in South Carolina.

CONTACTS:
- Dave Cable, Executive Director
- Tonya Harris, Paralegal
- Lindsey Dunevant, Public Resources Director
- Amanda Anderson, Volunteer and Grants Coordinator
- Ann Browning, Carolina Thread Trail Project Director
- Dean Thompson, Communications and Community Partnerships Director
- Travis Morehead, Carolina Thread Trail Community Coordinator
- Randi Gates, Carolina Thread Trail Community Coordinator
- RoxAnne Smith, Associate Director
- Sharon Wilson, Stewardship Director
- Heike Biller, Administrative Director

CUMULATIVE LAND PROTECTION TOTALS: Protected 8,981 acres in 130 places. Own fee simple title to 2,475 acres. Placed 6,124 acres under conservation agreements; transferred conservation agreements to governments on 58 acres.

2010 LAND PROTECTION TOTALS: Protected 1,436 acres in 11 places. Own fee simple title to 95 acres. Placed 1,058 acres under conservation agreements.

CONSERVATION TRUST FOR NORTH CAROLINA

MISSION STATEMENT: To protect our state's land and water through statewide conservation and cooperative work with land trusts to preserve our natural resources as a legacy for future generations.

MAIN OFFICE:
ADDRESS: 1028 Washington St. Raleigh, NC 27605
PHONE: 919-828-4199
FAX: 919-828-4508

BOONE OFFICE:
ADDRESS: PO Box 481 Boone, NC 28607
PHONE: 828-989-8010

EMAIL: info@ctnc.org
WEB: www.ctnc.org
ESTABLISHED: 1991
BOARD MEMBERS: 17 (2 ex-officio)
STAFF: 11 F/T, 2 P/T
GEOGRAPHIC AREA: Statewide

CONTACTS:
- Reid Wilson, Executive Director
- Margaret J. Newbold, Associate Director
- Melanie Allen, Diversity Project Coordinator
- Alberto Alzamora, Staff Accountant
- John Bell, Development Director
- Richard Broadwell, Land Protection Specialist (Boone)
- Lisa Creasman, Conservation Project Manager
- Wendy Howard, Finance Director
- Margaret Lillard, Communications Director
- Edgar Miller, Government Relations Director
- Rusty Painter, Land Protection Director
- Jan Pender, Development Associate
- Megan Smith, Office and Membership Administrator

CUMULATIVE LAND PROTECTION TOTALS: Protected 34,287 acres in 94 places. Own fee simple title to 1,194 acres; transferred fee simple title to governments on 2,626 acres. Placed 27,556 acres under conservation agreements; transferred conservation agreements to governments on 1,989 acres and to other organizations on 85 acres.

2010 LAND PROTECTION TOTALS: Protected 457 acres in four places. Own fee simple title to 301 acres. Placed 156 acres under conservation agreements.

DAVIDSON LANDS CONSERVANCY

MISSION STATEMENT: To provide the citizens of Davidson and surrounding areas alternatives for protecting natural lands and other open spaces for ecological and aesthetic purposes.

ADDRESS: PO Box 1952 Davidson, NC 28036
PHONE/FAX: 704-892-1910
EMAIL: dlc@davidsonlands.org
WEB: www.davidsonlands.org
ESTABLISHED: 2001
BOARD MEMBERS: 18
STAFF: 1 P/T
GEOGRAPHIC AREA: Town of Davidson and adjoining areas of Cabarrus and Iredell counties.
CONTACT: Roy Alexander, Executive Director

CUMULATIVE LAND PROTECTION TOTALS: Protected 159 acres in three places. Placed eight acres under conservation agreements.

Appendix To Chapter Eight

ENO RIVER ASSOCIATION (ASSOCIATION FOR THE PRESERVATION OF THE ENO RIVER VALLEY)

MISSION STATEMENT: To conserve and protect the natural, cultural and historical resources of the Eno River Basin.

ADDRESS: 4404 Guess Rd. Durham, NC 27712
PHONE: 919-620-9099
FAX: 919-477-0448
EMAIL: land@enoriver.org
WEB: www.enoriver.org
ESTABLISHED: 1966
BOARD MEMBERS: 19
STAFF: 4 F/T, 1 P/T
GEOGRAPHIC AREA: Eno River Basin in Durham and Orange counties

CONTACTS:
- Robin Jacobs, Executive Director
- Kurt Schlimme, Director of Conservation
- Kathy Lee, Director of Education
- Greg Bell, Festival Coordinator
- Cynthia Satterfield, Development Director

CUMULATIVE LAND PROTECTION TOTALS: Protected 5,845 acres in 131 places. Own fee simple title to 257 acres; transferred fee simple title to governments on 787 acres. Transferred conservation agreements to governments on 60 acres.

2010 LAND PROTECTION TOTALS: Protected six acres in two places. Own fee simple title to one acre.

FOOTHILLS CONSERVANCY OF NORTH CAROLINA

FOOTHILLS CONSERVANCY OF NORTH CAROLINA

MISSION STATEMENT: Foothills Conservancy of North Carolina works cooperatively with landowners and public and private conservation partners to preserve and protect important natural areas and open spaces of the eastern Blue Ridge Mountains and their foothills, including watersheds, environmentally significant habitats, and forests and farmlands for this and future generations.

ADDRESS:
Street: 135 ½ West Union St., Morganton, NC 28155

Mailing: PO Box 3023 Morganton, NC 28680
PHONE: 828-437-9930
FAX: 828-437-9912
EMAIL: info@foothillsconservancy.org
WEB: www.foothillsconservancy.org
ESTABLISHED: 1995
BOARD MEMBERS: 15
STAFF: 5 F/T, 1 AmeriCorps, 2 P/T
GEOGRAPHIC AREA: Alexander, Burke, Caldwell, Catawba, Cleveland, Lincoln, McDowell and Rutherford counties, and the majority or significant portions of the upper Catawba, Broad and Yadkin river basins

CONTACTS:
- Capt. Michael "Squeak" Smith, Board Chairman
- Susie Hamrick Jones, Executive Director

- Tom Kenney, Land Protection Director
- Andrew Kota, Protection and Stewardship Associate
- Lynn Allen, Development Director
- Mary Braun, Office Manager
- Brian Sewell, AmeriCorps Member, Communications and Outreach
- Edward Norvell, Legal Counsel
- Suzi Berl, Development Counsel

CUMULATIVE LAND PROTECTION TOTALS: Protected 45,694 acres in 39 places. Own fee simple title to 1,487 acres; transferred fee simple title to governments on 28,707 acres. Placed 1,758 acres under conservation agreements; transferred conservation agreements to governments on 471 acres.

2010 LAND PROTECTION TOTALS: Protected 535 acres in four places. Own fee simple title to 153 acres; transferred fee simple title to governments on 306 acres. Placed 76 acres under conservation agreements.

HIGHLANDS-CASHIERS LAND TRUST

Highlands-Cashiers LAND TRUST
"Saving Special Places since 1909"

MISSION STATEMENT: To protect valuable land resources for all generations.

ADDRESS: PO Box 1703
348 South 5th St.
Highlands, NC 28741

PHONE: 828-526-1111
FAX: 828-526-0066
EMAIL: hltrust@earthlink.net
WEB: www.hicashlt.org
ESTABLISHED: 1883, as the Highlands Improvement Society
BOARD MEMBERS: 20
STAFF: 2 plus 1 Americorps member
GEOGRAPHIC AREA: Southern Macon and Jackson counties

CONTACTS:
- Gary Wein, Executive Director
- Julie Schott, Development Director
- Kyle Purel, Stewardship Coordinator

CUMULATIVE LAND PROTECTION TOTALS: Protected 2,023 acres in 71 places. Own fee simple title to 241 acres; transferred fee simple title to governments on 110 acres. Placed 1,672 acres under conservation agreements.

2010 LAND PROTECTION TOTALS: Protected six acres in three places. Own fee simple title to six acres.

4 • 2011 North Carolina Land Trust Directory

Everything You Need To Know About Buying Mountain Property

Land Trust for the Little Tennessee

MISSION STATEMENT: The mission of the Land Trust for the Little Tennessee is to conserve the waters, forests, farms and heritage of the upper Little Tennessee and Hiwassee river valleys.

ADDRESS:
Street: 88 E Main St., Franklin, NC 28734
Mailing: PO Box 1148, Franklin, NC 28744
PHONE: 828-524-2711
FAX: 828-524-4741
EMAIL: pcarlson@ltlt.org
WEB: www.ltlt.org
ESTABLISHED: 1999
BOARD MEMBERS: 11
STAFF: 6
GEOGRAPHIC AREA: Watersheds: Hiwassee (North Carolina only); Little Tennessee (North Carolina and Georgia). Counties: Cherokee, Clay, Graham, Jackson, Macon and Swain, N.C.; portion of Rabun, Ga.

CONTACTS:
- Paul J. Carlson, Executive Director
- Sharon F. Taylor, Deputy Director

CUMULATIVE LAND PROTECTION TOTALS: Protected 12,819 acres in 66 places. Own fee simple title to 1,423 acres; transferred fee simple title to governments on 358 acres and to other organizations on 4,467 acres. Placed conservation agreements on 3,903 acres; transferred conservation agreements to governments on 2,666 acres and to other organizations on two acres.

2010 LAND PROTECTION TOTALS: Protected 280 acres in four places. Own fee simple title to 166 acres. Placed 114 acres under conservation agreements.

LandTrust for Central North Carolina

MISSION STATEMENT: The LandTrust for Central North Carolina is a private, nonprofit conservation organization working with private and public landowners to protect the special natural areas, family farms and rural landscapes of Anson, Cabarrus, Davidson, Davie, Iredell, Montgomery, Randolph, Richmond, Rowan and Stanly counties.

ADDRESS:
Street: 215 Depot St., Salisbury, NC 28144
Mailing: PO Box 4284, Salisbury, NC 28145-4284
PHONE: 704-647-0302
FAX: 704-647-0068
EMAIL: landtrust@landtrustcnc.org
WEB: www.landtrustcnc.org
ESTABLISHED: 1995
BOARD MEMBERS: 17
STAFF: 4
GEOGRAPHIC AREA: Lower Yadkin/Pee Dee Watershed; Anson, Cabarrus, Davie, Davidson, Iredell, Montgomery, Randolph, Richmond, Rowan and Stanly counties.

CONTACTS:
- Jason A. Walser, Executive Director
- Dyke Messinger, Board President
- Andrew B. Waters, Director of Operations
- Barbara M. Lawther, Director of Development
- Crystal J. Cockman, Uwharrie Conservation Specialist

CUMULATIVE LAND PROTECTION TOTALS: Protected 19,171 acres in 144 places. Own fee simple title on 4,933 acres; transferred fee simple title to governments on 1,282 acres. Placed conservation agreements on 11,667 acres; transferred conservation agreements to governments on 271 acres.

2010 LAND PROTECTION TOTALS: Protected 563 acres in four places. Placed 96 acres under conservation agreements.

Lumber River Conservancy

MISSION STATEMENT: To preserve the Lumber River as one of the nation's Wild and Scenic rivers by conserving land along it and its tributaries.

ADDRESS: PO Box 1235, Pembroke, NC 28372
PHONE: 910-522-5751
FAX: 910-522-5754
EMAIL: patricia.sellers@uncp.edu
WEB: www.lumberriverconservancy.org
ESTABLISHED: 1991
BOARD MEMBERS: 14
STAFF: 1 P/T
CONTACT: Dr. Patricia P. Sellers, Executive Director

GEOGRAPHIC AREA: Lumber River corridor (118 miles) in Columbus, Hoke, Robeson and Scotland counties.

CUMULATIVE LAND PROTECTION TOTALS: Protected 3,909 acres in 56 places. Own fee simple title to 2,678 acres; transferred fee simple title to governments on 474 acres. Placed 678 acres under conservation agreements; transferred conservation agreements to governments on 80 acres.

2010 LAND PROTECTION TOTALS: Protected 40 acres in one place. Own fee simple title to 20 acres. Transferred conservation agreements to governments on 20 acres.

Appendix To Chapter Eight

NATIONAL COMMITTEE FOR THE NEW RIVER

MISSION STATEMENT: NCNR envisions a permanently protected New River as a treasured national resource. The mission of NCNR is to advocate for successful protection of the New River, to restore eroding river and stream banks and enhance riparian habitat, and to permanently protect land along the River.

ADDRESS: PO Box 1480
West Jefferson, NC 28694

PHONE: 336-982-6267
FAX: 336-982-6433
EMAIL: info@ncnr.org
WEB: www.ncnr.org
ESTABLISHED: 1974 (1991 as a land trust)
BOARD MEMBERS: 13
STAFF: 5 F/T, 3 P/T
GEOGRAPHIC AREA: The New River Watershed in North Carolina, Virginia and West Virginia, including Ashe, Alleghany and Watauga counties in North Carolina.

CONTACTS:
• Laura Green, Administrative Assistant
• George Santucci, Executive Director

CUMULATIVE LAND PROTECTION TOTALS: Protected 2,873 acres in 25 places. Own fee simple title to 47 acres; transferred fee simple title to governments on 1,005 acres and to other organizations on 149 acres. Placed 1,673 acres under conservation agreements.

2010 LAND PROTECTION TOTALS: Protected 189 acres in three places. Transferred fee simple title to governments on 75 acres. Placed 114 acres under conservation agreements.

NORTH CAROLINA COASTAL LAND TRUST

MISSION STATEMENT: The Coastal Land Trust's mission is to enrich the coastal communities of our state through acquisition of open spaces and natural areas, conservation education, and the promotion of good land stewardship. We are active throughout the coastal plain of North Carolina: its beaches, river corridors and marshes, its sandhills and savannas, its public parks and greenways. We aspire to bring together citizens and landowners, natives and newcomers, to set aside lands for conservation.

MAIN OFFICE:
ADDRESS: 131 Racine Dr., Suite 201
Wilmington, NC 28403
PHONE: 910-790-4524
FAX: 910-790-0392

NEW BERN OFFICE:
ADDRESS: 3301-E Trent Rd.
New Bern, NC 28562
PHONE: 252-634-1927
FAX: 252-633-4179

EDENTON OFFICE:
ADDRESS: 112 W. Eden St.
Edenton, NC 27932
PHONE: 252-449-8289
FAX: 252-482-0239

EMAIL: info@coastallandtrust.org
WEB: www.coastallandtrust.org
ESTABLISHED: 1992
BOARD MEMBERS: 19
STAFF: 8 F/T, 3 P/T
GEOGRAPHIC AREA: Beaufort, Bertie, Bladen, Brunswick, Camden, Carteret, Chowan, Columbus, Craven, Currituck, Dare, Duplin, Edgecombe, Gates, Greene, Hertford, Hyde, Jones, Lenoir, Martin, New Hanover, Northampton, Onslow, Pamlico, Pasquotank, Pender, Perquimans, Pitt, Sampson, Tyrrell, Washington and Wayne counties.

CONTACTS:
• Camilla Herlevich, Executive Director, camilla@coastallandtrust.org
• Janice Allen, Deputy Director, janice@coastallandtrust.org
• Lee L. Leidy, NE Region Director, lee@coastallandtrust.org

CUMULATIVE LAND PROTECTION TOTALS: Protected 47,328 acres in 158 places. Own fee simple title to 6,012 acres; transferred fee simple title to governments on 5,494 acres. Placed 23,592 acres under conservation agreements; transferred conservation agreements to governments on 6,459 acres and to other organizations on seven acres.

2010 LAND PROTECTION TOTALS: Protected 2,075 acres in three places. Own fee simple title to 135 acres. Placed conservation agreements on 45 acres; transferred conservation agreements to governments on 994 acres.

NORTH CAROLINA RAIL-TRAILS

MISSION STATEMENT: The mission of North Carolina Rail-Trails is to protect rail corridors for trail and rail-with-trail use, providing non-motorized transportation, recreation environmental education and historic preservation.

ADDRESS: PO Box 61348
Durham, NC 27715
PHONE: 919-428-7119
EMAIL: execdirector@ncrailtrails.org
WEB: www.ncrailtrails.org

ESTABLISHED: 1990
BOARD MEMBERS: 15
STAFF: 1
GEOGRAPHIC AREA: Statewide
CONTACTS: Carrie Banks, Executive Director
919-428-7100

CUMULATIVE LAND PROTECTION TOTALS: Protected 308 acres in nine places. Transferred fee simple title to governments on 61 acres. Placed conservation agreements on 52 acres.

Everything You Need To Know About Buying Mountain Property

NORTHEAST NEW HANOVER CONSERVANCY

MISSION STATEMENT: To establish the quality, by scientific research, of the natural resources within a 20-square mile coastal area; to take steps to protect healthy resources and to upgrade quality of those impacted.

ADDRESS: 1513 Futch Creek Rd.
Wilmington NC, 28411
PHONE: 910-686-1554
EMAIL: bushardt@bellsouth.net
ESTABLISHED: 1982
BOARD MEMBERS: 7
STAFF: All volunteer
GEOGRAPHIC AREA: Northeast New Hanover County – 13,000 acres between US Highway 17 and Atlantic Ocean ending at the Pender County line

CONTACT: Paula Bushardt
CUMULATIVE LAND PROTECTION TOTALS: Protected 1,876 acres in eight places. Own fee simple title to 1,053 acres. Placed conservation agreements on 823 acres.
2010 LAND PROTECTION TOTALS: Protected 49 acres in one place. Own fee simple title to 49 acres

PACOLET AREA CONSERVANCY

MISSION STATEMENT: Protecting and conserving our area's natural resources to create a community living and growing in harmony with a legacy of our natural heritage.

ADDRESS: 850 N. Trade St.
Tryon, NC 28782
PHONE: 828-859-5060
FAX: 828-859-5074
EMAIL: info@pacolet.org
WEB: www.pacolet.org
ESTABLISHED: 1989
BOARD MEMBERS: 14
STAFF: 3

GEOGRAPHIC AREA: Polk County, N.C., adjoining parts of Greenville and Spartanburg counties, S.C., with holdings in Transylvania, Polk, Rutherford and Henderson counties in North Carolina and in Spartanburg County, S.C.
CONTACTS:
- Sally Walker, Executive Director
- Pam Torlina, Land Protection Specialist

CUMULATIVE LAND PROTECTION TOTALS: Protected 8,065 acres in 79 places. Own fee simple title to 441 acres. Placed conservation agreements on 4,040 acres; transferred conservation agreements to governments on 124 acres.

PIEDMONT LAND CONSERVANCY

MISSION STATEMENT: Piedmont Land Conservancy permanently protects important land to conserve our region's rivers and streams, natural and scenic areas, wildlife habitat, and farmland that make the Piedmont a healthy and vibrant place to live, work and visit for present and future generations.

ADDRESS: PO Box 4025
Greensboro, NC 27404-4025
PHONE: 336-691-0088
FAX: 336-691-0044
EMAIL: info@piedmontland.org
WEB: www.piedmontland.org
ESTABLISHED: 1990
BOARD MEMBERS: 18
STAFF: 4 F/T, 7 P/T
GEOGRAPHIC AREA: Alamance, Caswell, Forsyth, Guilford, Randolph, Rockingham, Stokes, Surry and Yadkin counties
CONTACTS:
- Kevin Redding, Executive Director
- Kalen Kingsbury, Associate Director and General Counsel
- Kenneth A. Bridle, Ph.D., Stewardship Director
- Mindy Mock, Land Protection and Outreach Specialist

- Kem Schroeder, P/T Development Director
- Lynne Dardanell, P/T Membership and Outreach Coordinator
- Palmer McIntyre, P/T Land Protection Specialist
- Ellen Driver and Jeri Donnelly, P/T Office Managers
- Chrissy Keyhko, P/T Database Manager
- Taylor Owens, P/T Database Specialist

CUMULATIVE LAND PROTECTION TOTALS: Protected 18,539 acres in 155 places. Own fee simple title to 3,156 acres; transferred fee simple title to governments on 3,485 acres. Placed conservation agreements on 9,901 acres; transferred conservation agreements to governments on 146 acres and to other organizations on 250 acres.

2010 LAND PROTECTION TOTALS: Protected 1,227 acres in 11 places. Own fee simple title to 578 acres; transferred fee simple title to governments on 389 acres. Placed conservation agreements on 247 acres.

Appendix To Chapter Eight

Sandhills Area Land Trust

MISSION STATEMENT: The Sandhills Area Land Trust is a community-based non-profit organization that offers assistance and education to help the public and landowners find ways to protect their lands and natural resources. We protect land, water, natural open space and farmlands. Our aim is to save the Sandhills landscape heritage for future generations.

MAIN OFFICE:
ADDRESS:
Street: 140 SW Broad St.
Southern Pines, NC 28387

Mailing: PO Box 1032
Southern Pines, NC 28388
PHONE: 910-695-4323
FAX: 910-695-1087

FIELD OFFICE:
ADDRESS: 831 Arsenal Ave
Fayetteville, NC 28305
PHONE: 910-483-9028

EMAIL: ntalton@sandhillslandtrust.org
WEB: www.sandhillslandtrust.org
ESTABLISHED: 1991
BOARD MEMBERS: 4
STAFF: 2 F/T, 2 P/T

GEOGRAPHIC AREA: Sandhills and mid Cape Fear region: Cumberland, Harnett, Hoke, Moore, Richmond and Scotland counties, and longleaf pine ecosystems in Lee County.

CONTACTS:
- Candace Williams, Executive Director
- Nancy Talton, Administrator
- Valerie Alzner, Land Steward
- Jessica Corean, Program Assistant

CUMULATIVE LAND PROTECTION TOTALS: Protected 10,824 acres in 73 places. Own fee simple title to 1,741 acres; transferred fee simple title to governments on 1,616 acres. Placed 5,163 acres under conservation agreements; transferred conservation agreements to governments on 1,217 acres.

2010 LAND PROTECTION TOTALS: Protected 270 acres in two places. Own fee simple title to 99 acres. Placed conservation agreements on 171 acres.

Smith Island Land Trust (A Subsidiary of Bald Head Island Conservancy)

MISSION STATEMENT: To acquire and preserve historically and ecologically significant lands on Smith Island for the benefit of current and future generations.

ADDRESS: PO Box 3109
Bald Head Island, NC 28461
PHONE: 910-457-0089
FAX: 910-457-9824
EMAIL: email@bhic.org
WEB: www.bhic.org
ESTABLISHED: 1996, merged with Bald Head Island Conservancy in July 2002 (BHIC established 1983)
BOARD MEMBERS: 8
STAFF: 9

GEOGRAPHIC AREA: The Smith Island Complex, the barrier spit that includes Bald Head, Middle and Bluff islands, in the mouth of the Cape Fear River in Brunswick County.

CONTACTS:
- Suzanne E. Dorsey, Executive Director
- Jene Douglas, President

CUMULATIVE LAND PROTECTION TOTALS: Protected 116 acres in 34 places. Own fee simple title to 20 acres; transferred fee simple title to governments on 70 acres. Placed conservation agreements on 27 acres.

Southern Appalachian Highlands Conservancy

MISSION STATEMENT: To conserve the unique plant and animal habitat, clean water, and scenic beauty of the mountains of western North Carolina and East Tennessee for the benefit of present and future generations. We achieve this by forging and maintaining long-term conservation relationships with private landowners, owning and managing land, and encouraging strong, healthy local communities.

ADDRESS: 34 Wall St., Suite 502
Asheville, NC 28801-2710
PHONE: 828-253-0095
FAX: 828-253-1248
EMAIL: sahc@appalachian.org
WEB: www.appalachian.org
ESTABLISHED: 1974
BOARD MEMBERS: 18
STAFF: 7 F/T, 3 P/T, 1 seasonal ecologist, 4 AmeriCorps members

GEOGRAPHIC AREA: Western North Carolina focusing on Avery, Buncombe, Haywood, Jackson, Madison, Mitchell, and Yancey counties, and East Tennessee, focusing on Carter, Johnson and Unicoi counties

CONTACTS:
- Carl Silverstein, Executive Director
- Kristy Urquhart, Associate Director
- Cheryl Fowler, Membership Director
- Michelle Pugliese, Land Protection Director
- William Hamilton, Farmland Program Director
- Hanni Muerdter, Stewardship & Conservation Planning Director
- Judy Murray, Roan Stewardship Director
- Gretchen Parlier, Finance Compliance Specialist
- Angela Shepherd, Office Administrator
- Nora Schubert, Seasonal Ecologist
- Valerie True, Program Coordinator, Blue Ridge Forever
- Ella Wise, AmeriCorps Land and Farmland Protection Member
- Allison Kiehl, AmeriCorps Stewardship Member
- Chris Coxen, AmeriCorps Stewardship Member
- Claire Hobbs, AmeriCorps Public Awareness and Outreach Member

CUMULATIVE LAND PROTECTION TOTALS: Protected 46,385 acres in 139 places. Own fee simple title to 22,153 acres; transferred fee simple title to governments on 23 acres and to other organizations on 265 acres. Placed conservation agreements on 15,600 acres; transferred conservation agreements to governments on 5,529 acres and to other organizations on 95 acres.

2010 LAND PROTECTION TOTALS: Protected 917 acres in 11 places. Own fee simple title to 611 acres. Placed conservation agreements on 297 acres.

Everything You Need To Know About Buying Mountain Property

COUNTY-BY-COUNTY INDEX OF LOCAL AND REGIONAL LAND TRUSTS IN NORTH CAROLINA

Numbers next to each county name correspond to the land trust(s) that serve that area.
(Land trusts are listed alphabetically by name inside; refer to Table of Contents on page 3 for page numbers of entries.)

LAND TRUSTS

STATEWIDE:
Black Family Land Trust
Conservation Trust for North Carolina
North Carolina Rail-Trails

1. Blue Ridge Rural Land Trust
2. Carolina Mountain Land Conservancy
3. Catawba Lands Conservancy
4. Davidson Lands Conservancy
5. Eno River Association
6. Foothills Conservancy of North Carolina
7. Highlands-Cashiers Land Trust
8. Land Trust for the Little Tennessee
9. LandTrust for Central North Carolina
10. Lumber River Conservancy
11. National Committee for the New River
12. North Carolina Coastal Land Trust
13. Northeast New Hanover Conservancy
14. Pacolet Area Conservancy
15. Piedmont Land Conservancy
16. Sandhills Area Land Trust
17. Smith Island Land Trust
    A subsidiary of Bald Head Island Conservancy
18. Southern Appalachian Highlands Conservancy
19. Tar River Land Conservancy
20. Triangle Greenways Council
21. Triangle Land Conservancy

CONSERVATION TRUST
FOR NORTH CAROLINA
1028 Washington St. • Raleigh NC 27605
919-828-4199 • www.ctnc.org

Data in this directory was compiled by the Conservation Trust for North Carolina from information provided by each local land trust.

COUNTY	LAND TRUST
Alamance	15
Alexander	6
Alleghany	1, 11
Anson	9
Ashe	1, 11
Avery	1, 18
Beaufort	12
Bertie	12
Bladen	12
Brunswick	12, 17
Buncombe	2, 18
Burke	6
Cabarrus	4, 9
Caldwell	6
Camden	12
Carteret	12
Caswell	15
Catawba	3, 6
Chatham	20, 21
Cherokee	8
Chowan	12
Clay	8
Cleveland	6
Columbus	10, 12
Craven	12
Cumberland	16
Currituck	12
Dare	12
Davidson	9
Davie	9
Duplin	12
Durham	5, 20, 21
Edgecombe	19
Forsyth	15
Franklin	19
Gaston	3
Gates	12
Graham	8
Granville	19
Greene	12
Guilford	15
Halifax	19
Harnett	16
Haywood	18
Henderson	2, 14
Hertford	12
Hoke	10, 16
Hyde	12
Iredell	3, 4, 9
Jackson	2, 7, 8, 18

COUNTY	LAND TRUST
Johnston	20, 21
Jones	12
Lee	16, 20, 21
Lenoir	12
Lincoln	3, 6
Macon	7, 8
Madison	18
Martin	12
McDowell	6
Mecklenburg	3
Mitchell	1, 18
Montgomery	9
Moore	16
Nash	19
New Hanover	12, 13
Northampton	12
Onslow	12
Orange	5, 20, 21
Pamlico	12
Pasquotank	12
Pender	12
Perquimans	12
Person	19
Pitt	12
Polk	14
Randolph	9, 15
Richmond	9, 16
Robeson	10
Rockingham	15
Rowan	9
Rutherford	2, 6, 14
Sampson	12
Scotland	10, 16
Stanly	9
Stokes	15
Surry	15
Swain	8
Transylvania	2, 14
Tyrrell	12
Union	3
Vance	19
Wake	20, 21
Warren	19
Washington	12
Watauga	1, 11
Wayne	12
Wilkes	1
Wilson	--
Yadkin	15
Yancey	1, 18

Appendix To Chapter Eight

Tar River Land Conservancy

MISSION STATEMENT: To protect the natural and cultural resources of Person, Granville, Vance, Franklin, Warren, Halifax, Nash, and Edgecombe counties by working in partnership with private landowners, businesses, public agencies and others to preserve rural landscapes and riparian corridors.

ADDRESS: 123 N. Main St., PO Box 1161
Louisburg, NC 27549
PHONE: 919-496-5902
FAX: 919-496-6940
EMAIL: info@tarriver.org
WEB: www.tarriver.org
ESTABLISHED: 2000
BOARD MEMBERS: 8
STAFF: 4
GEOGRAPHIC AREA: Edgecombe, Franklin, Granville, Halifax, Nash, Person, Vance, and Warren counties
CONTACTS:
- Derek E. Halberg, Executive Director, dhalberg@tarriver.org
- Amy R. Edge, General Counsel/Business Manager, aedge@tarriver.org
- Eric V. Jenkins, Land Protection Specialist, ejenkins@tarriver.org

CUMULATIVE LAND PROTECTION TOTALS: Protected 16,401 acres in 152 places. Own fee simple title to 445 acres; transferred fee simple title to governments on 195 acres. Placed conservation agreements on 9,040 acres; transferred conservation agreements to governments on 9,173 acres and to other organizations on 193 acres.

2010 LAND PROTECTION TOTALS: Protected 210 acres in three places. Transferred fee simple title to governments on nine acres. Placed conservation agreements on 201 acres.

Triangle Greenways Council

MISSION STATEMENT: The mission of the TGC Land Trust is to conserve land and water corridors connecting the culture of our cities and countryside; past, present and future.

ADDRESS: 520 Polk St.
Raleigh, NC 27604-1960
PHONE: 919-828-8322 (Bill Flournoy)
EMAIL: bflournoy@nc.rr.com
WEB: www.trianglegreenways.org
ESTABLISHED: 1985 (1998 as a land trust)
BOARD MEMBERS: 19
STAFF: All volunteer

GEOGRAPHIC AREA: Triangle area: Chatham, Durham, Lee, Johnston, Orange and Wake counties.
CONTACT: Bill Flournoy, Land Trust Committee

CUMULATIVE LAND PROTECTION TOTALS: Protected 449 acres in 20 places. Own fee simple title to 339 acres; transferred fee simple title to governments on three acres.

2010 LAND PROTECTION TOTALS: Protected 104 acres in six places. Own fee simple title to 87 acres.

Triangle Land Conservancy

MISSION STATEMENT: Triangle Land Conservancy's mission is to protect important open space – stream corridors, forests, wildlife habitat, farmland and natural areas – in Chatham, Durham, Johnston, Lee, Orange and Wake counties to help keep our region a healthy and vibrant place to live and work.

ADDRESS: 1101 Haynes St., Suite 205
Raleigh, NC 27604
PHONE: 919-833-3662
FAX: 919-755-9356
EMAIL: info@triangleland.org
WEB: www.triangleland.org
ESTABLISHED: 1983
BOARD MEMBERS: 18
STAFF: 13
GEOGRAPHIC AREA: Wake, Durham, Orange, Chatham, Johnston and Lee counties. River basins: Neuse River, Little River, Marks Creek, Deep River, Haw River and Rocky River.
CONTACTS:
- Kevin Brice, President
- Alberto Alzamora, Staff Accountant
- Donnie Lee Barnes, Land Steward
- Ellica Church, Annual Giving Manager
- Leigh Ann Clenek, Conservation Planner
- Robert Howes, Conservation Project Manager – Orange & Durham Counties
- Tandy Jones, Director of Special Projects
- Jeff Masten, Director of Conservation Strategies
- Aime Mitchell, Development Operations Manager
- Jennifer Peterson, Communications Coordinator
- Jessica Poland, Business Manager
- Tabitha Roberson, Conservation Project Manager – Chatham & Lee Counties
- Jonathan Scott, Conservation Project Manager – Wake & Johnston Counties
- Walt Tysinger, Land Manager

CUMULATIVE LAND PROTECTION TOTALS: Protected 14,638 acres in 132 places. Own fee simple title to 4,038 acres; transferred fee simple title to governments on 1,439 acres and to other organizations on 114 acres. Placed conservation agreements on 5,042 acres; transferred conservation agreements to governments on 112 acres.

2010 LAND PROTECTION TOTALS: Protected 1,476 acres in 14 places. Own fee simple title to 838 acres. Placed conservation agreements on 638 acres.

CHAPTER NINE

Epilogue

Some closing thoughts

The heart and soul of this book is about providing consumers with the tools and information that they need in order to make informed and educated decisions regarding the acquisition of land for their future residences in the mountains. However, in a more indirect manner, the book is about the need for the ongoing compromise and balance between oftentimes competing interests:

- those of the real estate developers, to create sustainable and attractive communities to address the growing demand for second homes, vacation homes, and retirement homes;
- those of the environmentalists and conservationists who are passionate about their sense of moral obligation to protect and preserve the area's biodiversity and considerable natural habitat;
- those of the regulatory agencies—federal, regional, and local—that strive to enact enough regulatory legislation to protect the natural resources and the consumers from the "bad apples" that inevitably comprise a small percentage of every sector of commerce, while not destroying the busi-

ness climate for the majority of those who operate from and within a sense of moral decency and ethical propriety;
- and finally, those of the consumers, who have a dream of finding their own pieces of heaven to eventually realize the lifestyles that they have fought so hard to achieve and that can't be found in environments that they are more than happy to leave behind.

None of these interests are going away anytime in the foreseeable future. In fact, any studied observer of demographic and social trends will tell you that the Blue Ridge and Smoky Mountain regions of Appalachia will continue to attract not only the retiring baby boom generation but also the successive generations who have the same desires as the baby boomers and are often able to realize them at an earlier stage in their lives.

There is nothing inherently wrong with real estate developers and builders who address the needs, desires, and demands of a population that has targeted a region for its natural beauty, enthusiasm for the outdoors, and the quality of life that accompanies those interests. The problem is when the motivation for developing real estate is predominantly to enhance a developer's personal financial statement at the expense of all other concerns. That is when things quickly deteriorate for the buyer, the land and natural habitat, and for the region in general. Ironically, as is often the case in business, when the primary motivation is a passion to pursue excellence—to "do the right thing"—personal wealth and other financial successes are simply natural by-products and windfalls from the passion, not from any desire for wealth.

There is nothing innately wrong with the desires of environmentalists and conservationists to protect and preserve as many acres as they possibly can from the negative impacts to the natural habitat and ecosystems that invariably occur as a direct result of real estate development. The problem is that those efforts are dramatically hindered by the restricted financial resources that are available to conservation groups and by the lack of a profit-making model that might better attract the interests of landowners and investment capital. In today's environment, the best they can do is to try to motivate private landowners with tax-based incentives to provide a minimally acceptable form of compensation. The hope is that these incentives, coupled with a sense of moral obligation to preserve the area's resources, are enough to convince the owners of substantial tracts of land to conserve their land in perpetuity, through conservation easement agreements or through outright property donations.

There is nothing intrinsically wrong with the efforts of regulators to bring about legislation that purports to instill an ethical "balance of trade" between the developers of real estate and the individual consumers who buy their developed end product. The problem is that many of the rural areas that are the subject of this book have a very short history and limited experience with multiple, large-scale residential developments. Their subdivision ordinances simply haven't caught up to the pace of development. Moreover, their relative lack of sophistication and modest tax bases preclude their ability to engage the appropriate consultants and hire the needed personnel to modernize and enforce the regulations that might have prevented some of the nightmares described in previous chapters.

Finally, there is nothing wrong with individuals who have their hearts set on buying parcels of land in the mountains to satisfy a burning inner desire to more fully enjoy their vacations, their children, their grandchildren, and their retirement years. The problem is that many, through no fault of their own, are completely unprepared to make an educated decision about making that purchase. Their process (or lack thereof) in making that decision is often badly flawed because they don't even know what the questions are, let alone the answers. You cannot protect yourself from the answer to a question that you didn't ask. If there are potential pitfalls that you are unprepared to avoid because you don't know they exist, there's a fairly decent chance that you may fall into one.

A fairly well known clothier, toward the end of the last millennium, made famous the line, "...where an educated consumer is our best customer." I read somewhere a quote from a marketing book that stated otherwise, something to the effect that the more informed a consumer or buyer is, the more difficult it is to sell to that consumer. I didn't read the book, but to that thought I would say, if a developer has a good product to sell, then you, as an educated consumer, will be his or her best customer; if a developer has a bad product to sell, you, as an educated consumer, may be his or her worst nightmare. If you have the choice, you might as well be someone else's nightmare in lieu of living your own. So be smart, take your time, ask all the right questions, get all the real answers, and achieve the dream.

Infrastructure — internet, etc.
Solar panels

Need Health Dept. Approval for Drain field & Improvement Plan

If plat approval is not dependent on Health Dept. don't buy lot until done

For water (p.148-149)
① Attempt to negotiate drilling, 10m's depth & flow as part of purcha
②

Well drilling ~~charges~~ charges
$8-10/lf
+ Casing: Plastic $8/lf Steel $15/lf — down to bedrock / Plastic is typica
+ Grout $200 (flat?)

Need to understand insuran expenses & how to reduce Klaims, concierge services, in home

LP Gas
500 gal is typical (Range 250-1K)

If water on property — find what's upstream

Trash Collection

Mail/UPS/FedEx — Mailbox like Mom & Dad's?

ICE/Snow Removal — ATV

→ Spend a month

OUTSIDE FACTORS

PROXIMITY TO FIRE IMPACTS INSURANCE PREMIUMS

What about surrounding land?

Travel the primary route — Visual population
SEE P 179 FOR LIST